Praise for *Mastering the Power of Self-Hypnosis*

The second edition of Roy Hunter's book is a comprehensive, practical, and stimulating guide to the use of self-hypnosis as a means of personal transformation. The author's decades of experience shine through in the depth and breadth of his coverage of the subject. He has the knack of making somewhat complex processes simple to follow through a "home-spun," light-hearted writing style, in which key points are illustrated by real-life examples. The sections on gateways to the subconscious, motivational mapping, and the correct use of affirmations are particularly outstanding. It is one of those rare books on hypnosis which serves equally well as an introduction for the novice and a dependable reference guide for the practicing hypnotist. It is highly recommended.

David Botsford, 4 Corners Hypnosis

Roy Hunter is one of the most highly respected professional hypnotherapists of our time. As well as being a prominent author he also teaches professional hypnosis and advanced techniques for professionals, and self-hypnosis to groups and clients for personal and professional motivation. His mentor was the late Charles Tebbetts whose work still gives him inspiration and a firm foundation upon which to build in his own inimical way.

Mastering the Power of Self-Hypnosis is the best book on self-hypnosis out there today. It is an excellent read as it is written by an expert communicator – clear, concise, informative, and immensely readable, as the author puts so much of himself into the volume.

Many books are dry textbooks which you read because you feel you ought to and come to the end of the reading with some relief and, very often, with as many questions as you have had answers! This book is written with such clarity and dynamism that it draws you in and takes you on an investigation into self-hypnosis that answers your questions and gives you the necessary confidence to use in an unparalleled way.

Whether you are a professional or a layperson this book is for you. It will be clearly understood by all who read it as the author leaves no stone unturned. This is an honest work and his use of personal anecdotes helps reinforce this honesty and immediacy. It is a must for anyone who uses or wishes to use hypnosis.

It was a delight to read a book which was entirely jargon-free. There were full explanations at every level and every necessary step was explained fully so that one traveled through the volume with confidence. Indeed the clarity of content makes it one of the best practical guides that I have come across in twenty years of working in this field. It is a truly masterful presentation of the fundamentals of self-hypnosis and of its associated techniques. This is a book that not only tells you *what* to change in order to transform your life in whatever way you desire, but actually tells you *how* to do it, step by step, point by point.

You learn the art and the power of self-hypnosis by discovering how to teach that most powerful part of you, the subconscious, to cooperate with your desires. The book reminds you that willpower will not work on its own. I have often said this to patients and have added that one's emotion and imagination are of more value than attempting to succeed with willpower alone. The author puts my thoughts into practice and shows you how to do just the same.

The empowerment exercises are fun to try out but powerful in their action. They deal with areas such as relaxation, stress management, and overcoming sleep problems. You are taught the vital yet often ignored skill of establishing clear priorities before you begin. Indeed, the author helps the reader to ensure that potential failure is avoided by this clear preparation.

Of great interest is the section on creative daydreaming to stop smoking, lose weight, improve performance, and so on. Prepare correctly, prioritize wisely, fine tune your use of language, learn the importance and relevance of affirmations, belief, expectancy, and conviction, and take on board the many suggestions the author makes and you will be in a position to journey on into the world of self-hypnosis and bring about changes such as you have not experienced before.

Here is the way ahead for you. I recommend it wholeheartedly to all who wish to gain the full benefit from self-hypnosis through which you WILL make the positive changes that you seek.

Roy Hunter is one of the most gifted guides that I have come across. He writes with first-hand knowledge, deep understanding of the subject, and conviction but also with undeniable humanity which helps make this book special!

This book receives my very highest endorsement; no person interested in using self-hypnosis can afford to be without it. It will not be a book on your shelf but on your desk as it will be constantly used for reference and inspiration.

David Slater, BA, DHyp, MHA(RegHyp), MASC, DCS, MGSCT, Clinical Hypnotherapist and Counsellor

This is one of the few books about empowerment and achievement that reveals the true secret of success: change that occurs at the unconscious level transforms lives forever. Roy Hunter shows you how to do this in a specific step-by-step process. This book is a gold mine of useful information that takes you to the next level. *Mastering the Power of Self-Hypnosis* has earned my highest recommendation. Buy this book. It will change your life.

Kevin Hogan, Ph.D., author of *The Psychology of Persuasion: How to Persuade Others to Your Way of Thinking*

Roy Hunter has written another authoritative and engaging book, *Mastering the Power of Self-Hypnosis*; this time it is a rewrite of an earlier volume on self-hypnosis that I somehow missed first time around. What an excellent book this is!

It has an enormous amount to offer many different types of reader; the person who wants to learn self-hypnosis, of course, will find it invaluable and will need no other. The hypnosis clinician, whether a novice or of many years standing, will find nuggets to include in their own hypnotic work which will enhance their effectiveness and increase their positive results. This book is absolutely ideal too for the clinician about to embark on giving a course on self-hypnosis. Everything you need is here, fully and systematically explained with lots of interesting, illustrative examples from Hunter's personal self-hypnosis experience and also that of his countless clients and trainees.

There is an excellent, interesting, and informative chapter on the origins of hypnosis for those who like to understand how it all began. For readers who can't wait to get started on their personal journey, and Hunter certainly creates a wonderful sense of eagerness, he directs them immediately to the chapters on the practical steps of learning.

Hunter not only explains how and why self-hypnosis works but also why it sometimes doesn't work and the pitfalls to avoid. This is invaluable and is an area not often addressed by other writers. The very good section on earlier suggestions received from perceived authority figures, possibly deeply embedded in the unconscious mind, alerts the reader to important work that needs to be done before newer suggestions can be accepted. There are no unrealistic claims that self-hypnosis is the one and only answer to all life's problems (although he rightly reassures us that it can be the answer to very many of them) so, very properly, the reader is also advised when it might be more appropriate to seek professional help.

This book is full of insights, self-hypnosis practice activities, scripts, powerful triggers, motivational mapping tools, stress relievers, and so much more. Do read it ... you will be so glad you did!

Lynda Hudson, BA (Hons) Psych D Hyp DBSCH D Strss Mgmnt, Clinical Hypnotherapist specializing in children's problems, author of *Scripts and Strategies in Hypnotherapy with Children* and *More Scripts and Strategies in Hypnotherapy* (for adults)

Roy Hunter's book is a masterful must-read for anyone who wants to learn the art of self-hypnosis. Straightforward, easy to read, and practical to use, Hunter has put together valuable and constructive information that can be used by all to improve their lives.

Hunter has done it again with this new work. The only difference is that this time he has focused on the needs of the individual rather than the professional. This is truly a step-by-step guide to self-hypnosis and includes scripts and tips that can be used in a number of situations that we all find ourselves in from time to time – whether that be stress reduction, motivation, confidence, memory recall, or even help with habits like weight or smoking. It really is a dip in and take what you need type of book.

It is fabulous and I highly recommend it for all who would like to learn the skill of self-hypnosis.

Terri Bodell, Deputy Chair, National Association of Counsellors, Hypnotherapists and Psychotherapists

Roy Hunter's writings, without exception, show a deep and passionate belief in hypnosis and in the power of the subconscious mind to effect change. This book carries on this tradition in style. Just one look at the contents page shows the reader that they are about to go on a journey of discovery into the world of mastering change through the use of creative hypnotic strategies.

From the first chapter Roy delivers what he tells you he will, showing you *how* this book will help you, not just *telling* you that it will. It does what every great book should do, which is put you into the right "frame" of mind before you start, which is where the most profound subconscious learning takes place. Roy further educates the reader in the states of mind which enable this change to take place, giving a real sense of solidity in his message which is backed up by scientific means.

A journey back to the roots of hypnosis shows a colorful array of historical figures involved in the shaping of modern practice hypnosis; in particular, the section on "hypnotherapy" which, apart from being a fascinating historical account, adds to the weight of this book as a "must read" for anybody seriously wanting to be informed from the top about the subject.

We are then introduced to the "gateways" to effective change and just what needs to be taken into account for ultimate transformation to take place. I have long been convinced that hypnosis *alone* is not enough; that to make a real difference, a process of education needs to occur. Roy offers the reader just that, a step-by-step process of what needs to happen to help somebody achieve what they desire. Exercises in planning, "clearing," and pure plain "mental muscle" help this process take effect and become part of the *how* to change that Roy promises at the start of this book.

He continues with the power of daydreaming, helping the reader appreciate at a conscious level just how powerful the book's message is and how important it is to address what one allows to journey through the mind from moment to moment. My own love of linguistics is captured in the exquisite way Roy educates us on the power of words, to a depth I have not seen in one book before.

Finally, if it wasn't enough to tell us in such a powerful way *how* to use hypnosis to its fullest extent, as he promised he would, Roy offers further ideas as to *what* to do with this knowledge once it is acquired.

I have had the pleasure of being in some of Roy's master classes a few years ago in California, and was impressed by the depth of his knowledge back then. More so I was mesmerized by the pure joy and passion he has in his work. This book is a real gem, and one which shows his commitment to the profession like few can or do. It will go to the top of our college's reading list without doubt.

If you really want to know your stuff in the world of hypnosis and empowerment, look no further than *Mastering the Power of Self-Hypnosis*.

Tom Barber, MA, DHp, Director, Contemporary College of Therapeutic Studies, UK

It is not often that one comes across a book which will be of such great use both to individuals who wish to improve their own lives and to professionals who wish to help others to do so. Roy Hunter's explanations of theory and technique, coupled with his approachable writing style make this such a book. His explanation of the use of positive visualization and affirmations serve to enhance the confidence-boosting effects of the methods he describes. This volume will also be an invaluable aid to those studying to become professional hypnotherapists and to those who are newly qualified. It is one of the most comprehensive guides I have come across in recent years.

Ursula Markham, Founder and Principal of the Hypnothink Foundation

Mastering the Power of Self-Hypnosis

Mastering the Power of Self-Hypnosis
A Comprehensive Guide to Self-Empowerment

C. Roy Hunter, M.S., FAPHP

2nd edition

Crown House Publishing Limited
www.crownhouse.co.uk
www.crownhousepublishing.com

Accompanying audio programmes available to download from
www.crownhouse.co.uk/featured/mastering-the-power-of-self-hypnosis

Originally published in paperback by
Sterling Publishing ISBN: 0806963514

This edition published by

Crown House Publishing Ltd
Crown Buildings, Bancyfelin, Carmarthen, Wales, SA33 5ND, UK
www.crownhouse.co.uk

and

Crown House Publishing Company LLC
PO Box 2223, Williston, VT 05495
www.crownhousepublishing.com

© C. Roy Hunter 2010

The right of C. Roy Hunter to be identified as
the author of this work has been asserted by him in accordance with
the Copyright, Designs and Patents Act 1988.

Transferred to digital printing 2016.

All rights reserved. Except as permitted under current
legislation, no part of this work may be photocopied, stored in a retrieval
system, published, performed in public, adapted, broadcast, transmitted,
recorded or reproduced in any form or by any means,
without the prior permission of the copyright owners.
Enquiries should be addressed to
Crown House Publishing Limited.

British Library Cataloguing-in-Publication Data
A catalogue entry for this book is available
from the British Library.

ISBN 978-184590465-4
LCCN 2010930996

To all who seek to attain their ideal empowerment.

Foreword

Here is a secret . . . Empowerment is not a process of the conscious mind. Empowerment is an experience that results from the unconscious mind successfully striving for goals and then experiencing at the conscious level a feeling of control. You can "try" to feel empowered. You can go to a seminar about empowerment and experience a feeling of greater control and focus, for a short period of time. However, you cannot be empowered at the conscious level if that empowerment is not supported at the unconscious level of the mind.

Your sense of empowerment is about to grow. You are about to embark on a journey with Roy Hunter, one of the world's greatest hypnotherapists. Roy will share with you how to make generative change at the unconscious level of awareness so that you begin to experience greater success, a feeling of control, and the ability to reach and maintain your goals in all aspects of life.

Many books about success and goal achievement fail because they address your mind at the conscious level. Roy Hunter is going to show you how be in touch with your unconscious mind. What does this mean to you? It means you will finally be able to have the necessary tools for personal growth and empowerment.

This book doesn't stop at this goal however. You get a few bonuses along the way! You are going to see how other people just like you have experienced success with hypnotic techniques. You are going to be instructed point for point on how to work with your unconscious mind.

There will be no guesswork involved. You will learn a brilliant mental confusion technique that will help you ease into sleep at night.

For each person who utilizes the powerful life-changing material in this book, I congratulate you in advance. *Mastering the Power of*

Foreword

Self-Hypnosis is the most important and most user-friendly book about self-hypnosis I have read in over a decade.

Your guide is eminently qualified in leading you on a journey through your mind. Along the way, he will show you how to make a few significant changes at that unconscious level we have been talking about. Your life is about to change. Enjoy the ride. It is going to be exciting!

Kevin Hogan, Ph.D., DCH
Author of *The Psychology of Persuasion:
How To Persuade Others to Your Way of Thinking*

Preface

As a clinical psychologist, I have conducted considerable research into the benefits of ethical hypnosis and hypnotherapy. That research validates the often overlooked value of trance as an effective modality to help people attain their full potential.

Roy Hunter, an internationally recognized leader in the field of hypnotherapy, has done much to elevate what many psychologists refer to as "lay hypnotherapy." Roy's work truly deserves to be called professional.

Although he did not have a doctoral degree when he wrote the first edition of this book, he was awarded one for his life's experience in the art of hypnosis. Also, I am personally familiar with this author's work. His presentations and training seminars at numerous national hypnosis conventions demonstrate his dedication to hypnosis as a profession; and he has taught college level hypnosis since 1987.

In 1994 Roy's comprehensive hypnosis text was published by another publisher, and received praise from the psychology profession as well as the hypnotherapy profession. He wrote and maintains the FAQs (Frequently Asked Questions) for the worldwide alt.hypnosis newsgroup, and has written numerous articles as well as two more hypnosis texts that are highly recommended around the world.

I believe you will find Roy's writing style easy to read, yet filled with valuable insight. Reading his self-hypnosis book will be well worth your time; and you just might learn some techniques that will change your life!

Don E. Gibbons, Ph.D.

Acknowledgments

First, I wish to thank the many thousands of readers who made the first edition of this book successful; and I am grateful for the many positive comments received from a number of readers over the years. Additionally, I wish to thank Crown House Publishing for choosing to publish the second edition.

My original inspiration for this book was my late mentor and teacher, Charles Tebbetts, who through both his teaching and personal example, convinced me that the power of the mind is the greatest power in the world, as well as God's greatest gift to the human race.

I would also like to thank the many hundreds of hypnosis professionals who have personally expressed appreciation to me over the years for my teaching of the concepts presented in this book and in my other books. This praise from my peers not only validates what I have already used and taught, it also honors my late mentor who taught me both the art of self-hypnosis and the art of hypnotherapy. I would also like to express my appreciation to my friends and family, and especially to Jo-Anne for her patience during the many nights she slept alone in the "wee" hours while I finished the first version of this book, as well as her continued patience during the additional evenings and nights I spent making revisions for the second edition.

Finally, I wish to thank you, the reader, for choosing this book as your tool to greater empowerment and freedom from old subconscious programming. It is my sincere hope that you find enough valuable information to help you feel an attitude of gratitude for your new awareness. May this book help you attain your ideal self-empowerment!

Roy Hunter
May 18, 2010

Contents

Foreword vii
Preface ix
Acknowledgments xi

Part I: Introduction to Self-Hypnosis 1
Chapter 1: The Purpose of This Book 3
    Subconscious Control 3
    Making the Commitment to Change 5
    Motivation and Responsibility 7
    What Makes This Book Different? 8
    How to Use This Book 10
Chapter 2: What Is Hypnosis? 11
    Altered Consciousness 11
    The Four States of Mind 12
    Who Has the Control? 14
    What about Stage Hypnosis? 15
    How We Enter Alpha 16
    Trance Ingredients 18
    Mental Exercises for Trance Preparation 19
Chapter 3: Hypnosis Then and Now 23
    Why Explore Hypnotic History? 23
    Possible Origins of Hypnosis 24
    The Hypnotic Pioneers 25
    Hypnotic Pioneers of the Eighteenth Century 27
    Hypnosis in the Nineteenth Century 32
    The Most Common Mistake of the Pioneers 37
    Twentieth Century Hypnosis 38
    The Art of Hypnotherapy: Birth of a Profession 40
    Legal Recognition of Hypnotherapy 44
    The Future of Hypnosis 45
Chapter 4: Entering Self-Hypnosis 47
    Progressive Relaxation 47
    Alternate Exercises 51
    Personal Observations 53

Part II: Subconscious Programming 57
Chapter 5: Why Program the Subconscious? 59
    Our Mental Computer 59
    Anchoring and Triggers 60
    Old Programs Can Be Changed 62

Contents

Chapter 6: Gateways to the Subconscious 65
    Gateway 1: Repetition 65
    Gateway 2: Authority 67
    Gateway 3: Desire for Identity (Ego) 69
    Gateway 4: Hypnosis/Self-Hypnosis (Alpha) 76
    Gateway 5: Emotion 78
    Summary 81
Chapter 7: The Quintuple Whammy 85
    Hypnosis Alone Is Not Enough 85
    Methods Working Against Desired Change 87
    Analysis 87
    Combining the Motivators to Quit Smoking 88
    Combining the Motivators for Weight Management ... 90
    What about Other Goals? 91
    Dealing with Inner Conflicts 92
Chapter 8: Exercises to Manage Stress 93
    What To Do When Your Buttons Get Pushed 93
    Stress Release Options: The Healthy Choices 95
    Using the Coping Technique 97
    The Mental Mini-Vacation 98
    Sleeping at Night 101
    Other People's Successes 105

Part III: Planning the Journey 107
Chapter 9: Clearing Obstacles 109
    The Failure Trap 110
    The Justification Trap 111
    "If Only . . ." 112
    Forgiveness and Responsibility 113
    Dealing with Criticism 115
    Self-Criticism 116
    Techniques for Releasing 117
    Additional Thoughts 121
Chapter 10: Define and Celebrate Your Success 123
    What Is Your Definition of Success? 123
    Love Yourself: Celebrate Your Success! 125
    Empowerment for Peak Performance 125
Chapter 11: Choosing Goals 131
    Goal Types 132
    Goal Categories 133
Chapter 12: Prioritizing Goals 137
    Step 1: Numbering the Goals 137
    Step 2: Entering Self-Hypnosis 139
    Step 3: Using the Chart 139
    Step 4: Making the Choice 140

Step 5: Scoring 141
Step 6: Assigning Priorities 141
Step 7: Evaluating the Results 143
In Conclusion 143

Part IV: Creative Daydreaming 145
Chapter 13: Preparation 147
    Cause and Effect 147
    Selling Success to Your Subconscious 149
Chapter 14: Creative Daydreaming Exercises 151
    General Guidelines 151
    Smoking Cessation/Reduction 154
    Weight Reduction 156
    Sales/Business Motivation 159
    Job Performance 161
    Memory and Study Habits 163
    Miscellaneous Habits 164
    Motivational Goals 165
    Confidence/Self-Esteem 166
    Sports Enhancement 166
    If Your Goal Isn't Included Above 173
    When to Consider Hypnotherapy 173

Part V: Adding Words of Power 175
Chapter 15: How Words Impact the Mind 177
    Sticks and Stones 178
    The Law of Expectancy 180
    The Law of Reversed Effect 181
    The Law of Awareness 182
    Be Careful What You Say 183
Chapter 16: Choosing Your Affirmations 185
    Affirm the Desired Result 185
    Present Tense vs. Future Tense 186
    Use Active Words 187
    Be Specific 187
    I Am 188
    Why Use Affirmations? 189
    Edit Your Affirmations 189
Chapter 17: Adding a Key Word 195
    Choosing the Best Word 196
    How to Use Your Key Word 197
Chapter 18: HypnoCise 199
    Review 199
    Doing It! 201
    Tips for Success 204

Chapter 19: Where Do We Go from Here?...207
        Helping Friends and Loved Ones.....................207
        Conclusion 210

Appendices..**213**
Appendix 1: When Might Hypnotherapy Be Needed? 215
Appendix 2: Choosing a Competent Hypnotherapist 220
Appendix 3: Questions and Answers about Self-Hypnosis...................222
Appendix 4: Motivation Mapping for Smokers......................231
Appendix 5: Motivation Mapping for Weight Management................245
Appendix 6: Script for Stress Management download...........258
Appendix 7: Affirmations and Scripts......................................262

Glossary..281
Bibliography 285
Index 287
About the Author...291

Part I
Introduction to Self-Hypnosis

Chapter 1

The Purpose of This Book

Have you ever tried to change a habit pattern, or become more self-motivated, only to find your subconscious mind resisting? Motivation programs and habit control seminars attract millions of dollars annually. People investing in these courses frequently feel frustrated, however, when they find themselves unable to apply what obviously works for others. All of us sometimes find ourselves feeling like slaves to our own subconscious programming. We often get frustrated trying to accomplish seemingly simple goals. We experience inner conflicts between conscious willpower and subconscious desires.

My clients frequently ask me why willpower seems insufficient for overcoming undesired habits. I respond by explaining that acceptance of any new habit pattern requires subconscious cooperation, otherwise subconscious belief in failure undermines your conscious decision to change. A basic law of the mind is at work: whenever the conscious and subconscious are in conflict, the subconscious invariably wins! Stated another way, imagination wins out over logic. Professionals call this the *law of conflict*, and this law represents a major reason for subconscious resistance to change.

Subconscious Control

Habits are controlled by the subconscious (often called the right brain) rather than by the conscious mind (often called the left brain). We must effectively motivate the subconscious in order to overcome subconscious resistance and permanently change a habit. All too often we tend to beat up on ourselves when the right brain refuses to buy any of the numerous logical solutions attempted by the left brain, compounding guilt on top of frustration.

Self-induced guilt became even more common after the movie *The Secret* took the world by storm, as many people are unable to get "The Secret" to work for them even though it seems to work for other people. Why?

All of our present habits, mannerisms, and thought patterns represent the results of past subconscious programming from parents, teachers, peers, coworkers, television, and a variety of other sources. We frequently try to change undesired habits through willpower and/or self-discipline, only to discover logic losing to imagination because of the law of conflict. While many people may convince themselves to take the logical course of action, they still *imagine* themselves following their subconscious desires.

For example, smokers trying to quit still imagine the taste or smell of cigarettes, or dieters imagine how good junk food would taste, only to backslide into old habits. The law of conflict has been proven repeatedly by smokers and dieters, as well as by anyone encountering difficulty in trying to attain a goal.

The only lasting solution requires that we reprogram the subconscious; otherwise it will maintain control over our habits. In other words, when we have a right-brain problem, we need a right-brain solution. Hypnosis and/or self-hypnosis can easily and effectively facilitate change at a subconscious level. Increasing numbers of people are realizing the benefits of trance.

Self-hypnosis helped me so much in changing my own life that I feel compelled to share its secrets with those who are ready to accept and use these valuable secrets. During my years of private practice, I have witnessed countless clients change their lives through self-hypnosis. I also believe in the win-win philosophy, so I teach clients both in private and group sessions how to sell success to the subconscious, with the personal goal of giving people far more value than they paid for in the first place.

Clients frequently leave my office with new self-help skills. Effective use of these abilities will help people feel good about themselves and become more motivated to attain both personal and professional goals. I teach how to *master the power of self-hypnosis* and to use a style of self-hypnosis which empowers the user to enjoy greater control over what goes into the subconscious mind. My goal is to help people attain greater self-empowerment.

Subconscious programming can either propel us into achieving our goals against all the odds, or keep us from success in spite of our best efforts. In order to succeed, then, it becomes vitally important for us to learn how to gain and maintain control of our own subconscious programming; otherwise it will control us.

First we must realize that the inner mind responds better to persuasion than to force. Virtually all of us have experienced the difficulty of changing a habit pattern at one time or another. Once the subconscious learns something, it does not like to change; and the more we try to force the change, the greater the resistance.

The subconscious is, in a sense, like a rebellious child who resents force. Yet people spend megabucks on various self-help books and motivation programs, only to wonder why the subconscious won't buy the wonderful methods that willpower can't seem to incorporate. Joe Vitale, author of *The Attractor Factor*, points out the fact that we tend to attract what we imagine with emotional energy. Unfortunately, many people affirm goals consciously while imagining failure, and they attract what they imagine even though they desperately desire change.

With millions of dollars invested annually by various organizations in motivational speakers, it is obvious that people (at least consciously) are ready for change. If you are among this group, this book is for you; but first, you must make a commitment to yourself.

Making the Commitment to Change

My own experience illustrates the importance of making the commitment to change your subconscious programming. I discovered this fact the hard way. Allow me to share my journey after success unexpectedly turned into failure.

First, I frustrated myself by reading all the excellent self-help books that worked for others, but somehow failed to work for me. My conscious mind totally accepted the ideas. I even used affirmations too numerous to count, yet justifying failure simply made matters worse. Negative beliefs inhibited me from making a decision to change, because I failed to understand the role of the subconscious. At the time I wondered why, and asked successful people for help. They simply told me to change my beliefs.

A typical response one frequently hears from a successful person is, "Whatever you believe, you will achieve." Of course, successful people frequently go on to expound that if you think positively, you will get positive results. Many people teach that you get exactly what you "program" for in life. Finally I desired in earnest to change my program, but my subconscious resisted. My past proved that I had the ability to succeed, because in 1979 my net worth boasted six digits; yet within two years I was broke and deep in debt.

Certainly extenuating circumstances cluttered my best intentions, yet they represented only excuses made up by my mind to justify the rapidly disintegrating motivation. My ego prevented me from admitting that my subconscious had become programmed for failure as indicated by a counselor. I felt victimized by other people's lack of integrity, and my fear of failure caused me to imagine more setbacks. Allowing others to influence my own mental programming took its toll; and negative daydreaming now defeated my positive thinking. It was time to make a commitment to change my subconscious programming.

That pledge challenged me clear to the soul! It proved difficult at best, especially with personal and family experiences perceived as failures. Letting go of the past is easier said than done. Adding to my frustration was the fact that people who told me *what* to change could not tell me *how* to change. Worse, some of my friends actually made me feel guilty for being unable to change. I had to make a commitment to change, and to accept responsibility for my own motivation to make the necessary adjustments. Are you ready to make that same commitment?

Motivation and Responsibility

It is easy to think positively when life fills our cup with positives. We can easily stay motivated while leading active, happy, and healthy lives, but how can one stay motivated and think positively when life seems full of negatives? Do you sometimes mistake the "light at the end of the tunnel" for that of an oncoming train? I have been there and done that! Such a setback proves the importance of staying motivated.

This book shares the secrets of motivating yourself so that you may get up again and keep on going, whether your goals are personal or professional.

Sometimes motivation involves patience. For example, certain career successes may precede their financial benefits by several years (as the 1980s taught me); so we must learn to maintain our self-motivation on a long-term basis. I have learned the hard way that a wall full of plaques and national awards will not pay the bills; but a greater income will eventually follow such successes if one stays motivated.

Even if we believe that someone else is responsible for throwing obstacles in our path, let us remember that *we* must accept responsibility for the way we respond to others. Do we allow another person to defeat us, or do we claim our own power of choice and make the best out of negative experiences? While we may not be able to control others, we most certainly can learn how to manage our own actions.

We can allow our minds to be either negatively or positively programmed by our own perceptions and responses to people, places, and things. In short, others most certainly can influence our external environment, but we have total responsibility for our internal responses. We can quit, or we can choose to learn from the experience. Regardless, the subconscious records everything, including our responses and any accompanying emotions; and our subconscious programming will be influenced accordingly.

Remember: you must first make the commitment to change your subconscious programming. Only you can make that decision; then you can use this book to help you along your journey.

What Makes This Book Different?

Countless self-help books tell you *what* to change, but very few teach you *how* to change. Many discuss positive thinking and goal setting, giving you pieces of a jigsaw puzzle, while often leaving you puzzled at how to effectively stay motivated or overcome negative programming. Some books teach visualization, while others emphasize affirmations. For example, many thousands of people attest to the benefits of practicing imagery techniques. Shakti Gawain teaches imagery in her book, *Creative Visualization*. Bernie S. Siegel also understands the value and power of visualization, as evidenced in his excellent book, *Love, Medicine & Miracles*. Napoleon Hill gave us a masterpiece in his classic book, *Think and Grow Rich*.

Do you seek affirmations? Go to any metaphysical bookstore and search through the self-help books. Affirmations abound in many of these titles, along with encouragement to read applicable affirmations many times daily.

The second half of the twentieth century exploded with hundreds of self-hypnosis books written by authors with varying credentials. You can find many to choose from in almost any bookstore. I don't discount any of the techniques mentioned above. In fact, this book discusses visualization, affirmations, and self-hypnosis as well as goals; but it teaches you *how to reprogram* your subconscious, and provides some possible answers for those who try "The Secret" and fail.

This is a *self-hypnosis handbook*. In Chapter 2 I explain self-hypnosis in simple language, and then step you through several creative self-hypnosis exercises, beginning with basic relaxation. I often refer to a mental exercise as an *empowerment exercise*. Chapter 3 is devoted to trance history – included in this book to satisfy the curious. In Chapter 4 I present several simplistic but effective methods for creating your own trance.

Part II explains how the subconscious mind is programmed, followed by some exercises for managing stress and going to sleep at night.

In Part III we explore various traps caused by negative thinking, and how to escape from them so that we may clear the obstacles from our journey through life. In Chapter 10 I also present a meditation into past successes in order to help build confidence and establish a trigger for peak performance. Additionally the reader will learn how to establish priorities for important goals through another creative self-hypnosis exercise in Part IV, as well as how to sell success to the subconscious through creative daydreaming. This lengthy chapter provides numerous self-hypnosis techniques for a variety of goals, followed by two important chapters concerning the power of words and affirmations.

After mastering the self-hypnosis exercises, in Part V you may combine creative daydreaming with the proper use of affirmations for a very effective form of creative self-hypnosis for self-empowerment and motivation. I call this final mental exercise HypnoCise (the original title for my first book about self-hypnosis).

Although I teach many concepts that others have practiced for decades, I blend them with important new information and valuable insights gained from over twenty-six years of professional experience with hypnotherapy. This book shows you how to put those pieces together in a way that really works.

You will learn how to motivate your subconscious to help you achieve your goals, and how to replace negative programming with positive programming. You are then responsible for how you use what you learn. Used properly, self-hypnosis enables you to put what you choose into your own subconscious mind. Self-hypnosis enables you to become more motivated to take control of your own life, so that you may enjoy self-hypnosis for empowerment.

How to Use This Book

You may have already noticed from the table of contents that I have divided this book into five parts in order to facilitate mastering the material presented. You may skim through the entire book in one sitting for an overview if you wish; but you will gain greater benefit by spending at least five self-help sessions at separate times to digest and use the material presented. Practice any appropriate exercises in each part at least once before moving on to the next part.

You will find numerous references to smokers and people wishing to reduce their consumption of cigarettes. I include these examples to help illustrate important concepts. Let me state for the record that I believe whether or not to smoke should be a matter of personal choice. Others might wish to convince you to overcome a habit; but you can either say yes or no. *You* must be the one who seeks to change in order for this book to serve you, because your journey through life belongs to you.

Numerous mental exercises enable you to discover the power of imagination. Rather than simply reading about them, *do* them! Also, take time to master those self-hypnosis exercises that pertain to your goals. These exercises can help you gain skills that will last a lifetime, and may benefit many areas of your life. If you don't follow this advice, this book could become one more "dust collector" on your bookshelf.

Other books tell you *what* to change; this one teaches you *how* to get your subconscious to buy the changes you choose. The primary purpose of this book is to help you *master the power of self-hypnosis* as a powerful tool to help you attain your goals along your journey through life. You could also say that another objective of this book is to teach you how to win with both sides of the brain!

Chapter 2

What Is Hypnosis?

Have you ever cried real tears during a powerful movie? Your conscious mind maintained awareness of your sitting in a theater watching actors and actresses, but your subconscious accepted the movie stars as real characters. Believe it or not, you probably entered a state of hypnosis. Since the subconscious doesn't know the difference between fact and fantasy, we respond emotionally to what happens on screen. People jump or scream during a scary sequence or get excited during a juicy romance scene – yet the conscious mind knows it is only a film. I can still remember the first time I saw the movie *ET*. Almost everyone in the theater cried, including me.

Altered Consciousness

Was I asleep when I saw *ET*? Not at all! Even though my conscious mind realized that a six-million-dollar puppet played the role of the extra-terrestrial, my subconscious accepted ET as a real character. I actually experienced hypnosis (right along with the others in the theater). While I remained very aware of the movie in progress, I tuned out the usually incessant coughing, straw slurping, and throat clearing among the theater audience. Even though I remained fully awake, I definitely experienced an altered state of consciousness . . . or hypnosis.

For the newer generation, the Oscar-winning movie *Slumdog Millionaire* created many emotions among viewers who were literally hypnotized during the film, identifying with one or more characters in various ways. If movies induce hypnosis, then what is hypnosis?

Introduction to Self-Hypnosis

The word hypnosis, coined by an English physician in the nineteenth century, still gives us an inaccurate impression of trance. Although derived from the Greek word *Hypnos*, meaning sleep, hypnosis is not a state of sleep. A better definition might be altered conscious awareness (as described above). We may more accurately describe hypnosis as the same relaxed state of mind we enter daily when our brain wave activity slows down to a frequency called alpha. Everyone passes through alpha on the way to and from sleep, so we have all experienced it many thousands of times.

Our bodies become physically relaxed during this state of mind, as in meditation, so an observer could perceive us to be asleep. Appearances can be deceiving, however, as the awareness of a person in hypnosis becomes heightened and/or focused rather than lessened. With the conscious mind also relaxed, the subconscious mind becomes accessible, thus giving us expanded possibilities for change. Hollywood leads us to believe that the hypnotist has control; however, the power actually resides within the minds of each one of us as we enter hypnosis (as explained more fully later in this chapter). All hypnosis could easily be called guided self-hypnosis. I also define hypnosis as guided meditation, or guided daydreaming. While professionals still debate over the definition of hypnosis, both my own experience and the experience of many clients validate this definition.

This same state of mental relaxation should already be familiar to you, because the hypnotic state usually occurs when we feel mellow, even though we may not recognize it as hypnosis. We regularly experience four different mental states of mind, which can be measured by an electroencephalograph (EEG).

The Four States of Mind

We remain in the *beta* state for most of our waking hours. Beta compares to high gear, and is a good place for decision making, reasoning, and logic. Brain waves are above 13 cycles per second, often higher, and may or may not be rhythmic.

When our brain waves slow to between 8 and 13 cycles per second, we enter the *alpha* state of mind. This opens the door between the conscious and subconscious, and it becomes easier to access our memory banks and/or store new information. We also enjoy enhanced creativity and a greater ability to imagine. We also become more suggestible, as Hollywood exploits in movies. Whenever we enter into the alpha state – whether guided by a movie, CD, MP3, or person – we are technically hypnotized.

Below the two conscious states are *theta*, the dream state, and *delta*, which is deep sleep or total unconsciousness. Whether or not you remember your dreams, you must pass through theta on the way to and from delta. Likewise, you must pass through alpha on the way to and from sleep, even if briefly; thus we all experience hypnosis daily.

According to Dr. Barbara B. Brown, author of *Stress and the Art of Biofeedback*, experts vary in their opinions on the exact range of alpha and theta waves. Within a month of my first self-hypnosis book hitting the press, a psychologist specializing in the study of brain waves informed me that recent discoveries had indicated that the brain still produces alpha waves even when we are in a total conscious state of beta. Initially that information bothered me, creating a concern that I might have included incorrect data. A psychiatrist soon clarified that the subconscious mind usually stays in alpha, at walking speed, while the conscious mind jogs along in beta. Then, when we enter hypnosis (or meditation), both conscious and subconscious slow down to alpha, enhancing communication between the right and left brain.

Opinions still vary, so I recommend that you draw your own conclusions regarding this debate. In my view, it is more important to learn how to make your subconscious become your servant rather than your slave master. This book can help you accomplish that objective by teaching effective use of self-hypnosis. Since I tell my hypnotherapy students that I teach hypnosis as an art rather than a science, I share my opinion with all who read this book: *self-hypnosis is an art*. To master the art, you must learn the steps and then practice the exercises described in this book.

Who Has the Control?

Before we explore self-hypnosis, let us take a few pages to rip away the Hollywood mysticism from the misrepresented arts of hypnosis and self-hypnosis.

Dr. James Braid, the English physician who coined the word "hypnosis," eventually acknowledged that the power is not with the facilitator, but with the person who enters the hypnotic state. Myron Teitelbaum, M.D., author of *Hypnosis Induction Technics*, came to the same conclusion, as is evidenced in Chapter 3 of his book: "The hypnotist is merely the guide who directs and leads the subject into the trance" (p. 18).

Simply stated, hypnosis does not put you under someone else's power. A female hypnotist proved this to me personally when she hypnotized me deeply and tried a number of different ways to suggest that I shave off my beard. After several minutes of her persistent prejudice, I brought myself out of hypnosis and gave her a lecture on ethics that I hope she remembers for the rest of her life. (Needless to say, I have never allowed her to hypnotize me since.)

My own experience with clients has also proven this many times. One deepening technique I frequently use involves asking a client to imagine that the left arm feels lighter than air. Yet sometimes, even while definitely in the hypnotic state, clients sometimes reject this suggestion – often just to prove to themselves that choice still exists.

The effective hypnotist does not try to control your mind; he/she serves as an artist who facilitates your ability to use your imagination and respond to simple suggestions. In other words, I do not put a client into trance. The client creates his or her own trance state by using me as a guide, and by allowing my voice to be the point of focus. People often ask, "If this is the case, then why do so many people make spectacles of themselves during stage hypnosis shows?" There are several reasons.

What about Stage Hypnosis?

First, a stage hypnotist often prefaces the show by stating that you cannot be made to do anything against your religious or moral beliefs. If you accept that statement literally before entering hypnosis, then you just gave yourself the autosuggestion that you will do anything else the hypnotist suggests. This creates an illusion of being under the hypnotist's control.

Another reason for the success of stage hypnosis becomes obvious by recognizing people's desire to have a good time. Frequently the volunteers for a stage show know little about hypnosis, but they expect to have fun. The stage hypnotist capitalizes on this fact. Even shy people may enjoy the opportunity to be part of the show while passing the buck to the hypnotist who "gave the suggestion." Most hypnotic volunteers become very creative in carrying out suggestions on stage. It becomes comfortable simply to respond and let the hypnotist be responsible. Most volunteers are aware of audience laughter, and are usually enjoying it themselves. (This represents my personal experience during the times I have volunteered for participation in stage hypnosis shows.) Some, though, merely follow suggestions even if they do not want to – because they somehow *believe* that they are under the hypnotist's partial control. (Some hypnotists trick their subjects into accepting this belief.) These hypnotized individuals act, or rather, *react*, according to their beliefs about hypnosis before entering that state.

Often a participant will reject a suggestion even during the show. The stage hypnotist isn't concerned with why someone rejects a group suggestion, but a good entertainer will definitely notice those who do not respond and promptly send them back to their seats in the audience. This leaves an unspoken suggestion: "If you want to stay in the show, do what I say."

The subject who believes that the hypnotist retains control responds accordingly; likewise, the participant knowing who has the power will also respond accordingly. Any volunteer realizing the latter might initiate the trance termination. In 1991 I saw a woman emerge from deep trance after a suggestion she obviously resented. She gave the stage hypnotist an obscene gesture in front of hundreds of people, and then immediately returned to her seat in the audience.

Occasionally someone will do things during the show that might feel comfortable only if consciously forgotten; so he/she conveniently forgets. Even if the hypnotist suggests amnesia, the volunteer can reject that suggestion if desired, but may still pretend to forget while discussing the show with a friend afterwards. I mentioned above, however, that many individuals enter hypnosis believing that they are "under the hypnotist's power" – and people tend to get whatever they believe.

I am not against stage hypnosis when done tastefully; but I am concerned that many stage hypnotists give the wrong impression about hypnosis in exchange for a few laughs. Hypnotherapy and self-hypnosis sparkle as powerful tools for making the changes we desire in our lives. As a member of National Speakers Association, I have endeavored to spread greater awareness of the benefits of hypnotherapy and self-hypnosis. It is time we woke up to the facts and fantasies of alpha – that state of mind which we all spend so much of our lives experiencing.

How We Enter Alpha

We enter the alpha state more often than most people realize. We can be guided into hypnosis by a thing as well as by a person. Remember my description of the effect of movies? The average person enters alpha very quickly after getting engrossed in a TV program.

Have you noticed how someone can be perfectly content watching television, only to have a sudden urge to raid the refrigerator during a commercial break? This demonstrates a hypnotic response to the sponsor's suggestions. Certainly, we can modify or reject the input just as someone in formal hypnosis can reject the hypnotist's suggestions. We might see a pizza commercial and ignore it; but the conscious mind knows where to find a bag of potato chips, so your conscious mind modifies the advertiser's suggestion.

Imagination becomes powerful at such times. If the subconscious produces a brief image of munching potato chips, you can be on your feet in a flash, headed for the kitchen! It is also very easy to check the refrigerator for something else to go with the chips. Does this scenario sound familiar? You demonstrate a response to hypnotic suggestion whenever this occurs, and television becomes your hypnotist. Occasionally I find myself refusing to buy certain products simply because the commercials insult my intelligence.

Perhaps you resonate to the next scenario along with many other parents (or grandparents) of small children. The Saturday morning cartoons can totally mesmerize a child, inducing a deep trance. I have literally stood directly between the child and the TV to gain acceptance of a simple suggestion such as taking a dirty cereal bowl to the kitchen. The young, impressionable mind ignores a parent's suggestion, while accepting the sponsor's suggestion to *get the cereal with the toy enclosed.* The response becomes so automatic that the little hand enters the grocery bag, finding and opening the box of cereal even before the groceries have been put away. I am certain that I am not the only parent to witness this frequent event.

Another example of our daily trip into the alpha state is in bed at night, just before falling asleep. Have you ever gotten irate at the local barking dog while trying to go to sleep? Some time back my neighbor got a noisy German Shepherd, and my bedtime thoughts were: "I can't sleep with that [bleep] dog barking!" After several nights it became apparent that I was giving myself negative self-hypnotic suggestions to be at the dog's mercy. The resulting insomnia motivated me to reverse the outcome by thinking, "Every sound I hear makes me sleepier and sleepier." Within one week I enjoyed the ability to sleep soundly with that dog still barking just thirty feet from my bedroom window.

We can enter alpha in numerous other ways: daydreaming while driving (stay alert), staring out the window in a reverie, getting lost in a good book, sitting in church engrossed in a sermon, listening to music, or whenever we find our imaginations running freely.

Even hard rock music induces alpha in some people (although not me). Others believe that music helps them to think well. Looking at the mountains, or a lake, a waterfall, or a meadow helps others to think and/or meditate. Remember that alpha enhances memory, creativity, and the ability to imagine. It also increases our subconscious ability to respond to whatever we imagine ourselves doing.

We also enter alpha at various times during our waking hours; and while there, whatever we imagine enters the subconscious immediately. Let us also remember our own vulnerability to suggestion, so it behooves us to be careful about whatever we imagine or daydream. Entering a state of meditation, alpha, or self-hypnosis is neither good nor bad; but rather, what we think and imagine during trance will produce either a positive, neutral, or negative result.

Trance Ingredients

Four important mental components help ensure success: *imagination, belief, expectancy,* and *conviction.* I consider these to be the important ingredients of a successful trance. (These trance ingredients are detailed in my *The Art of Hypnosis: Mastering Basic Techniques.*) Let us briefly examine them now.

Imagination is the language of the subconscious. You may easily demonstrate this fact by simply imagining your favorite food when you are hungry. A smoker imagining a cigarette soon wants one, especially if trying to quit. A runner imagining exhaustion will quickly tire. A dieter imagining junk food will soon splurge. The exercises at the end of this chapter will help you discover the power of imagination.

Belief adds to the power of imagination. Whatever we believe will happen influences both our imagination and our actions. The ex-smoker who believes he/she will backslide succumbs to intensifying urges. The dieter who believes he/she will successfully reduce will succeed. Belief also applies to self-hypnosis. If you believe it will work, you are right. Hopefully the realization that you have already experienced trance will help you believe in your ability to enter trance at will. If you experience any difficulty believing in your ability to enter self-hypnosis, then I suggest that you practice the exercises in this chapter several times if necessary, as they will help prepare you for your journey into self-hypnosis.

Expectancy and *conviction* are like twins. If one expects to succeed (or fail), and becomes totally convinced of an expected outcome, that conviction virtually guarantees personal actions that match the expectation. In order to change the expectation, we must first deal with imagination and belief.

Imagination leads to belief, or vice versa. These both lead to expectation and conviction regardless of the conscious desire; and this principle applies with habits as well as the state of hypnosis. Building a positive presence of these ingredients creates a greater probability of success. The acronym is BICE (belief, imagination, conviction, and expectancy).

Let us start the process with the following mental exercises.

Mental Exercises for Trance Preparation

Stage hypnotists often take a lemon and peel it in front of an audience, pretending to suck the juice. Imagine how you might feel if you saw someone sucking on a lemon. Does your mouth react? Isn't it interesting how we can react to fantasy?

Now enjoy a more relaxing exercise. Sit back comfortably in a chair or on a couch. Either have someone read the three following paragraphs, or record the script in advance into a recorder and play it back.

> Stretch your arms out in front of you and close your eyes, and take a deep breath . . .

Introduction to Self-Hypnosis

> *[Pause briefly . . .]*
>
> Imagine that a cord is tied to one of your wrists, and a large balloon is tied to the other end of the cord, tugging your arm upward. SEE the balloon and FEEL it tugging . . .
>
> Now, imagine that you're holding an empty bucket in your other hand, and someone pours water into the bucket. SEE the water pouring, HEAR the water splashing, and FEEL the bucket getting heavier as it gets fuller and fuller . . . heavier and heavier . . . pulling your arm down . . . heavier and heavier, fuller and fuller . . . as your other arm gets higher and higher . . .

When you feel obvious movement in one (or both) arms, open your eyes. How well did you respond to the above exercise? Even a slight movement of one arm indicates the power of your imagination. The conscious mind knows that we are pretending; yet we respond to what we imagine or fantasize as though reacting to reality.

Here is another exercise demonstrating our ability to respond to fantasy.

> Clasp your hands together, interlacing your fingers. Now extend both index fingers outward, and separate them by about an inch . . .
>
> IMAGINE that you have magnets on each fingertip, with opposite poles attracting each other. SEE the magnets, and FEEL the magnetic attraction . . .

Almost all of my clients respond to at least one of these exercises. Sometimes a hypnosis student in my college class refuses to imagine what I suggest, just to test my reaction. My usual response is to put my hand near the blackboard and pretend that I am going to scratch the blackboard with my fingernails!

Did the sentence in that last paragraph give you a reaction? It is amazing how quickly my students yell out, "Don't do that!"

Even the imaginary scratch on the blackboard demonstrates how we react to imagination. In other words, *imagination is the language of the subconscious.* Practice the exercises of imagination until you find yourself responding to at least one of them. If you need to increase your belief in the power of thought, simply remember the last time that you saw someone else eating your favorite food. Did it make your mouth water? Or consider your emotional responses during a powerful movie. We are moved emotionally because of the power of imagination. Your awareness of how we respond to thoughts will help build *belief in the power of imagination,* which is important for successful self-hypnosis.

When you learn how to take control of your own imagination, self-hypnosis will feel more natural to you, making self-motivation a far greater reality for establishing positive success habits. Naturally, the two exercises with the scripts provided above will serve you with the best comfort as you prepare for self-hypnosis. Before you create your own trance, however, let us spend one chapter exploring the history of hypnosis.

Chapter 3

Hypnosis Then and Now

Even before the first edition of this book, certain experts argued over who is qualified to use professional hypnosis. Some of those same controversies still exist today, jeopardizing your freedom to choose a hypnotherapist. Understanding the history of hypnosis may help spread enlightenment, and provide greater insight into what might be behind some of these controversies.

Why Explore Hypnotic History?

Since I wrote this book primarily to be a "how to" presentation about learning and mastering the art of self-hypnosis rather than as a scientific study, some people might wonder why it includes a chapter on the history of hypnosis. Some readers might wish to skip this section and move right on into the instructional chapters. If you are among them, go to Chapter 4; but I believe that most people can benefit from understanding how and why trance today still remains under the influence of yesterday's misunderstandings.

We can gain important insight regarding the hotly debated question of who has the power during a trance. Does the hypnotist have the power, or do we all have the power inside ourselves? People still debate this issue even now. An understanding of history helps spread the enlightenment of truth; so I believe this chapter will give you greater confidence in your own use of trance work both now and in the future, whether self-induced or facilitated by another.

The long and often unhappy history of hypnosis demonstrates the roles of belief, imagination, expectation, and conviction (outlined in Chapter 2). History also reveals how ignorance of these vital ingredients of hypnosis resulted in faulty theories, some of which

Introduction to Self-Hypnosis

prevail to this day. By considering the origin and historical background of some of those early ideas of hypnosis, the resulting confusion becomes evident.

The information below comes partly from my own studies, partly from personal knowledge of certain individuals, and partly from material I received from some unpublished typed notes from research done by the late Charles Tebbetts. (I have rewritten this section from a more detailed chapter on the history of hypnosis which appears in my hypnosis text *The Art of Hypnosis*.)

Possible Origins of Hypnosis

How old is hypnosis? Believe it or not, trance may be older than history itself. As early as 3,000 BC, the Egyptians used a form of hypnosis, as proven by hieroglyphics found on tombs of that period. The Greeks also understood trance, as did the Mayas of South America. Research reveals trance artists to include Hindu fakirs, Chinese teachers of religion, Persian magi, the Celtic druids, African and American witch doctors, Shamans, and more.

Some believe that hypnosis was spontaneously discovered in each civilization of the world as its history unfolded, and that trance work will always become known in any group of people, in any setting. Why, then, does hypnosis still remain such a mystery? Contrary to the opinions of some, we cannot totally blame Hollywood.

First, consider the greedy side of human nature shared by many of the pioneers of trance. Throughout history, the elite few jealously guarded the knowledge of trance, shrouding it in mysticism and religion.

Another reason for the lack of knowledge may relate directly to another side of human nature. We tend to have fear, anxiety, or skepticism at that which we don't understand; even if that which is feared is based on scientific fact. For example, consider how people laughed at the Wright brothers. Most people in the early

1900s thought that if God had intended man to fly, he would have given us wings. Now airplanes are a part of life. Even electricity received the label of "demonic" power in the not too distant past!

Should we be surprised that hypnotism, misunderstood to this day, is only now beginning to gain recognition and wide-scale acceptance? Since the dawn of history, the selected few have hidden the secrets of trance from the average person; and certain elitists would like to again hide the power of trance from the public. My inclusion of this history chapter may help to prevent the darkness of ignorance from sending hypnosis back into the Dark Ages again.

The Hypnotic Pioneers

Hypnosis is considered both as a science and as an art. Thousands of people have contributed to the advancement of hypnotism. Those recognized by the medical community normally took a more scientific approach; but others also deserve their places in history. Some researchers categorize the hypnotic pioneers into four groups. This chapter overviews each group first, and then examines all but the first group in greater depth.

The Early Unscientific Group

This group includes most of those who experimented with trance without knowing hypnosis by that name. This group includes Genghis Khan, who used group suggestion to create hallucinations and to motivate his men to fight. While some names are remembered, many pioneers of trance never found their way into the history books. The early group also includes the seers and sages of Greece, ancient Egyptians, and tribal "witch doctors" dating back to prehistoric times. Additionally, some hypnotherapists (including myself) believe that Jesus used hypnosis with many whom He healed.

The Semi-Scientific Group

This group began researching hypnotism as a science, although some of the people in this set never heard the term "hypnosis" during their lifetimes. Some theories and research remained in esoteric realms.

The Scientific Group

The scientific group includes those who first removed hypnosis from the realms of "mysticism" and started experimenting with what hypnosis could actually do. Their efforts almost brought hypnosis out of the Dark Ages during the nineteenth century, until Sigmund Freud sent the art of trance backward many years, altering the history of hypnosis. The second and third groups are classified together in this chapter in chronological order.

The Modern Groups

The modern groups, starting in the twentieth century, include both those who teach and promote hypnotherapy as an art and/or a profession, as well as those who research hypnosis as a science. There seems to be a gulf today between the scientific community and the many thousands of dedicated full-time hypnosis professionals who successfully help clients change their lives. So you could say that the modern groups are divided between the *scientific* community and the *artistic* community.

Now let us look more closely at some of these pioneers of both the science and art of hypnotism, and explore their contributions to hypnosis. As you read these pages, be sure to look for our friends: *imagination*, *belief*, *expectation*, and *conviction*.

Hypnotic Pioneers of the Eighteenth Century

Franz Anton Mesmer

Hypnotherapists consider Mesmer to be the most famous name in the entire history of hypnosis, even though he never knew it by that name. As the first man ever to try to explain scientifically what he did, Mesmer received the title of the "Father of Hypnosis" (a name he shares with Johann Joseph Gassner and the Marquis de Puységur). Even today we speak of "mesmerizing" someone; and the hypnotherapy community still bears many references to him and his work. This undeniable tribute warrants a somewhat lengthy exploration of Mesmer's accomplishments.

Mesmer's life began in Iznang, Germany, on May 23, 1734, on the *Bodensee*, or Lake of Constance. He first studied medicine in Vienna, where he became a practicing physician. After seeing a demonstration of magnetic cures by Father Maximilian Hell in 1774, Dr. Mesmer started experimenting with magnets. He apparently borrowed his first magnets from Father Hell. (Can you believe this priest's last name?) Then, in 1766, Mesmer wrote his doctoral dissertation, *De planetarum influxu in corpus humanum* (On the Influence of the Planets on the Human Body). He believed that a general sort of magnetic fluid pervaded nature and the human body, and that this solution must be evenly distributed throughout the body for wellness. This theory received the label of "animal gravitation" and eventually became known as "animal magnetism." Although his theories intrigued many, he also blended them with astrology and metaphysics, which widened the credibility gap with the skeptics.

At first, Mesmer experimented primarily with magnets. His patients enjoyed profound results; but before long, Mesmer discovered that he could help people obtain a "cure" without the magnets. He came to believe in an invisible, voluminous fluid, which permeated everything. He believed that the liquid could be influenced by the position of the planets, as well as by his own energies. He soon modified his magnetism theories to include the fact that he somehow became endowed with more "magnetic fluid" than other people, although he believed that everyone did have a certain amount.

Mesmer's fame grew quickly, but other practicing physicians became furious and labeled him a quack. Yet in spite of the persecution, the good Dr. Mesmer just kept right on doing his work. Unfortunately, he did not know that his "cures" resulted from his artistry in inducing guided self-trance. Mesmer actually helped patients to use the power of their own subconscious minds for their cures; but his ignorance of this important fact left him without a good response after his first failure.

In attempting to cure a neurotic blind girl, beloved by the empress, he managed to help her restore her sight but found himself unable to explain her loss of equilibrium, which angered her parents greatly. The girl's father came to Mesmer's clinic demanding that he release her immediately. She begged to stay, but her father drew his blade with his demand, and she went into convulsions and lost her sight again, never to regain it.

Mesmer's critics used this incident as an excuse to drive him out of Vienna. He then moved to Paris, where he invited leading scientists to witness his demonstrations. The persecution persisted, so Mesmer turned away from the science of magnetizing people and became a showman and practiced his cures as an "art."

Mesmer's clinic became a showplace in Paris, where getting mesmerized became as popular as going up in hot air balloons. Mesmer developed the legendary *bacquet*, a round contraption, roughly a foot high, which had a seating capacity of about thirty. Holes in the top allowed subjects to grasp iron rods and receive the "magnetic flow" and *go with the flow*. The magnetic doctor enhanced the entire scenario with music, unusual lighting, and the presence of highly suggestible subjects, so that even a skeptic generally found it easy to trance out into convulsions by grasping one of the iron rods.

All this show business again brought public criticism, even from the press. Paris newspapers published cartoons depicting Mesmer with the face and ears of a donkey while magnetizing a woman. Some cartoons became demeaning and depicted both Mesmer and his followers as dogs.

Eventually King Louis XVI appointed a commission headed by Benjamin Franklin (my great (seven times) uncle) to investigate Mesmer's work. Subjects tranced out drinking water from cups that Dr. Mesmer had magnetized, so Franklin had the old doctor magnetize a cup that he gave to a woman – along with another cup of ordinary water. However, my Uncle Ben pulled the old-fashioned switch-a-roo! When the woman drank Mesmer's water, Franklin told her that the water was ordinary, and nothing happened. She then drank the water that she believed to be magnetized, and tranced out. One does not have to be a scientist to realize that the woman had the power of trance, not Dr. Mesmer.

Another experiment involved trees which Mesmer had magnetized. Again, a male subject failed to trance out at the correct tree, but instead he went into convulsions when touching the tree that he believed was magnetized. Franklin proved that Mesmer did not have the power, and correctly concluded that all his cures and theatrical results were caused by imagination. Any of us could have come to the same conclusion; yet the question of who has the power is still being debated today. I wonder if Franklin had any idea that a day would come when ethical hypnosis professionals would rely so heavily on this true observation of his.

Mesmer failed to understand the role of imagination in his successes, and went into retirement in Switzerland, where he lived quietly and sadly, occasionally treating his neighbors, until his death in 1815. Long before his death, he lost control of mesmerism, as spiritualists blended it with spiritualism. Had Anton Mesmer really understood the vital role of even just some of the ingredients of the hypnotic formula – belief, imagination, expectation, and conviction – the entire history of hypnosis may have changed course. Personally, I consider it to be tragic that both the nineteenth-century pioneers and some of the twentieth-century researchers have failed to learn from Mesmer's mistake.

Johann Joseph Gassner

Johann Joseph Gassner, a Catholic priest contemporary with Mesmer (1727–1779), worked actively with trance states. Father Gassner mastered the art of suggestion as a means of faith healing, and became perhaps the first of the modern faith healers.

His followers believed that God had endowed the priest with heavenly powers; the psychological advantage he gained from this resulted in a tremendous conviction that something would happen. As a religious authority, Gassner worked under the most favorable conditions possible for hypnotic response. People believed that he represented God's authority over them, and therefore expected things to happen when he spoke. (Does this sound familiar?)

Imagine this scenario and its dramatic affect: Father Gassner performed his trance induction in a dimly lit cathedral, muttering suggestions in Latin and circling his subjects while carrying a candle-lit, diamond-studded crucifix. The belief held by the priest's subjects caused them to easily imagine the power of God at work. Thus, he sent even difficult subjects into instant trance just by the touch of the glittering cross. The mere presence of this crucifix frequently hypnotized most subjects even before being touched. Gassner's average trance induction time was an almost unbelievable seven seconds, again proving the effectiveness of belief, imagination, expectation, and conviction.

The question remains: Who had the power? Perhaps some might believe that the power came from God, while others believe that Father Gassner used the God-given power of trance inherent in all of us. My opinion is that the power remained both with the individuals and with God; and the priest was merely the trance artist. Regardless of your own personal opinion, however, this priest got results. Many of the people Father Gassner sent into trance became well.

Marquis de Puységur

A former student of Mesmer's, Armand-Marie-Jacques de Chastenet, the Marquis de Puységur (also spelled Purségur), lived and experimented in Buzancy, France. He expanded on Mesmer's theories, and soon decided that magnets were unnecessary – so he would "magnetize" an elm tree and get results from people visiting the tree. The local populace could enjoy the latest in convulsions even in the Marquis's absence (while he apparently did more important things). Would you agree that the hypnotic formula worked here in the minds of people "magnetized" by a tree? If one were to believe that a certain tree had been magnetized, and he/she could easily imagine becoming magnetized by that same tree – and therefore expected to be magnetized – wouldn't hypnosis occur even if tied to the wrong tree? (Remember that Franklin previously observed someone trancing out after touching the wrong tree.)

Hollywood could create an interesting movie scene with the Marquis making his magnetic passes around an ominous looking elm tree. Add in some mysterious music, a few dark clouds, some lightning, and so on, and I am certain the effects would appear quite dramatic. (Sometimes my motion picture family heritage influences my methods of telling stories!)

Unfortunately, Puységur emulated Mesmer's mistake by assuming that subjects fell "under his power." Does that sound familiar? Why didn't some of these early pioneers recognize mesmerism as guided self-mesmerism?

Other Practitioners of the Eighteenth Century

All the way into the first part of the nineteenth century, many men studied and practiced hypnosis with different approaches, even though the word "hypnosis" had not yet been coined. Commissions were often formed to investigate their findings and works, writing reports just as unfavorable as Mesmer's review. Most, including Puységur, experimented with clairvoyance and extrasensory perception (ESP), thus further fueling the fires of the skeptics. But isn't it interesting that so many of these scientists explored ESP?

Hypnosis in the Nineteenth Century

Many advances to enhance trance contributed to hypnosis during the nineteenth century. I will only discuss the most important ones here.

Abbé Jose Castodi de Faria

Abbé de Faria was one of the first scientific experimenters in hypnosis, operating in Paris around 1815. He first formulated many of the theories later rediscovered by (and credited to) other men. He taught that a trance could not be induced against one's will. He also developed the "fixed-gaze method" of induction, leading to numerous induction techniques used both then and now that incorporate eye fixation.

Faria's reputation faded when several jealous doctors hired some people to pose as subjects for him at a public demonstration. The bogus subjects pretended to go into trance very quickly and easily. At a predetermined moment, they jumped up and announced that they were shamming, and falsely claimed that Faria had paid them. This disgusting product of jealousy discredited Faria, and he lost all of the recognition he justly deserved. Today one of Faria's direct descendents is involved with hypnosis.

John Elliotson

John Elliotson, born in 1791, served as a professor of theory and practice at University Hospital in London, England. Beginning his experiments in 1837, Elliotson found that his patients could undergo major surgery without pain, and he applied these techniques whenever possible. This incurred the wrath of his fellow physicians. Elliotson also believed in clairvoyance, so the envious doctors used this as extra ammunition and put his hypnosis work into the same dubious category.

Certain skeptics escalated their opinions into open controversy, demanding that Elliotson discontinue his trance work. After a stormy scene, he left the hospital and university, never to return. As you might expect, officials formed a specially appointed commission and "cleaned away" all traces of mesmerism behind him. The scientific community of the time dealt another tragic blow at the heart of hypnotism, targeting its leading scientific practitioner. Apparently at that time most people with scientific minds wanted facts, but not alternative ideas; even if the unorthodox theories provided profound benefit to some individuals.

James Braid

James Braid (1795–1860), a prominent Scottish surgeon, became famous for coining the word "hypnosis" (derived from *Hypnos*, the Greek god of sleep). He performed numerous experiments with trance, formulated theories, and wrote about them.

Braid's work helped advance hypnosis greatly, as he became the first man to be recognized for scientific experimentation into the "why's" of mesmerism. He also developed another eye-fixation type induction technique with the use of bright light, and discovered how to enhance the trance with much more emphasis on vocal suggestions. He also believed that trance depended on the suggestibility of the subject, which could be influenced greatly by vocal suggestions from the hypnotist.

Braid made one glaring mistake that still impacts hypnosis today. He assumed that something physiological took place as a result of the fixed-gaze techniques, which created an absence of volition; thus Braid failed to realize that all hypnosis is self-hypnosis. (Some of my peers believe that Braid eventually recognized where the true power resides.)

Most of us acknowledge Braid primarily for giving hypnotism its name, which remains to this day in spite of many efforts to change or disguise the word. Even some modern day practitioners attempt to mask the practice of hypnotism with other names (such as "group meditation," "programmed imagery," "guided relaxation," "guided imagery," "creative visualization," etc.), but the word "hypnosis" is obviously here to stay.

James Esdaile

While Braid made quantum leaps with hypnosis, another Scottish doctor, James Esdaile (1808–1859), experimented and gained permanent recognition in the history of hypnosis. Stationed in Hooghly, in West Bengal, India, Esdaile used hypnosis in surgery with astounding results; even today many would say that his work with applied hypnosis almost borders on the fantastic. Reports he submitted at the end of 1846 indicate that he performed several thousand minor operations and about 300 major ones, including nineteen amputations, all painlessly. Due mostly to the removal of post-operative shock through hypnosis, he cut the 50% mortality rate of the time down to less than 8%. (One book even reported less than 5%.) His report to the Medical Association received acceptance, and he continued his "mesmerist" operations at the Calcutta hospital.

While the Association considered mesmerism taboo at University Hospital, mesmerism could quite easily be expected to work for the uneducated masses in India, long known as the home of the occult sciences. Esdaile had assurance of success from the very beginning because of the common belief system. When Esdaile returned home, he was unable to duplicate his work because of lack of belief and negative expectation; so his career went down the same dark path of discouragement taken by Elliotson.

The Nancy School: Bernheim and Liébeault

In 1864 a country doctor, Ambroise-Auguste Liébeault, settled in Nancy, France. He established his practice there, treating patients either hypnotically or with medicine.

Liébeault offered his hypnotic treatments for free, which naturally made them popular. These treatments lasted only about ten minutes, and the doctor stated quite clearly that he had no supernatural power. He became the first man we know of to have taught that hypnosis is purely a matter of suggestion – so he courageously took the first step on a new path.

Hippolyte Bernheim, a professor of medicine at the Nancy Medical School, wrote an article discrediting Liébeault as a fraud; but a visit to Liébeault's clinic convinced him otherwise. Liébeault's methods gained results, so the two men eventually joined forces and founded history's most renowned center for hypnotic healing: the Nancy School became an institution both in actuality and in thought.

The art of hypnosis had taken another giant leap forward. Perhaps the biggest mistake at the Nancy School, however, resulted from the belief that once a person entered hypnosis, the physician had the power rather than the patient.

The School of Salpêtrière: Charcot

At the same time as Bernhiem and Liébeault were engaged in their studies of hypnotism in Nancy, Dr. Jean-Martin Charcot was experimenting with hypnosis in his clinic at the Salpêtrière Hospital in Paris. He became the first person to identify and label the various levels of hypnotic depth.

Although one of the most advanced neurologists of his day, Charcot made several mistakes when he approached the new subject. Basically, he believed that hypnosis was a phenomenon that could best be studied with patients of hysteria, and taught that hypnosis was a pathological state. Even though Charcot's primary ideas about hypnosis may have been incorrect, he made an important discovery in recognizing the various levels of hypnosis.

Charcot named the three stages, in order, as lethargy, catalepsy, and somnambulism. Various hypnotists use other scales comprising four, five, seven, or even more stages of trance depth, but the three-step scale devised by Charcot continues to be the most practical.

Nineteenth Century Hypnosis at Its Height

By the late nineteenth century, both public and medical acceptance of hypnotism as a science throughout Europe had become a reality. Great strides became evident in almost every medical field through the application of hypnosis by the scientific pioneers who explored various therapeutic uses of hypnotism. However, most of these early successes resulted from the mistaken belief that people experiencing hypnosis were subject to the suggestion of the practitioner.

Since this became the expectation on the part of both the subject as well as the hypnotist, we can only speculate on how many successes might actually have resulted from the "placebo" effect – especially since most of these pioneers used suggestion alone. As most patients were convinced that the physician understood the use of hypnotism, they could easily imagine being under the sway of a powerful medical authority. The hypnotized person who believed in results frequently enjoyed the cure that was expected.

Apparently many of the cures lasted permanently; then along came Freud.

Hypnosis Regresses

Sigmund Freud, attracted to the research of Joseph Breuer, studied hypnosis at both the Nancy and Salpêtrière schools, but disagreed with Charcot in two important areas. First, Freud discarded the theory about hypnosis being useful only for hysterics. Second, he did not believe that deep levels of hypnosis were necessary for change; but, rather, taught that suggestions could be accepted and past events recalled even in a light state of trance. Unfortunately for the future of hypnotism at that time, Freud apparently was a poor artist in the skill of induction. According to Billa Zanuso, author of *The Young Freud: The Origins of Psychoanalysis in Late Nineteenth-Century Viennese Culture*, Freud admitted that he wearied quickly of the "monotony of the sleep suggestions."

While working with one patient, Freud failed to induce a hypnotic trance. He had almost reached the point of despair when, in desperation, he hit on the idea of trying free association in the waking state. The case proved to be successful, and Freud apparently welcomed the opportunity to drop hypnosis from his methods, creating and publicizing the technique of psychoanalysis. He then taught that psychoanalysis was now "the executor of the estate left by hypnotism," and led a general abandonment of its use. He now discouraged many practitioners from using hypnosis by teaching that psychosomatic symptoms served an important economic function in the psychic life of the patient; and he labeled the use of hypnosis as irrational. From literally thousands of articles written about hypnotism annually, the number dwindled to several dozen. (Perhaps it is a great blessing that the good doctor could not control his subjects, otherwise hypnosis might be totally controlled by psychologists and/or the medical profession.)

Despite hypnotism's terrific advancement, Freud managed to give hypnosis a hypnotic regression backward in time, leaving its flames of interest just barely flickering.

The Most Common Mistake of the Pioneers

A familiar thread runs through the accounts discussed so far in this chapter: all of the researchers believed that *they* held the power, and that the individuals subject to their experiments gave up their free will and subjected themselves to the operator (hence the word subject). Nicholas Spanos and John Chaves write, in *Hypnosis: The Cognitive-Behavioral Perspective*:

> The history of hypnosis contains repeated references to the so-called classic suggestion effect, the apparent absence of volition in the performances of hypnosis subjects. This apparent lack of agency was not problematic to those scientists and practitioners who subscribed to the mental state theory. Given that the person was regarded as an object or organism, the scientific observer would merely record evidence of purported happenings within the organism. It was thus irrelevant to raise the question whether the subject willfully performed a particular action. (p. 403)

Note carefully that last statement: "It was thus irrelevant to raise the question whether the subject willfully performed a particular action." The authors also point out in the same work the fact that both Mesmer and Puységur claimed that results depended upon the "special prowess or supernatural skills" of the hypnotist, causing the "magnetized" person to behave as a virtual automaton (p. 79).

Perhaps if any of our pioneers had understood all the components of the hypnotic formula, they might have come to the conclusion that all hypnosis is guided self-hypnosis, or vice versa. Also, had Freud taken a quantum leap forward and realized this, both the history of hypnosis and the history of psychology would have been forever altered. Instead, the twentieth century dawned with hypnosis virtually in the Dark Ages again; but this century would find an amazing hypnotic evolution taking place in its latter decades.

Twentieth Century Hypnosis

During the time between Freud's discoveries and the First World War, only the efforts of a few interested men kept hypnosis from vanishing entirely. Émile Coué de Châtaigneraie (1857–1926) made some lasting contributions, especially with his theories of waking hypnosis and autosuggestion. He took a totally new and innovative approach for his time. Coué explained the law of conflict (briefly mentioned in the Chapter 1), calling it "will and imagination." In his work *Self-Mastery through Conscious Autosuggestion*, he stated:

> *This will that we claim so proudly, always yields to the imagination. It is an absolute rule that admits of no exception.*
>
> *"Blasphemy! Paradox!" you will exclaim. "Not at all! On the contrary, it is the purest truth," I shall reply . . .*
>
> *Suppose that we place on the ground a plank 30 feet long by 1 foot wide. It is evident that everybody will be capable of going from one end to the other of this plank without stepping over the edge. But now change the conditions of the experiment, and imagine this plank placed at the height of the towers of a cathedral. Who then will be capable of advancing even a few feet along this narrow path?* (p. 7)

Even this explanation of the law of conflict remains a very significant contribution by Coué, as he seemed to realize where the power resides. Many hypnotherapists to this day use various metaphors to illustrate the law of conflict; I wonder how many trance artists appreciate that Coué gave us this important contribution. His understanding of the law of conflict is vital to anyone practicing hypnosis or self-hypnosis.

A few others made scientific contributions in the early twentieth century; but perhaps those who entertained with stage hypnosis did more than most people realize to keep the flames of interest flickering. Throughout time these entertainers and masters in the art of stage hypnosis have preserved the general interest in hypnosis through compelling public demonstrations.

After the First World War, trauma caused by the anxiety of conflict resulted in an acute need for a fast method of therapy. In desperation the medical profession turned again to hypnosis. In the Second World War, history repeated itself. Reports of the successful treatment of these men became available after the war, and young doctors, unafraid of the new techniques, began applying hypnosis in dentistry, obstetrics, dermatology, and other fields. Once again, the use of medical applications of hypnosis started its journey on the upswing.

By the middle of the twentieth century, Dave Elman was helping the growing trend in the medical community by teaching hypnosis to many doctors and surgeons. Then, in 1958, the Council on Mental Health of the American Medical Association finally accepted the use of hypnosis.

Among the later twentieth century scientific researchers, one name shines out brilliantly above all others: Milton Erickson. He became recognized as the most important contributor to the acceptance of both medical uses of hypnotism and the art of hypnotherapy. This late psychiatrist, often called the grandfather of hypnotherapy, forever changed the history of hypnosis. People with outstanding professional credentials have examined, analyzed, and written books about the work of Milton Erickson. Meanwhile, many professional hypnotherapists who approach hypnotherapy as an art consider Dr. Erickson to be a master of hypnosis who worked intuitively. Erickson's success speaks loudly regardless of one's perception of his methods.

The names of many other twentieth century hypnotic researchers and experimenters appear in scientific books and articles from this period; but let us consider an important development in the history of hypnosis.

The Art of Hypnotherapy: Birth of a Profession

As Erickson began his vitally important work, the seeds had already began to grow for the birth of hypnosis as an *art*, a profession composed of men and women dedicated to the use of hypnosis and hypnotherapy to help people improve their lives.

These many dedicated professionals employ hypnosis for numerous non-medical uses – such as motivation, habit control, and so on. However, with a medical referral, many professional artists of hypnosis can also treat problems such as pain management.

This legitimate profession of men and women dedicated to helping people almost exclusively with hypnosis and hypnotherapy has produced its own superstars. Names like Ormond McGill and Charles Tebbetts became legends before their passing. Both of these men were considered masters of the art. Ormond McGill traveled the world performing stage hypnosis during much of the twentieth century and wrote numerous books on hypnotism and meditation. Charles Tebbetts started out as a stage hypnotist, eventually using hypnosis as an avocation alongside an advertising career. Eventually he returned to full-time hypnotherapy and went on to become an outstanding teacher of hypnotherapy. Some masters of hypnosis in the artistic group have formed professional hypnotherapy associations and/or devoted themselves to helping people through the art of hypnosis.

Rexford L. North was a stage hypnotist during the 1940s, who eventually lost his hearing. In spite of being deaf, he became a teacher of professional hypnosis and founded the National Guild of Hypnotists, which grew to become the world's largest hypnosis association before the end of the twentieth century. Additionally, according to Dwight Damon in *The Amazing Stone-Deaf Hypnotist: Dr. Rexford L. North,* North trained some notable names in the scientific community, including Dr. Martin Orne.

Countless numbers of clients validate the benefits of the hypnotherapy profession. Hundreds of thousands of former smokers can attest to this fact, as well as countless more whose lives have been improved by other non-medical uses of hypnosis. Yet now, in a strange twist of history repeating itself, some of the worst criticism of professional hypnotherapists comes from the very same psychological and medical communities researching and advocating the scientific uses of hypnotism.

Even though many doctors and psychologists acknowledge the hypnotherapy profession, a small few would like to suppress and outlaw the use of hypnosis by "lay hypnotists" and gain legal control of its use. (Isn't this reminiscent of how the elite in ancient times sought to preserve the secrets of trance inductions?)

Unfortunate hypnotherapists in Texas woke up one morning in 1995 only to find their livelihoods legislated out of existence. A change in the legal definition of the practice of psychology made it illegal for even a well-trained veteran hypnotherapist to practice in the state. Meanwhile, a licensed mental health counselor could practice hypnosis after only a three-day course, or even if only self-taught in the art of hypnosis – simply because of the counselor credentials.

On the flip side of the coin, many so-called hypnotherapists do engage in practice with only a few days of training. These people unwisely give ammunition to our critics by making mistakes and refusing more comprehensive training. Yet many of us believe that we can build better bridges with the scientific group by upgrading our training standards within the profession. Both the scientific and hypnotherapy communities must find ways to enhance communication and cooperation to bridge the gulf and keep hypnotherapy alive.

Bridging the Great Gulf

Some people within the medical and academic community believe in crossing the gulf, wisely basing their opinions on the fact that results are more important than academic credentials.

A modern pioneer, Arthur Winkler, bridged the gulf by establishing a professional training program for hypnotherapists without discriminating against those who lack advanced degrees. He obtained his doctorates in clinical psychology and in theology, but then chose to become a hypnotherapist instead of a clinical psychologist.

Bernie Siegel, M.D., who has done wonders with hypnosis in the treatment of cancer, has gone so far as to recommend hypnotherapy in his book, *Love, Medicine & Miracles*:

> *A hypnotherapist can be valuable in the beginning, especially if the patient has trouble entering the state of deep relaxation. No matter who sets the course for the first meditative sessions – doctor, counselor, hypnotherapist, or the patient . . .* (p. 230)

Dr. Siegel has helped to bridge the gulf by evidencing public acceptance of the hypnotherapy profession, both in his book and elsewhere. In addition, increasing numbers of physicians, psychiatrists, and psychologists refer some of their patients to hypnotherapists when it is deemed to be helpful; and ethical hypnotherapists who know their limitations refer clients back to other professionals as appropriate. Dr. Siegel has also demonstrated his professionalism by example: speaking at hypnosis conferences that a few might consider to be "lay hypnosis" conventions.

Where Is Hypnotherapy Today?

In the latter decades of the twentieth century, hypnotherapy finally came into its own both in the USA and abroad. Skyrocketing as a profession, hypnosis enjoys more popularity than at any other time. Numerous state, national, and international professional hypnosis associations have sprung up in recent years. These associations promote hypnotherapy as a career to people outside the medical community who wish to devote themselves full time to the practice of the art.

Charles Tebbetts became a living legend during his lifetime. He taught client-centered techniques, and also taught emphatically that all hypnosis is guided self-hypnosis, truly making hypnosis an art. Ormond McGill, author of numerous hypnosis books, earned the title "Dean of American Hypnotists" even though he was not exclusive to any one hypnosis association. Here are the names (in alphabetical order) of other individuals who deserve to go down in hypnosis history: Harry Aarons (founder of the Association to Advance Ethical Hypnosis), Gil Boyne (founder of the American Council of Hypnotist Examiners), Dwight Damon (current president of the National Guild of Hypnotists (as of 2009) and charter member of NGH), John Kappas (founder of the Hypnosis Motivation Institute), Al Krasner (founder of the American Institute of Hypnotherapy), Sol Lewis (hypnosis instructor with decades of experience), Anne Spencer (founder of the International Medical Dental Hypnotherapy Association), and many others.

Legal Recognition of Hypnotherapy

One of the biggest breakthroughs for the hypnotherapy profession came in 1987 in Washington State, which passed a law legally recognizing the hypnotherapy profession. This happened through the combined efforts of Charles Tebbetts, Fred Gilmore (a director of the Washington Hypnosis Association), and Bill Kiskaddon, M.S.W. (a certified hypnotherapist as well as a credentialed family and marriage counselor), a state senator at the time.

The passage of Substitute House Bill No. 129 in Washington made history. This bill provided two great benefits for hypnotherapy within the state: (1) It provides a greater degree of public safety by requiring all hypnotherapists to register with the professional licensing division and to adhere to the Uniform Disciplinary Code requiring certain professional ethics and (2) this legal recognition has helped hypnotherapy take a quantum leap within Washington.

The Hypnosis Motivation Institute in California, founded in 1967 by Dr. John Kappas, has one of the best hypnosis training programs in the country. Additionally, and perhaps more significantly, Dr. Kappas became instrumental in obtaining legislative assistance from an affiliate of the American Federation of Labor and Congress of Industrial Organizations (AFL-CIO) to help keep hypnotherapy legal.

The National Guild of Hypnotists eventually jumped on board by forming the Office and Professional Employees International Union (Local 104 OPEIU-ALF/CIO), and played a key role in stopping detrimental legislation in Florida and other states. Also, a unifying organization called the Council of Professional Hypnosis Organizations (COPHO) was organized to create a greater unity and national acceptance of hypnotherapy. COPHO has other goals designed to help raise the professionalism of hypnotherapy and help assure its survival and acceptance as a self-regulating profession.

As of the writing of this book, the hypnosis profession unfortunately still remains divided; but it is my hope that we can find a greater unity during my life. We are still a relatively new profession with growing pains.

The Future of Hypnosis

Many thousands of hypnotherapists specialize in non-medical applications of hypnosis, as well as some therapeutic applications under medical referral and/or supervision. Furthermore, increasing numbers of people with medical backgrounds and other more advanced degrees support the various professional hypnosis organizations, working to help promote hypnotherapy in a way that will finally bring trance work out of the Dark Ages once and for all.

Just recently I saw a network news program presenting the importance of the spiritual connection in healing – or, put into other words, the importance of the mind–body–spirit connection. The program went on to explain that some hospitals now recognize the value of spiritual faith and prayer in the healing process. Additionally, they employ chaplains to help their patients accelerate the healing process. Furthermore, medical programs in some universities now offer classes on the spiritual aspects of healing. Personally, this makes me rejoice; because it is my personal opinion that hypnotherapy is a spiritual profession that can help heal this planet. However, the hypnotherapist must be competently trained, and must work from a sincere desire to help the client (or patient). He/she must be willing to cooperate with the medical community as well as to work for the best interests of the client. In so doing, we can finally build a bridge between hypnotherapy and traditional health care. If hypnotherapy is to survive, then this bridge must be built.

During my research of twentieth century hypnosis, it became obvious that many important discoveries regarding the use of hypnosis actually originated from the artistic community; so I thank God that we have survived into the twenty-first century.

The future of hypnosis finally looks bright – perhaps bright enough to grow into its true full potential and reach total enlightenment.

Chapter 4

Entering Self-Hypnosis

Now that you know something about the alpha state, are you ready to experience it? The first self-hypnosis exercise, called progressive relaxation, represents only one of thousands of methods of entering an alpha state. If you have learned a different method from another book (or from a seminar) use whatever method you prefer as long as it works for you.

I suggest that you read through this exercise once or twice to become familiar with the content before you begin using the technique. The specific words you use can vary from the typical session suggested here; but you should always follow the basic format.

Progressive Relaxation

Find a comfortable place to recline or lie down. If you wear hard contact lenses, remove them. If you chew gum, throw it away. Also ensure that your clothing feels comfortable. If possible, unplug your phone or turn on your answering machine, and make certain to put your pets in another room. Some animals seem to sense the mental peace you feel in the alpha state, and they may want to be close. (Experience has taught me that a cat suddenly pouncing on your stomach during relaxation can come as quite a shock!)

Now that you are comfortable, take several deep breaths. Close your eyes if you wish. Imagine yourself letting go of all of your cares and tensions as easily as you let go of the air from your lungs.

Background music is optional, but recommended if you meditate in an area where there may be distracting background noise.

Introduction to Self-Hypnosis

Think to yourself words like the sans-serif script on the following pages while fantasizing being in a peaceful place. That serene place can be a beach, the woods, a waterfall, lake, stream, meadow, and so on.

Note: The grammar is often imperfect, because the words are intended for the subconscious rather than the conscious mind. Three dots (. . .) indicate a pause.

> As I now imagine a relaxing sensation entering my toes, my breathing continues to be free and easy, just as when I sleep. The relaxation becomes more and more real with each breath I take, moving up into my feet . . .
>
> It feels sooooo good to relax that it becomes easy, comfortable, and automatic for the relaxation to move up into my ankles . . . The relaxing sensation becomes more and more real with each breath I take. It now moves up into my calves. All my nerves and muscles just let go, responding to my desire to relax . . . The relaxation moves right on through my knees, going up into my thighs . . . all the nerves and muscles letting go into a deeper and deeper state of relaxation.
>
> My hips relax. It feels sooooo good to relax, that the feeling continues right on into my stomach muscles and up around my rib cage.
>
> With each breath I go deeper and deeper relaxed. The relaxation moves on into my lower back, going right up into my shoulders, just as though gentle fingers have just given me a soothing back rub. The soothing feeling of relaxation moves down through my elbows, going right on out through my hands and fingers . . . With each breath I take, I just go deeper and deeper . . .
>
> The back of my neck relaxes . . . My scalp relaxes . . . It feels sooooo good to relax that the feeling of soothing comfort moves into my forehead and temples. With each breath I just go deeper and deeper. My cheeks relax. My jaw muscles relax . . . My entire body now feels completely relaxed . . .

Entering Self-Hypnosis

At this point you may very well be in a light or medium state of alpha consciousness from this sample induction. If you practice self-hypnosis at night before going to sleep, you may find yourself sound asleep long before you finish the exercise. Some of my clients tend to fall asleep before getting past their knees. If you still feel considerable awareness, however, you may wish to deepen the relaxation by using additional self-talk as follows:

> As I now count from ten down to one, I become deeper and deeper relaxed with each number. . . just drifting down into a very soothing tranquility.
>
> Number ten: deeper and deeper, relaxing physically . . .
>
> Number nine: deeper and deeper, relaxing mentally . . .
>
> Number eight: deeper and deeper, relaxing emotionally . . .
>
> Number seven: deeper and deeper, relaxing totally . . .
>
> Number six: every nerve and muscle relaxes completely . . .
>
> Number five: each number taking me deeper and deeper . . .
>
> Number four: the deeper I go, the easier it is to go deeper . . .
>
> Number three: just drifting into total relaxation . . .
>
> Number two: just drifting into deeeeep hypnotic peace . . .
>
> Number one: waaaaay down deep . . .

Again, some people may benefit by also fantasizing a peaceful place with pleasant sights, sounds, and feelings. Others may prefer to use the script as written, without the added "safe place." Make your own choice. If you prefer, you can record this script, changing all the "I" and "my" words into the second-person format.

You may experience time distortion, finding that time seems to condense or expand (ten minutes seems like two or twenty).

Also, you may notice that your mind tends to wander. In fact, your thoughts may drift considerably as you go deeper into the alpha state. You may have to keep bringing yourself back to each new number, sometimes forgetting the last number counted. If this happens, just go on with the first number that comes to your mind. Some of you may have to count down twice to get deeper, or count from a higher number. Many people start the countdown with twenty, and some even start with 100. You make the choice.

You may return to full beta awareness by simply telling yourself that you feel wonderful and wide awake at the count of five. Then count from one to five either mentally or out loud. If you wish, use the following script as a guide.

> Now, I am going to count from one up to five and then I am going to say "fully aware." At the count of five, my eyelids open and I feel calm, refreshed, relaxed, fully aware, and normal in every way.
>
> One . . . Slowly, calmly, easily, and gently returning to full awareness once again.
>
> Two . . . Each muscle and nerve in my body is loose, limp, and relaxed, and I feel wonderfully good.
>
> Three . . . From head to toe I am feeling perfect in every way . . . physically perfect, mentally alert, and emotionally serene . . . and when I get behind the wheel of my vehicle, I am totally alert in every way, responding appropriately to all traffic and road situations.
>
> Number four . . . My eyes begin to feel sparkling clear, just as though they were bathed in fresh spring water. On the next number now, my eyelids open and I am then calm, rested, refreshed, fully aware, and feeling good in every way.
>
> Number five . . . Eyelids open now. I am fully aware once again.
>
> Take a deep breath, fill up your lungs, and stretch.

While some clients find that they can enjoy progressive relaxation during the first attempt, most others find that they must practice the technique several times first. A minority of clients may also need other techniques; so some readers may be asking an important question: "What if I don't respond to progressive relaxation?" I can best answer that question by providing additional options.

Alternate Exercises

A minority of people may find their patience wearing thin when trying to enter self-hypnosis with the technique described above. Although you certainly have the option of choosing a hypnotherapist to help you, one of the following alternate inductions may help you attain an alpha state.

Eye Fixation

Get comfortably seated, reclining or lying down. Stare at an object, such as a candle or dim light. A candle works well because the flickering produces eye fatigue (although you may use any object if your eyes are sensitive to light). Take two or three very deep breaths before you begin. Now stare at your chosen object, and imagine your eyelids are getting heavier and heavier with each breath you take. Say to yourself:

> As I try to keep my eyes focused on the candle *[light, or other object]*, my eyelids become heavier, droopy and drowsy . . . The harder I try to keep my eyes open, the more they want to close . . . As I breathe deeply and slowly, my entire body just wants to relax and let go . . . relax and let go . . . until my eyes just want to close all by themselves . . .

Repeat this until you find your eyes getting so tired that they have to close. Once your eyes finally close, continue with the deepening described in the progressive relaxation script.

Introduction to Self-Hypnosis

This eye-fixation technique works well as an alternative for those who do not respond to progressive relaxation. A Boeing employee told me some years ago that he could stare at a candle and simultaneously imagine his arm feeling lighter than air. Within seconds his arm floated with an apparent weightless feeling. He demonstrated his ability in my office, putting himself into a deep trance within a minute. Naturally, his ability made my work with him much easier. He combined eye fixation with a variation on mental misdirection, which is discussed next.

Mental Misdirection

Some hypnotherapists use the imagination to create a physical response, *misdirecting* the conscious attention in order to produce a trance. You can do this for yourself by taking one of the exercises described in Chapter 2 and holding the imaginary water bucket a little longer.

Get comfortably seated or reclined. Now hold your arms up in front of you and imagine the bucket and balloons as mentioned in the earlier exercise.

> I now imagine that a cord is tied to my wrist, and a hundred helium balloons are tied to the other end of the cord, tugging my arm upward. I can SEE the balloons and FEEL them tugging . . .
>
> I'm holding an empty bucket in the other hand, and someone pours water into the bucket. I can SEE the water pouring, HEAR the water splashing, and FEEL the bucket getting heavier as it gets fuller and fuller . . . heavier and heavier . . . pulling my arm down . . . heavier and heavier, fuller and fuller . . . as my other arm gets higher and higher . . .
>
> As the bucket gets heavier and fuller, my arm just wants to release the bucket as I release myself into trance . . . The harder I try to hold up the bucket, the heavier it gets . . . until I release the bucket and release myself into trance . . . When I release the bucket, my arm drops and I just drop off into deep,

> hypnotic peace . . . or I can release myself into total relaxation . . .

If you feel responsive to your imagination at this point, you can drop both arms down and proceed with the counting as described earlier in this chapter; otherwise continue as follows.

> Someone DOUBLES the number of helium balloons, while someone else drops a rock into my bucket . . . The bucket is getting SO HEAVY that it would be so easy to just release the bucket and release myself into trance . . . It's so easy to release the bucket and just release myself into trance . . .

Drop your arms into your lap now, and proceed with the counting previously described for deepening your trance. Use the awakening technique described above when you are ready to return to beta consciousness.

Very few of my clients use mental misdirection to enter self-hypnosis; but some of my professional hypnosis students report satisfying results. You may wish to try all the techniques described in this chapter several times, and choose the one you like the best.

Personal Observations

Some people drift off to sleep practicing self-hypnosis, so be sure to set an alarm unless you have time for a nap. Many people remain very aware and start noticing distracting sounds or physical feelings, such as uncomfortable clothing, an itch, and so on. When you enter a light state of alpha, you have an increased awareness of anything perceived through the five senses. Rather than thinking that you might not be in hypnosis because of hearing background noise and so on, recognize your increased awareness as a signal that you have already reached a light trance state.

If the counting fails to deepen you to your satisfaction, you may try other helpful techniques involving the additional use of your imagination. For example, if desired, you can use an imaginary elevator to help you go deeper. If you don't like elevators, use an escalator, slide, or steps. You could also be floating into a cloud, walking into the woods, lying on a beach listening to waves of relaxation, or you may be getting into an imaginary jacuzzi. (Note: Do not do this exercise while sitting in a real jacuzzi!) Again, you may incorporate these deepening techniques with any of the induction exercises described in this chapter; another deepening technique involves adding a peaceful place to the meditation. (Chapter 8 contains an empowerment exercise to help you enjoy your peaceful place.)

The degree of success varies from person to person. Some of you may find the progressive relaxation technique works great the first time. Others may have to practice all the above techniques (as I did) until finding the best one. In fact, I had so much stress when I first tried self-hypnosis that I had to go to a hypnotherapist for post-hypnotic suggestion to help me learn self-hypnosis. Even simple meditation had proven difficult previously because others instructed me to simply "blank out" my mind. Well, that is difficult if not almost impossible for me to do, because even when I relax, my mind still runs a thousand miles per second. (That is why I create my own safe place in my mind when relaxing; you may find benefit in doing likewise.) Remember that imagination is the language of the subconscious; so *imagine* your peaceful place even if your conscious mind is thinking many times faster than the spoken voice.

Practice entering self-hypnosis through each of the exercises in this chapter at least once before attempting any of the other self-hypnosis exercises in this book. As you develop your ability to relax, you may find yourself able to enter an alpha state easily by taking two or three deep breaths and thinking the word "relax" each time you exhale. Numerous clients create what they call a "centering" technique to help them enter the alpha state more easily each time; and some of my students refine their centering into a signal for quickly entering the alpha state. Employing such a trigger for instant self-hypnosis has many benefits.

If you feel you need help, find a qualified hypnotherapist in your area to work with you. (Refer to Appendix 2 for tips on finding a qualified hypnotherapist.) If you wish, you may make a recording of your voice for any of the above scripts and listen to the suggestions to relax. If you prefer this method, remember to change "I am" to "you are" rather than keeping the first-person format. Good luck!

Part II
Subconscious Programming

Chapter 5

Why Program the Subconscious?

What do motivational seminars and New Year's resolutions have in common? Most people forget them by the following week. Why does this happen? We may set ambitious goals, but often the desire to change remains only at the conscious level. Remember the law of conflict discussed in Chapter 1? In a battle between the conscious and subconscious, the subconscious invariably wins, because our minds resemble computers.

Our Mental Computer

A computer terminal accepts input; and a computer always gives the same output until either we change the input or change the program. This also holds true for the subconscious mind. When we try to change a habit pattern or a way of thinking by simply changing the input – without changing the subconscious program – replaying the original program will trigger the old habit pattern.

For example, a friend of mine left the country for an extended period of time. She decided to stop smoking, and simply did not buy any more cigarettes. Two months after returning home to her old environment, she unintentionally picked up a friend's lit cigarette while having a cup of coffee. The old input of the smoking trigger resulted in a subconscious response based on an old subconscious program. My friend believed she had "blown it," and consequently started smoking two packs a day almost immediately.

Several diet counselors have told me that 97% of people who pay money to lose weight gain all the lost pounds in less than two years.

In other words, diets work on the body but not the mind. Unless we change the subconscious programming, willpower works only for a short time – and the dieter almost always backslides. The temporary input of the diet counselor may cause temporary changes; but when one returns to the old input, the behavior corresponds to the previous subconscious programming. The sight of favorite foods frequently triggers the desire to relapse. Friends can also blow the dieter's best intentions by helping to execute the old subconscious programs. In my business, we refer to subconscious programming as "old tapes" since our minds retain everything. Some therapists prefer the terms *anchoring* and *triggers*. Either is correct.

Note that many people still call these "old tapes" even though CDs have now replaced most tapes. Perhaps in time we might call them "old recordings" rather than old tapes.

Anchoring and Triggers

Anchoring compares to the act of *programming* the subconscious. The *trigger* is the signal that *plays* or *executes the program*. Many therapists today utilize anchoring and triggers to help clients gain empowerment; and I do too. Triggers influence much of what we do every day of our lives.

Do you need to think about every step when tying your shoes? Your conscious mind sends a quick signal to your brain that triggers your subconscious into action. How about opening a door? We do this automatically; yet a parent often laughs while observing his or her small child learning how to open doors for the first time. We find ourselves subconsciously stopping at red lights, braking and accelerating automatically, picking up the phone and answering appropriately whether at work or home, and doing many small tasks on "autopilot."

Can you relate to these examples? Our mental programs influence our actions, whether at home or work, in sports, and in social circumstances. This is true whether we are alone or with others. For the most part, I consider it a blessing that we can learn to respond automatically to triggers, because this makes doing many of life's mundane chores much simpler by freeing our minds to think about whatever else we choose.

The specific influence triggered by activating an old tape (or old program) depends on the program previously anchored into the trigger. Over a period of time repetition anchors the habitual response to a trigger in the subconscious. Contrary to what some people believe, however, triggers sometimes become anchored suddenly. Such anchoring often happens during an intense emotional experience, but it can also happen during a hypnotic trance.

When dealing with habits, remember that nature dislikes a vacuum; so I recommend a new response to an old trigger to replace the undesired one. For example, one deep breath of air in response to a light-up trigger has no calories and no side effects. Frequent snackers can substitute water for snacks.

Certain events can trigger desires as well, such as a smoking urge. Dieters might immediately crave to eat something sweet upon seeing someone else eat candy. The mere act of passing a vending machine often triggers the appetite; so someone who overeats may be vulnerable to snacking without consciously deciding to eat. We might prefer to call this *temptation*; but regardless of the definition chosen, our mental computer responds to old programs previously anchored (or programmed) in the past.

We can also anchor emotions into the mind, or use emotion to make a trigger more powerful. When an emotional event anchors a tape (or program) into the subconscious, the same emotions can easily surface by any type of trigger reminding the subconscious of that same event. Phobias provide evidence of the anchoring of emotions. For example, a vicious dog attack could easily make a child afraid of dogs for many years. Afterwards, the mere sight of a dog triggers fear in that person, even into adulthood. Good emotions can also become anchored into the mind. It becomes very beneficial to rehearse desired events in your imagination during self-hypnosis, and to fantasize good emotions while establishing (or anchoring) a trigger.

While we can accept most tapes as beneficial, the question remains: How do we deal with undesired triggers or tapes?

Old Programs Can Be Changed

Unfortunately, we can't just erase an old program. Instead, we must record a new program over the old one and replace it. Had my friend changed her response to the old smoking trigger to a deep breath instead of a light-up, her chances of long-term success would have been better. Instead, she tried to delete the response altogether; yet she eventually reacted to her old triggers and smoked.

Some old programs relate to attitudes. We may be programmed to say "thank you" when appropriate and act according to certain social standards. We accept these good attitude programs without even thinking about them. But bad attitude programs enter our minds as well, such as "I have my father's temper," or "I'm lousy with math," or "All my relatives are overweight, because it runs in the family."

One important fact deserves emphasis here: once opened, the subconscious mind does not permit us to keep program files blank. Either *you* remain in control of your own programming, or you end up turning control over to somebody or something else. This seems even truer with attitudes. For example, dieters often have ups and downs with weight because others influence them subconsciously. (Some people call this the yo-yo effect.) I have seen clients get stressed, only to use food to stuff the stress into the subconscious. Smokers trying to quit frequently backslide after listening to negative remarks from a friend or relative, because of the impact on their attitude or self-esteem.

Have you ever given someone else the power to influence your subconscious programming? Some people have the ability to let other's opinions roll off of them without any emotional reactions. Most of us, however, seem to be vulnerable occasionally to negative input from relatives, or from people whom we consider close.

Such negativity seeps into the subconscious much more quickly whenever we do not actively maintain control over our own minds.

During my experience as a sales manager, one colleague on my unit always fired up his enthusiasm after an inspiring motivational seminar. He would make several sales calls and close a sale, only to take a tailspin into a slump at the first sign of criticism. My consistent good producer believed in success at a subconscious level, and programmed herself to release a lost prospect and go on to another. The first sales rep worked twice as hard and twice as many hours, but getting only half the results of the woman who enjoyed the benefits of positive programming. Both individuals had equal talents and ability; but each had dramatically different results.

Any athlete experiencing extended bad luck demonstrates how the mind influences results. If a baseball player believes he/she will make an out, that out usually gets recorded. Watch a bowler who believes that he/she went into a slump, and the ball just seems to keep missing the right pins. Golf serves as a prime example of mind over matter, with the matter being the club and ball! Just fantasize where you do not want the ball to go, and watch how often the club seems to know just how to hit the ball into that dreaded location. (I speak from personal experience!)

Attitude has a profound impact on the subconscious, so we must do whatever possible to avoid running pessimistic attitude programs. When the subconscious mind gets filled with negative triggers or programs, we have great difficulty staying in a positive frame of mind unless we change those programs at the subconscious level. We must decide which programs need changing, and then begin replacing them with new programs. What is needed, then, is a simple way to accomplish this. Additionally, the subconscious must accept the new programs in order for us to stay motivated and realize permanent habit change. My own professional experience proves that this process involves more than visualization alone, and more than affirmations alone.

I have successfully taught people this process for years, both in private sessions and business seminars. The key lies in mastering the power of self-hypnosis, and building upon the important information presented in this book thus far. The remaining chapters provide step-by-step instructions; but first, we need to understand the five methods of subconscious programming, explained in Chapter 6.

Chapter 6

Gateways to the Subconscious

According to my late mentor, Charles Tebbetts, there are five basic ways to change our subconscious programming. He discussed them thoroughly in his hypnosis course and summarized them in his book, *Self-Hypnosis and Other Mind Expanding Techniques*. I suggest that you memorize these five gateways to motivating the subconscious: *repetition, authority, desire for identity* (ego), *hypnosis*, and *emotion*. A good acronym is HEARD (although it changes the order of these motivators): hypnosis, emotion, authority, repetition, and desire for identity.

While I believe in the value of mastering self-hypnosis, I also accept that other means can be beneficial. Clients come to me for help in achieving goals, so I give them a variety of tools to use.

I have devoted considerable time over the years to developing a workable approach to habit control around these five gateways, or subconscious motivators. We could also compare these gates to directories in a computer, or highways into the mind. You may already recognize some of these methods as familiar ways of effecting a change. Used alone, each gateway has a chance of success with little or no opposing input, with varying degrees of effectiveness. Used harmoniously, these five motivators open wide the doors of subconscious motivation to help you implement your conscious desire for change. Let us examine them now.

Gateway 1: Repetition

Metaphorically speaking, we walk slowly on a dirt path through Gateway 1.

How often have you heard that practice makes perfect? Everyone knows that you can learn a new habit by practicing. The piano teacher insists on practicing scales; the baseball coach insists on batting practice; the elementary school teacher drills students on multiplication tables. Any skill or sport improves with practice. Repetition does work, but it takes time. The amount of time can vary from person to person based on other subconscious beliefs as well as one's own natural and/or developed ability.

While repetition can create a new habit pattern or way of thinking, have you ever tried to delete an old habit by the repetition of avoidance? Many people riding a bicycle for the first time in years seem surprised at their ability to stay balanced. The subconscious still remembers this skill, as well as all learned habits. These habits can be replaced, but not easily erased.

If you find that difficult to believe, consider the smoking habit again. Numerous resolutions to quit smoking literally go up in smoke! For example, the smoker I mentioned in Chapter 5 simply tried to delete an old habit by ignoring old smoking triggers. She did avoid buying cigarettes, but the subconscious patterns remained dormant, waiting to be activated once again. The old smoking triggers became strongly anchored into her subconscious over time. Consequently, when a situation occurred that used to trigger her light-up urge, she immediately grabbed her friend's lit cigarette without even consciously realizing what she had done.

This same principle holds true for dieters as well, as the best intentions get consumed along with the junk food. Whether the food trigger is the vending machine at work, or simply eating junk food as a response to seeing another person indulge, old responses tend to remain. Common smoking triggers are: turning a key in the ignition, picking up a beverage, walking through the front door, and so on. Common weight triggers are: frequent snacks, eating too quickly, and/or cleaning up the plate even if feeling full.

Sometimes you can successfully replace an old habit with a new one by repetition. If repetition alone does not work, however, other subconscious resistance may be working against you; and if so, you must use more than repetition to replace the undesired habit. Now let us find out why, and take a look at the more powerful ways of reaching the subconscious.

Gateway 2: Authority

Suggestions or commands presented by an authority figure often go straight into the subconscious mind (even from impersonal authority, such as proven laws of health). Such statements will either push an "obey" button or create a desire to rebel. Even ideas or concepts taught by someone in authority often impact the subconscious. We see this more easily in children than in adults. Third graders, for example, may believe anything that "Teacher says." If the teacher tells a child that he/she excels in math, the compliment motivates the student to do well. Conversely, a child labeled "accident-prone" (as I was) may continue getting frequent bumps and bruises even into adult life.

People with severe weight problems often clean their plates automatically because of childhood programming from authority figures. Even today, many parents teach their children to eat everything, whether hungry or not, until the plate is empty. This programming haunts many people wishing to reduce, making weight reduction more difficult until they resign from the clean plate club.

During my original training in Advanced Hypnotherapy, I watched a videotaped regression of an engineer whose teacher told him during fifth grade that he couldn't spell. The boy's mother then reinforced the new belief; and he spent the next thirty years of his life spelling no better than the average fourth grader. Two authority figures programmed him with the belief that he did not have the ability to spell well; and that belief remained until he finally released the feelings and allowed his subconscious to receive positive beliefs. Within a month, he started spelling as well as the average adult.

Sales people often face difficulty when making prospecting calls because of negative comments heard repeatedly from parents about salesmen. Smokers sometimes smoke because their parents told them to wait until adulthood; then, after reaching maturity, they light up.

Perhaps you can remember certain ideas presented by your parents and teachers. As adults, we may feel less vulnerable to new subconscious programming by authority figures. Our parents no longer run our lives, nor do our former teachers and college instructors; but the power of authority that they once held over us can still exert tremendous impact in certain situations. Evidence of this appears frequently during hypnotic regressions.

Certain current authority figures (or authority "wannabes") may also directly impact the subconscious, creating an immediate "obey" or "rebel" response. Typical authorities may include: deity, individual (employer, minister, professional authority), organization (government), or non-entity (laws of health).

Some teenagers demonstrate the flip side of authority by smoking out of rebellion against authority figures; and some smokers find difficulty in quitting because they resent being told by employers not to smoke. I have had clients tell me that their smoking actually increased when their doctor told them to quit. In short, we sometimes have an illogical desire to do something simply because an authority figure forbids it. We may also find ourselves rebelling if a would-be authority tries to force us to abide by his/her opinions, such as a stranger telling someone to put out a lit cigarette or a smoker seeing a "No Smoking" sign.

One example demonstrating such impact happened to a very dear friend of mine whom I worked with during the 1970s. Any time someone even hinted that he shouldn't smoke, he argued for smokers' rights and lit up at the first opportunity. He smoked for over twenty years; and while he considered quitting, he tried and failed. He finally just decided to go on enjoying the habit. (Of course, this happened before my professional entry into hypnotherapy!)

After surgery for a collapsed lung, his doctor came into the hospital room and said: "If you want to live longer than six months, throw your cigarettes away!" My friend respected the doctor as a medical authority, so his subconscious opened Gateway 2 totally for any health-related suggestions planted there by his physician. He remained a non-smoker for over ten years, right up until the day he died.

Of course, when we give credibility to any outside authority, negative programming can be just as powerful. The subconscious doesn't know the difference between right and wrong. Rather, the subconscious merely accepts whatever the conscious mind allows to enter; so we must monitor what goes into the subconscious through the five gateways.

Common *positive* authority motivators for smoking cessation and weight control are: health benefits, medical advice, and prayer. Common *negative* motivators are: desire to rebel, past painful encounter with authority figure, and compulsion to clean the plate (weight control only). Your own attitudes determine whether you have a dirt road or a paved street through Gateway 2.

Gateway 3: Desire for Identity (Ego)

Whether we like it or not, we have an ego which craves belonging, acceptance, recognition, and love. My late mentor Charles Tebbetts called this motivator "Desire for Identity." I prefer to simply refer to this subconscious gateway as the ego, which opens up to several avenues.

Peer Pressure

Virtually all of us have experienced the power of peer pressure, both as children and adults.

How many parents have heard your child beg you for a particular style of clothing merely because other kids at school already wear that style? When my son turned eighteen, he felt that he needed $50 jeans instead of $25 jeans of like quality (a different brand name) simply because of concern over the opinions of his classmates.

Children can do very illogical and dangerous things simply because of a "dare" from a sibling or a friend. The movie *Stand by Me* shows a scene where young boys run across a train bridge; and that scene gave me an instant hypnotic regression to childhood. My cousin dared me to walk across a similar bridge, but an oncoming train made it a life-threatening situation. Had I been four inches closer, my life would have ended right then – and you would not be reading this book. Also, that dare proved to be the last one I ever accepted from my cousin.

How many smokers started the habit while growing up because of peer pressure? Most of my clients wishing to quit smoking list peer pressure as the reason given for having started in the first place. These clients originally bought into the identity of a smoker because of their friends and/or perceptions of adulthood. More than one client has described practicing smoking in front of a mirror in order to look mature! We can justify peer pressure because of youth, right? But does age close this gateway to the subconscious?

To answer that question, consider how many billions of dollars the cosmetics and fashion industries generate by catering to the desire to look good. Lest you men think that applies only to women, what about our habit of dressing in a long-sleeved shirt, coat, and tie on a hot summer's day? On one hand, it is absurd to be uncomfortable and inappropriately dressed for the weather; yet I personally choose to buy into the peer pressure of wearing a business suit because I feel more acceptable, especially during a public speaking engagement. A friend of mine, a former senator, appeared in the State Legislature on a hot day in a short-sleeved shirt. Other legislators asked him to go home and dress properly! These lawmakers chose custom over comfort, even though their personal discomfort may have clouded their mental skills and judgment while considering legislation that impacted taxpayers in Washington State. Perhaps someday tens of millions of businessmen will get wise and change an outdated tradition. Until then, we will continue to be hot and uncomfortable by overdressing on summer days, while justifying our actions because of a subconscious acceptance of tradition. Those who attempt to change first will be criticized and judged by those who still cling to old subconscious programming.

Mentor

We love to admire heroes. Many celebrities relish this fact, and enjoy receiving huge sums of money from sponsors who recognize our need for mentors.

People of all ages emulate sports heroes. While umpiring a little league baseball game years ago, I wiped a teenager's spit from my face while he was at bat. When I asked him why he needed to spit, he said he wanted to be just like his favorite baseball player, who spat incessantly while at bat.

When we choose to emulate a friend, sports hero, or movie star, we tend to soak up that person's habits and mannerisms like a sponge; and, of course, the easy ones come first. Perhaps you sometimes laugh like someone else you know; or maybe you occasionally use a slang expression that a friend or work associate uses frequently. Often, whether or not your conscious mind likes the new behavior, the subconscious already emulates your mentor. Years ago a smoker discovered during deep hypnosis that his inability to quit smoking was because he emulated John Wayne, who was a chain smoker.

We also have gurus in the business world. A management trainee may look up to a professional mentor and start using the same "power phrases" and business jargon. The new employee may even hold a coffee cup the same way as the mentor (as I found myself doing when I became an insurance agent), consciously and subconsciously assuming that the path to success lies in totally imitating another successful person. In reality, the ego desires the praise and recognition that we perceive the other person worthy of receiving. Such emulation may evolve into something good, provided you choose your tutor wisely and monitor out those traits you wish to exclude; but beware. When the subconscious opens, what you do not filter out may come in and stay permanently. Certain professional organizations even offer formal mentor/

mentee programs, so that newer people in a given profession can learn from those who have more experience and are worthy of emulation.

Group Identification

Do you know someone who justifies having a temper because it runs in the family? Perhaps an acquaintance looks down on you because you don't belong to the same church, political party, or race.

People tend to identify easily with groups: *my* team, *my* fraternity, *my* country, and so on. A special feeling comes along with belonging to a group or in identifying with a cause. The desire to belong seems closely related to peer pressure, and appears to be universal. Some organizations often capitalize on this common desire to belong by encouraging members to surrender individual identity to a greater group identity; people with low self-image are especially vulnerable to this. Such organizations frequently use this motivator to further group goals, even to the detriment of its members.

Again, as with mentors, I consider group identification to be neither positive nor negative, until proven by individual results. Members make themselves susceptible to subconscious programming based on group goals, methods, and the degree of individual involvement (as well as what the member of the group chooses to accept or reject). Many people belong to an organization, a minority race, a faith group, and so on, and somehow learn to accept the good from the group while rejecting any negative input before it takes root in the subconscious. The risk grows with those who get so caught up in group causes that their minds become prejudiced and closed to other points of view.

People of my generation reeled in shock when Jim Jones motivated almost a thousand of his Peoples Temple followers to commit suicide in South America in 1978. Many have wondered how that tragedy could possibly have happened; but most members had such a strong desire to be part of the group identity of this religious organization that anything the group spokesman said went right into the subconscious. This event forever serves as an extreme example of group identification. Religious cults often combine authority programming with peer pressure and group identity, doing a double whammy on the subconscious by speaking in God's behalf. Ministers of religious cults frequently use the phrase: "I didn't say this, God did!" Then the personal opinions that follow go right into the subconscious minds of all those in the congregation who believe the first phrase. The unfortunates who believed that Jim Jones spoke in God's behalf became part of a tragic lesson in history. Some cult leaders also employ group hypnosis, creating a triple whammy.

I recommend that you make your own decisions rather than giving a representative of any organization carte blanche to program your mind as he/she chooses. If you have any remaining doubt about my advice, consider the tragedy of the Heaven's Gate cult during the 1990s. These suicides shocked us all. The cult victims unknowingly allowed their leader to gain total access to their subconscious minds, resulting in his ability to lead them to a terrible end.

Recognition

The "child inside" loves recognition and rewards as much as acceptance. Sales organizations utilize ego recognition with numerous programs for rewarding good performance. During my time in sales management, I found that some of my reps worked harder for a recognition award than for the monetary reward. Some people drive themselves to great lengths for recognition in the business world, politics, sports, and so on, often at great personal sacrifice. Many over-inflated egos frequently don't care who gets stepped on; yet some people motivated by desire for recognition remain loving and likable. Somehow these considerate people learn how to use their ego for personal motivation without becoming a slave to it, thus making their ego a positive motivator and friend.

Alcoholics Anonymous also recognizes the motivation of good strokes. Some of my clients who quit drinking through the help of AA have indicated great pride in receiving their sobriety pins. Often food serves as a reward. Clients seeing me for weight control frequently recognize both their successes and failures with food, and then feel bad about having used food to feel good. Needless to say, this creates inner conflict.

I recommend that my clients choose the positive side of ego by planning both short-term and long-term rewards for themselves when working toward a goal. Whether or not we believe in rewards and recognition, these "warm fuzzies" influence us; so we might as well work with incentives. Even the most negative person will sometimes do things in order to get attention, regardless of the benefits or consequences of that attention. Most of us still prefer "warm fuzzies" over cold criticism. Positive strokes, genuine appreciation, and positive recognition tend to bring out the best in most of us.

Some people, unfortunately, never seem to learn the value of positive recognition. These negative critics continually tear other people down or find fault. Many parents harm their children's self-image (or self-identity) with statements such as: "You'll never amount to anything," or "You can't do anything right." I urge parents to stop putting such destructive programming into tomorrow's adults. Many people today seek therapy because of their own parents' negative criticism and abuse.

Employers, managers, and supervisors frequently fail to appreciate the importance of giving good strokes to employees. They seem to demand loyalty without earning it, and then wonder why there are morale problems. Some major businesses actually have unwritten codes against giving a common employee an "outstanding" rating on yearly appraisals. I strongly disagree with this bias.

In my professional opinion, frequent employer criticism is dangerous to employee morale and loyalty. If a worker does an outstanding job, the employer should give both praise and a raise. Professional faultfinding takes its place as one more example of why so many individuals have self-esteem problems. We live in a

Gateways to the Subconscious

world where many people seem to be afraid of giving another person a kind word. The critic would rather punch away at another's self-esteem, and then justify putting the other person down. Why aren't we more willing to look for the good in others and compliment them?

We cannot control what others may or may not recognize in us, so I give clients the following three recommendations:

1. Don't give your power away by always depending on others to recognize you.
2. Learn to recognize your own strengths.
3. Celebrate your own successes and love yourself as much as your neighbor. (There's more about this in Chapter 10.)

God created us with ego. Unfortunately, trying to ignore our ego will not make it go away; but we can use ego positively while keeping a balance. The inner child will seek recognition whether that attention comes in a positive or negative way. We can either serve the ego, or make it serve us.

Left ignored, the ego can trip us up. By learning to use the energy of the ego in a positive way, however, we can enjoy a powerful ally for self-motivation. While exploring the good side of ego, let us learn to find positive things to say to others as well as to ourselves.

If you employ other people who help you earn your income, stroke their egos. Be sure to give the good employee appropriate compensation and recognition for contributing to your success. In the long run the investment is worth it, especially when you consider the cost of recruiting and training new staff to replace the seasoned ones.

Common *positive* ego motivators are: desire for greater social acceptance (weight and smoking cessation), look good (weight control), greater social acceptance, better self-image, and pride of success or sense of accomplishment. Common *negative* ego motivators are: peer pressure (smokers), rewarding self (with food or cigarettes), resentment of social pressure, and shame (because it causes us to fantasize the problem rather than the solution).

Depending on your ego, you may have either a paved highway or a freeway passing through Gateway 3.

Gateway 4: Hypnosis/Self-Hypnosis (Alpha)

When your mind enters the alpha state, the subconscious opens up for new programming. As pointed out above, we can best describe hypnosis as guided self-hypnosis. Also, remember that all hypnosis may also be called guided meditation, or guided daydreaming. Furthermore, imagination is the language of the subconscious; and hypnosis facilitates one's ability to use the imagination.

Remember that the subconscious responds to what we imagine, whether or not the input originates from an external source. For example, if a stage hypnotist suggests that you go to the North Pole and feel cold, you might be very distracted by focusing on how hot the stage lights make you feel. If you imagine being in a blizzard, as suggested, your body might even produce goose bumps. You could just as easily be sitting in a movie theater watching a film of a snow scene, and feel a desire to put on your coat.

The person in hypnosis can imagine one hand in a bucket of ice and can actually feel the numbness. Better yet, the person in hypnosis can imagine achieving a goal, and the belief of possible achievement takes root in the subconscious. Sometimes you can exclusively control what you imagine. At other times, it is easier to allow someone or something else to guide you into creative imagination.

When you visit a hypnotherapist or utilize a self-hypnosis CD, imagine the goals suggested to you rather than dwelling on the problems you wish to avoid. For example, if you listen to suggestions for weight control while imagining the taste of some goodies, your subconscious simply accepts what you frequently imagine. People who don't realize this may find themselves wanting to eat upon emerging from hypnosis.

Increasing numbers of people around the country give testimony to the benefits of hypnosis for personal or business motivation. Many thousands of ex-smokers use hypnosis only as a last resort after exhausting other methods to kick the habit. People have learned how to control weight and eating habits through hypnotherapy. Sales people have enjoyed significant increases in income after only a few sessions. Others have improved at sports.

Among my own clients, I have helped many hundreds of former smokers successfully quit. Numerous clients have reduced and kept the weight off. Former nail biters have long fingernails. A black belt immensely improved his timing in the martial arts. A swimmer won a silver medal in a national competition. Some bowlers have improved their averages by more than a mark. Golfers have taken some strokes off their game. Sales people have doubled their incomes. One realtor turned his income into a six-digit figure. A hypnotherapist increased her practice by more than double. One salesperson ended the year at 245% of quota just three months after her sessions; and within eighteen months became the branch manager. Shortly after, she became product manager for the entire company. Last time I saw her she had attained one of their top executive positions. Hypnosis works.

Common *positive* hypnotic motivators for habit control are: previous success with hypnosis (works at a subconscious level), hypnotherapy, and frequent use of self-hypnosis. Common *negative* hypnotic motivators are: eating or smoking while watching TV, smoking in bed, midnight snacks, and frequent negative visualization of problems.

Entering the subconscious through the alpha gateway compares to driving on a superhighway (except that some highly analytical people sometimes create detours). While you may travel through that gate quickly, you still have the ability to steer provided you realize that *you* are the one in the driver's seat. Make certain that you travel on the right road.

Gateway 5: Emotion

Emotion is the motivating power of the mind. It compares to the ace of trumps, serving as the most powerful way possible to impact the subconscious. We don't walk through this gateway; we fly through it as though on a jet. Sometimes, however, we fly so fast that we miss important places along the way.

One minute of intense emotion can permanently impact the subconscious, as evidenced by one of my clients with a fear of water because she almost drowned during childhood. A former hypnotherapy student spent over thirty years hating dogs because of a vicious attack during childhood. Another student spent most of his life fighting claustrophobia because his older brother tormented him by trapping him inside a box for an hour when he was only six.

Whenever we enter into an emotional state of mind, we become very vulnerable to subconscious programming. Furthermore, as the emotions intensify, that emotional energy drives the imprints deeper into the subconscious. One doesn't have to be a psychologist to know that severe emotional traumas contribute to serious mental problems. It is dangerous to experience prolonged fear, sadness, or anger. If the emotions go to an extreme, the owners of these intense feelings can enter a state of deep depression and become totally unable to cope.

The results of deep emotional pain can take months or years of professional help to correct, such as war veterans with post-traumatic stress disorder who find themselves having flashbacks. Such scars may require far more therapy than hypnosis alone can provide. How many people spend literally years of therapy dealing with the emotional aftermath of childhood traumas or past abuse? Many books have been written on this topic; and widespread emotional trauma keeps the mental health profession quite busy. Stephen Parkhill, hypnotherapist and author, believes that cancer can usually be traced back to intense negative emotions; and he has specialized in releasing people from their buried feelings.

Many of his clients have enjoyed profound improvements in their health.

Although I neither treat nor diagnose physical or mental illness, I recognize the importance of being careful what we imagine whenever we experience emotion, especially because emotion serves as the most powerful of the five methods of subconscious programming.

Much has been said and written about the importance of controlling our feelings; but I believe in going one step beyond this concept. We must monitor our thoughts when we experience any kind of emotion, whether it is positive or negative. For example, if you get frustrated at your boss or work associate and fantasize how you would like to respond, you may someday indeed find those same words jumping out of your mouth before you can stop them. When you rehearse certain words or actions mentally while experiencing emotion, your subconscious records these impressions. This rehearsal creates the potential for the imagined words or actions to come out automatically at a time or place you might regret.

Does this mean we should never have feelings? I don't think so, because our emotions serve us. Our ability to feel gives us wonderful abilities: to love, to enjoy, to appreciate the beauty of a sunset, to feel inspiration from wonderful music, to experience ecstasy with someone dearly loved, to know the contrasts between good times and sad times, or to taste life. Even negative feelings help us to appreciate the positive ones, as long as we remain in control. Controlling our emotions, however, means choosing *when* and *how* to express those feelings rather than simply stuffing them. In my opinion we must find a balance. Feel the feelings; express them, and then release them. Obviously, we should avoid loss of control during stress; but pretending to be calm and stuffing it can be risky as well. For this reason, I encourage you to master the exercises for reducing stress in Chapter 8.

Emotion makes us even more vulnerable to suggestion than hypnosis, so it behooves each of us to learn what to do when our buttons get pushed. Also, be aware that a positive emotion does not necessarily guarantee a helpful result, nor does a negative emotion always produce a harmful result.

For example, a new private challenged by his drill sergeant in boot camp could get angry, or he could channel the energy into a desire to be a man and prove it. In my opinion, however, motivation by negative emotion can be dangerous in the business world. I knew a sales manager for a large corporation whose use of anger and fear motivation techniques backfired as a large percentage of his staff resigned in disgust. A veteran insurance professional with fifteen years of experience walked out of this manager's office one day, slamming the door behind her. She failed to produce to his satisfaction, so he "motivated" her by accusing her of being lazy and worthless. This insensitive man sprinkled his admonition with unprofessional language and threats, and spoke loudly enough for the rest of us to overhear. She resigned immediately, and then upper management asked for her former manager's resignation as well. The allegedly "lazy" woman became very successful selling real estate.

Some managers unwisely use fear and threats in order to increase employee productivity, and then wonder why they experience high employee turnover. One of my former Yellow Page representatives decided to quit in protest after his manager used fear tactics to try to motivate the sales staff. Management apparently threatened to fire anyone who didn't come within a few percentage points of sales quota. Fear and anger sometimes motivate people to improve their work habits temporarily; but these methods often backfire and destroy morale in the process. If you are a sales manager, think twice before using fear to motivate your sales people. Negative feelings usually create destructive results that may even go beyond loss of employee morale, coming back to bite the employer in the rear.

Strangely enough, we can sometimes find examples of negative results from positive feelings – evidenced partly by the divorce courts. And we have all given in to enjoyable emotions and overindulged in food, drink, or some other pleasure more times than we care to share. On a more serious note, consider the fact that people who followed Jim Jones to their deaths found themselves originally drawn into his cult by warm emotional feelings of acceptance and perceptions of love. People who manipulate others frequently use love and positive emotions as well as guilt and fear.

We live in a manipulative world, with people constantly pushing our buttons. Whether the buttons trigger positive emotions or negative ones, we must accept responsibility for choosing whether or not to buy into the manipulation. Loved ones often know exactly which buttons to push. Those who attempt to exploit someone through guilt take a risk that may miscarry. Many good relationships deteriorate quickly because of this dangerous game of manipulation through guilt: "If you really loved me, you would . . ."

We tend to have a greater degree of control over the imagination while experiencing positive feelings; but any emotion felt in the extreme opens us wide to sudden and lasting subconscious imprints. This points to a very real need for us to control our feelings instead of allowing them to control us. Additionally, we need to be aware of what happens at a subconscious level when experiencing emotions, so that we may monitor the input.

Common *positive* emotional motivators for achieving goals are: loving the benefits, and excitement at the realization of the goal itself. Common *negative* emotional motivators are: guilt (damages the self-esteem), and using food or smoking to cope with stress. Also, people wishing to reduce must contend with the fact that food tastes good and gives us emotional satisfaction; but we wouldn't have it any other way!

Summary

Lots of success techniques work; but unless the subconscious mind accepts the changes we desire, the old habits almost inevitably return. How do we gain that acceptance?

Repetition alone takes too long. Authority is faster for some people, but is less effective for self-starters who often resent being told what to do. Furthermore, your own subconscious does not recognize you as an authority over yourself, which explains why we often rebel at attempts to use willpower. Remember that an immediate subconscious desire to obey or rebel serves as an example of how authority motivates the subconscious.

Desire for identity, used alone, has drawbacks; yet we can certainly supplement any plan by choosing a mentor wisely. Furthermore, we can gain improved self-esteem by learning to recognize our own successes.

Hypnosis and/or self-hypnosis (alpha) shines as the easiest to use of the five subconscious motivators. The alpha state increases your ability to consciously plan the proper road and monitor what takes place subconsciously. However, even hypnosis (of and by itself) might not be sufficient to break old habit patterns.

Emotion is the motivating power of the mind, and can propel you to success when used wisely. I highly recommend using self-hypnosis in combination with positive emotion for success. Realize, however, that people prone to the many emotional highs can also be subject to states of depression, thereby negating positive programming. Most setbacks perpetuate themselves simply because of the emotional state of mind accompanying the setback. (When you imagine another failure while feeling emotion, you energize that failure deeper into your subconscious.)

Since emotion is the energy (or motivating power) of the mind, I recommend that we use hypnosis and/or self-hypnosis to learn to gain more control over our feelings, particularly negative ones. Of course, we remain in control of our emotions more easily while feeling calm. This is logical. When feelings of anger, anxiety, or fear suddenly flood our awareness, however, we usually have difficulty staying in control without previous practice! We all have the ability to practice appropriate emotional responses in the rehearsal ground of our imagination while in the alpha state. Emotion plays such an important role in making or breaking our success, therefore emotional control becomes vital.

The self-hypnosis exercises described in Chapter 8 will give you straightforward methods to help you take more control of your life and become less vulnerable to manipulation by others who push your buttons. That chapter also discusses ownership and control of negative emotions as an important part of using a stress-coping technique. Many clients over the years have told me that learning to manage stress with self-hypnosis ranks very high among the most valuable skills ever learned. Your emotions can serve you, or you can serve them. The choice is yours.

You'll find even more information concerning emotion in Part IV on creative daydreaming; but for now let us look at how all the subconscious motivators can be utilized to stimulate the subconscious and change a habit.

Chapter 7

The Quintuple Whammy

Now that you have read about the five subconscious gateways, let us consider their combined impact on the subconscious. I also call these gateways (or subconscious motivators) the five methods of subconscious programming, and I have developed my own original approach to motivation.

Obviously, the greater any of these motivators impacts the subconscious mind, the stronger the program becomes. The idea, belief, trigger, or program goes deep into the subconscious; but each gateway can allow both positive and negative input to enter. This causes inner conflicts. We may have a strong desire to change a habit while simultaneously experiencing subconscious resistance to change. While we continue to experience subconscious motivation to make changes, we also respond to contradictory subconscious programming.

Consider the importance of recognizing all five subconscious gateways, and creating what I call a motivation map. Put in other words, we may often find it necessary to use all five motivators in order to overcome the strength of the negative input working against us. I also call this the quintuple whammy.

Hypnosis Alone Is Not Enough

Although self-hypnosis or hypnotherapy may be used to remove negative programming (as well as to enhance one's ability to regularly visualize desired changes), hypnosis alone fails to outweigh several negative subconscious motivators. If you have already tried hypnosis and failed to achieve your goal, this chapter may give you valuable insight.

Clients have often come to me over the years telling me that they failed to respond to hypnotherapy. In some cases they experienced hypnotic regression and so on, to help release the original cause of overeating. Then, even with a follow-up of positive suggestions, some clients continue to eat junk foods and wonder why. Negative input previously planted by an authority figure sometimes needs to be removed by hypnotherapy; but other negative subconscious input often continues to work against some individuals.

Also, many smokers have tried and failed the "30-Minute" stop smoking programs. Some advertise unbelievable success rates, which are just that: unbelievable. One might suppose that these programs would work for most people; but several years ago a reporter told me that only 20% of attendees that he surveyed lasted even one week. Let us look at why people get drawn to these seminars.

In this fast food society, people want something quick, cheap, and guaranteed; and many smoking cessation programs "guarantee" success in only one session. Over the years many of them have advertised a 97% success rate, when in reality four out of five smoke again within seven days (as that reporter told me). While 20% would still be an acceptable success rate, truthful advertising probably would not draw nearly as many people to these groups. Yet while these seminars work for some of the people some of the time, they do so only because more than one method of subconscious programming already makes the subconscious receptive to change. The hypnotist just makes enough difference to tip the scales toward success. (Even some smokers who manage to succeed in one session never stop grieving for the loss of what they describe as a "friend," and often take up another addiction such as eating sweets.) Many who fail after trying these one-shot programs unfortunately become skeptical of hypnosis, and that need not be.

Hypnosis remains very effective; but trance alone will never be a panacea to all of life's problems. Rather, we must use hypnosis in conjunction with other solutions.

Methods Working Against Desired Change

Now let me illustrate the use of all five motivators with a case history of a smoker wishing to quit. I call this analytical information process "motivation mapping" and have taught this unique technique to hypnotherapists on both coasts. Before proceeding, however, let me state that I honor the freedom of those who choose to smoke; and I only help a client quit when *he or she makes the choice*.

John (name changed) failed at ten previous attempts to quit smoking. Two of his previous tries involved hypnosis, with one hotel seminar and one private session.

Repetition: He had years of practice at smoking when certain old triggers occurred (the ringing telephone, etc.). In the past he had tried to ignore those triggers. The urges persisted, making it almost impossible for him to give up the habit.

Authority: He started smoking to make a statement of rebellion against parental authority. He also resented his doctor telling him to stop.

Identity: John identified with smokers and resented increasing peer pressure to quit.

Hypnosis (alpha): John regularly smoked while watching TV, completely unaware of most hypnotic puffs until emptying his full ash tray after the 11 o'clock news (TV induces hypnosis).

Emotion: John always responded to stress buttons by using another light-up as an emotional distraction to help him stuff his feelings.

Analysis

With this much working against John subconsciously, he had virtually no way to change without using all five methods of subconscious programming in a positive way.

Hypnotherapy could release him from the past rebellion of old authority figures. Trance could also enhance creative imagery for success; but John needed more, because he had too many other subconscious factors motivating him to keep on smoking. Furthermore, he had already failed at two previous hypnosis programs. The quickie one-session hotel seminar increased his belief that he would get a major disease, yet that fear failed to make him quit. The one private session incorporated only post-hypnotic suggestion to avoid smoking, but failed to help him replace his cigarettes. John's motivation map indicated that he would have to use a quintuple whammy in order to stop smoking for good.

Combining the Motivators to Quit Smoking

A smoker wishing to give up smoking may use the quintuple whammy, using all five gateways of the subconscious to quit permanently. Appendix 4 includes a self-directed guide to help smokers create their own motivation map, which may be used to increase the probability of stopping permanently.

Here is how I helped John combine all five programming methods. Since his case is similar to many, my recommendations illustrate the quintuple whammy.

Repetition: I suggested that he get into the habit of taking one deep breath of air whenever one of the old smoking triggers occurred. (Refer to the section on anchoring and triggers in Chapter 5.) One deep breath has no calories and can be done anywhere.

Remember that we can often *replace* a habitual conditioned response (light-up) with another conditioned response (deep breath); but trying to *erase* that habit proves far more difficult. People who simply try to delete the smoking habit frequently use food or another addiction as a substitute for smoking.

Authority: John recognized the medical authority of proven health statistics. Health was his primary motive for quitting, so authority was already part of his positive motivation. In spite of his acceptance of medical statistics, however, he always resisted his personal physician's advice to give up the habit.

The subconscious tends to rebel against force. Rebellion is, in a simplistic form, resistance against manipulation regardless of the consequences. John resented others trying to manipulate him into quitting; but, in reality, he allowed the actions of others to manipulate him into smoking! He decided to claim his own power of choice and do as he chose, regardless of whether someone was being manipulative. He could now use his desire to rebel by resisting cigarettes. Furthermore, John believed in God and decided to use prayer power to obtain help from the highest authority.

Desire for identity: John decided to enjoy the sense of accomplishment obtained by successfully quitting. He allowed this sense of accomplishment to become part of his new identity as a totally tolerant non-smoker. To help him with this new identity, I suggested that he reward his successes with the money that used to go up in smoke. We established his reward levels at one week, one month, three months, and one year.

Hypnosis (alpha): To help John become less vulnerable to the hypnotic influence of television, I recommended that he replace TV-smoking with water or a non-caloric beverage of his choice. In addition, I gave him a non-smoking self-hypnosis tape designed to help him imagine his desired success. (Today it would be a CD rather than a tape.) When we frequently imagine ourselves behaving in a particular way, we often behave as we imagine.

Emotion: To help minimize stress, I taught John the stress-coping technique described in Chapter 8. I also had him imagine his personal benefits and bond emotionally with them.

Combining the Motivators for Weight Management

As with any type of motivation program, I recommend that people wishing to stop overeating also use a quintuple whammy. Here is some additional information that might be helpful.

Emotion benefits us when we fantasize the benefits of being at an ideal weight. Enjoy that sense of satisfaction at looking good and feeling good. Allow yourself to fall in love with the benefits. You must create an emotional desire to succeed to offset the emotional bond to food. If your weight makes you feel guilty, forgive yourself. The fastest way to release guilt is through forgiveness. The chapters you have read thus far should be sufficient to help you realize that the deck might be stacked against you, thus you have no reason to hang on to any guilt.

Hypnosis (alpha) serves us more effectively when combined with the other motivators.

Some people requiring only minimal motivation may find sufficient help by mastering the self-hypnosis exercises in this book. Remember that TV induces trance, so avoid snacking while watching television. If needed, replace the snacks with water or a low-caloric beverage. When strong subconscious resistance exists, however, we may need a combination of group or private sessions along with a self-hypnosis CD. In either event, weight reduction usually requires the quintuple whammy for long-term success.

Desire for identity is a motivator that enables the ego to serve us rather than vice versa. Find a mentor. Admire someone who does well at controlling his/her weight, and then emulate your mentor's strengths. Also, reward yourself for your successes along the way (every 5 pounds, etc.) and celebrate your successes. When you succeed at motivating yourself for a change of habit, the little child inside will strongly desire attention and recognition. Make certain that you remember to do this. Honor your inner child! If you have difficulties, then you may need to work on self-esteem (see the exercise in Chapter 10).

Authority is important, because you need a proven plan that really works. Some fad diets are dangerous, yet many so-called authorities stretch the truth about their knowledge of nutrition. Belief in God also opens up the subconscious in certain situations. If you believe in a higher power, pray for help. If you have a healthy "rebel" button, use it as an ally to fight against junk food.

Repetition of any and all of the above programming methods reinforces impact at a subconscious level. Using all five gateways to input positive programming into the subconscious remains almost essential in long-term weight control because of the strength of past programming, as well as the continual subconscious bombardment from society to activate old programs. If you are a member of the clean plate club, get into the habit of leaving a little food on the side. If you eat too quickly, remind yourself frequently to eat slowly.

Make Your Own Motivation Map

If you wish to manage your weight, you can create your own motivation map using the information provided in Appendix 5.

What about Other Goals?

For goals other than weight control or quitting smoking, this process can often be easier because the forces working against you may not be as severe. A number of motivation maps have validated this. Yet some people have old habits and thought patterns that may be even harder to change, especially if energized with negative emotion during unpleasant experiences.

One of my goals is to teach my clients to be aware of what is imagined whenever the subconscious mind opens up. Awareness of these five gateways to the subconscious (or subconscious motivators) serves as the foundation to understanding this process. With this understanding, you can maintain greater control of the changes you choose to make in your life.

Chapters 11 and 12 discuss establishing goals and assigning priorities for your goals. Later chapters in Part V discuss the power of words, and provide exercises to help you achieve your goals. Once you start doing these exercises, you may wish to refer back to both this chapter and the preceding one so that you may identify sources of negative subconscious input and start monitoring them carefully. Next, you can look for ways to incorporate as many of the five subconscious motivators as possible to give yourself positive input, thereby improving your chances for success.

Feel free to photocopy the motivation mapping pages in Appendix 5 for your own use if desired.

Dealing with Inner Conflicts

Sometimes a client has numerous subconscious motivators making it difficult to overcome the undesired habit. This is because excessive negative motivators usually result in inner conflicts (conflicting subconscious desires). If you find yourself experiencing these inner conflicts, you may wish to seek out a hypnosis professional who is experienced in parts therapy or one of its variations.

Parts therapy is a powerful hypnotic technique designed to help clients resolve inner conflicts. The facilitator of parts therapy acts like a mediator, assisting objective mediation with the parts of your subconscious that are in conflict. Handled properly, clients can experience great breakthroughs; but this technique (or any variation) must be facilitated by someone who has received specialized training in order to maximize the probability of lasting success.

If you believe you need this type of hypnosis, refer to Appendix 2. For now, however, let us explore some empowerment exercises to help manage stress.

Chapter 8

Exercises to Manage Stress

This chapter contains three self-hypnosis empowerment exercises designed to help with three different phases of stress: coping at the moment stress occurs, calming down after stress with a mental mini-vacation, and sleeping at night (rather than worrying) during times of stress.

Let us start by considering our options when things seem fine, until somebody pushes the wrong buttons.

What To Do When Your Buttons Get Pushed

Many professionals with outstanding credentials can provide excellent advice to help you reduce stress both at work and at home. In addition, many books and seminars offer assistance with stress management; but what do you do when someone still happens to cause you stress? As long as we have the "three T's" (teenagers, traffic jams, and telephones), our buttons will get pushed. In other words, it is not a question of whether we buy into unwanted emotions, it is only a question of *when* . . . and then what?

The first empowerment exercise helps you create a simple coping technique to help you during a situation of emotional anxiety. This exercise comes with an audio download on managing stress. You will find the stress management script in Appendix 6; but in order to maximize the benefit from the download, be sure to read the rest of this chapter as well as the next one.

Since emotion is such a powerful door to the subconscious, I teach the importance of learning how to control our feelings by making a positive choice at the time our buttons get pushed. (For healthy choices follow the directions for the exercise below.) We must also accept ownership of our emotions (even negative ones). So if you tell yourself: "X made me mad," you just gave your power away. Rather, you should perceive that X sold you some stress. You bought it, and now you own it – but you have the power to decide what to do with the stressful emotion.

Let me illustrate further from my own experience as a former parent. When a teenager demonstrates their temper, I *just might occasionally* buy into some anger. While growing up, some children prove to be quite effective at selling stress. Reaching their teens somehow seems to enhance their skills at selling negativity to parents; but sometimes I refuse to buy into their negative emotions. In simple terms, while I cannot control the actions of my child, I (and I alone) must accept responsibility for my responses to my teenager's actions. Believe me when I tell you that my children provided me with numerous opportunities to practice what I teach. (Often it seems that those we love the most are those most easily able to trigger our emotions.)

Now let us get on with the instructions for the first stress management exercise.

To maximize the benefits of the stress-coping technique, you must practice the coping skill several times in the rehearsal room of your imagination while in a state of self-hypnosis. This helps your subconscious mind accept the desired technique at a quiet time when your emotions remain calm. The exercise compares to the rehearsal that any musician believes to be essential before a good performance.

Before you begin, get relaxed and comfortable. (If you have not already done so, practice the simple self-hypnosis inductions given in Chapter 4 until you gain success with at least one of them. Also remember to remove contacts if you wear hard lenses, and remove any chewing gum.) Read and understand the instructions before proceeding, so that you don't have to refer to them once you begin.

Next, read the affirmations on stress management in Appendix 7. Read them slowly and deliberately, either silently or out loud.

Now you may enter self-hypnosis through the method described in the first practice session. Daydream that you are in a totally peaceful place. Imagine pleasant and peaceful sights, sounds, and/or feelings. As you do, take a deep breath and think the word "relax" as you exhale. (Some readers may need to first master the mental mini-vacation exercise described later in this chapter.)

Daydream your ability to remain calm in a scenario you rehearse in your mind where someone tries to make you mad. Physically take a deep breath, thinking the word "relax" as you exhale; and imagine your ability to actually feel calm, confident, and composed – totally in control of your feelings. Fantasize making one of the three choices described under the heading "Stress Release Options" below. Imagine yourself feeling calm, confident, and in control of your emotions. Imagine the situation through to a desirable conclusion. Practice the other two choices in the same manner.

When you are ready, come back to the beta state by counting from one to five.

Stress Release Options: The Healthy Choices

As mentioned above, we may choose from among three healthy options whenever we feel stress or anxiety over a situation:

Express yourself immediately but appropriately

Some situations, such as your child doing something dangerous (or a sales professional getting an unexpected objection during a closing interview), require an immediate response. You may find emotion reflected in your voice in the first example, and you may have to wait until you have yelled "No!" before taking your deep breath. In the second example, you may wish to take a deep breath first; and then simply express yourself calmly and confidently. In some situations, you may wish to find the humorous side of the situation. Laughter can be a good release; sometimes tears; sometimes one word spoken firmly; sometimes sarcasm; and so on.

Express yourself later at a more appropriate time and place

This option might be in your best interest if an associate at work pushes the wrong button in the presence of others. Some people will accept your opinion much more readily in private over a coffee rather than in front of peers. Furthermore, parents frequently find meals more enjoyable by instructing their children to wait until after dinner to solve their arguments.

Release and let go – or, forgive!

If you don't choose either of the first two options, then practice this one (you do not have to condone). If you think someone else owes you an apology, you place yourself in bondage to that belief. By freeing others from their emotional debts, you actually free yourself. The key to forgiving involves the ability to release the other person from the apology formerly owed, and to also forgive yourself for buying the stress in the first place. Release might be the wisest option if your boss says or does something that is annoying.

Most people use other options for stress control, such as stuffing bad feelings or internalizing. The results vary from person to person. We might take out our stress on friends or loved ones. We could take it out on strangers. We might also take it out on the same person at a later date through blowing something up all out of proportion. Worse yet, some people take it out on themselves through sickness, escapism, or addiction, or by becoming accident-prone. Some people react to stress with an uncontrolled, immediate emotional expression. All these options are hazardous to our health and wealth.

In going through the healthy scenarios during self-hypnosis, remember to rehearse each of the three choices. Your rehearsal during self-hypnosis influences your performance during real-life stress, like post-hypnotic suggestions. You will now allow your subconscious to respond to a given signal, and *you decide when to give the signal.* Practicing during the trance state anchors the power of choice into your signal, creating a trigger for choice. As an added benefit, your trigger for choice becomes a form of empowerment at a subconscious level.

This simple technique alone can improve family and social relationships. Emotion can transfer from subconscious to subconscious in any discussion where opinions might differ, compounding the anxiety of all parties concerned. Confidence can also transfer from subconscious to subconscious, increasing the probability of peaceful resolution.

Businesspeople may discover that the use of this technique increases their income. If someone in a sales interview fears losing a deal after an unexpected objection, the prospective customer may subconsciously pick up on that fear. While the sales rep might fear losing the sale, the prospect fears making a decision, and will want to think it over instead of giving you the real objection. Confidence also comes across at a subconscious level, making the customer more prone to either buying confidently or revealing the real objection.

Using the Coping Technique

The deep breath becomes your trigger for choice: *now, later,* or *release.* The deep breath trigger becomes a reminder to you that you own your emotions, and you have the power of choice.

Understand, too, that your degree of success in coping may vary according to the situation at hand, as well as the frequency of use of your new technique. Exercising a muscle creates strength; so you could think to yourself: *"As a muscle that is used becomes stronger with use, my power of choice becomes stronger with use."*

When you have completed this practice session, take note of your opportunities to practice this new skill. Next time you drive and someone turns left in front of you, take a deep breath and think the word "relax." If you feel like calling him a jerk first, go ahead, as long as you still take the deep breath before or afterwards.

The work place is another great place to practice this skill. Suppose you want to go home after a hectic day on the job, but suddenly find out you have to stay late because someone else didn't finish an assignment. Take one deep breath, think relax, and then say and do what seems most appropriate. Many of my clients have reported to me an improvement in their own self-confidence simply from mastering the art of this technique.

Let us suppose you have a day riddled with stress. You have a few moments alone in your office, or you've already come home feeling overloaded with the day's strains. Perhaps you might wish to calm down by taking a short mental mini-vacation.

The Mental Mini-Vacation

Your imagination is like the rehearsal room of your mind, where you have the ability to practice being the person you wish to be. You can imagine what you plan on doing tomorrow, or you can replay what happened yesterday by reliving those experiences in the imagination.

We use the imagination quite frequently to imagine our anticipated pleasure for a planned long-weekend – when we finally get out to the lake, or the golf course, or the campground, or the beach. Dating couples can attest to the fact that anticipation influences both mind and body. I'll avoid describing what frequently takes place in the imagination during a date; yet I'll remind the reader that both mind and body will respond to the imagination! Mind and body also respond to fantasized places of peace and beauty.

Consider your imagination to be your own private place, where you can travel through time and space. *Star Trek* fans can compare the imagination to the *holodeck* of the mind, because you can create your own program. You can *be* anywhere you wish, and *do* anything you wish ... in your imagination. You can relive any memory

Exercises to Manage Stress

(happy or sad), or you can experience any fantasy. Although many of our parents taught us not to daydream, we can't avoid daydreaming occasionally. The question is whether you control your daydreams, or vice versa.

The mental mini-vacation utilizes your ability to daydream. You may enjoy going back in time to a favorite holiday spot, or you may imagine going forward in time to a future vacation. You have the choice! Remember that you have total power, total freedom, and total privacy in your imagination. You can do anything you wish, and go anywhere you wish. Are you ready?

Enter self-hypnosis using your chosen induction, and then adapt the following script to your own words. If you record your voice, change the first-person format to the second-person. Again, notice that the simple wording means more to the subconscious than good grammar.

> I'm going to count backwards now from ten to one. As I do, it becomes easier and easier for me to imagine sights, sounds, and feelings in my beautiful, peaceful place . . .
>
> Number ten: deeper and deeper, relaxing physically . . . With each breath, it's easier to imagine my peaceful place . . .
>
> Number nine: deeper and deeper, relaxing mentally . . . With each sound, it's easier to imagine pleasant sights, sounds, and feelings . . .
>
> Number eight: deeper and deeper, relaxing emotionally . . . The deeper I go, the better I feel, and the deeper I want to go . . .
>
> Number seven: deeper and deeper, relaxing totally . . . The deeper I go, the easier it is to go even deeper, imagining my peaceful place . . .
>
> Number six: every nerve and muscle relaxes completely . . . as if I'm becoming a part of the peace that I imagine . . .

Number five: each number making it easier and easier to go deeper and deeper . . . and it feels SO good to just relax . . .

Number four: as I go deeper, it becomes easier and easier to imagine sights, sounds, and feelings that are so calm, and so peaceful . . .

Number three: just drifting into total relaxation . . . into my place of total peace . . . where I can enjoy being anywhere I wish now . . .

Number two: just relaxing at my ideal peaceful place now . . .

Number one: waaaaay down deep . . . Relaxing into a very deep, inner peace . . . a very deep, inner peace . . .

As I touch my finger to my thumb, or take a deep breath and think the word RELAX, it's an automatic reminder of my inner peace. *[Touch a finger to your thumb, and take a deep breath.]* Whenever I do this in the waking state, I feel calm and composed, free to think with a clear mind . . . but for now, I can just enjoy going even deeper into relaxation . . . deeper and deeper . . .

With each breath I take, it's easier and easier to enjoy my freedom of imagination, to go to a favorite vacation spot now . . . and imagine my IDEAL vacation . . . doing what I enjoy doing, and relaxing as well . . .

In my mind, as much time as I wish can pass . . . and I feel as though I've enjoyed an hour's nap . . . I feel like I enjoyed an hour's nap . . .

Before emerging from trance, imagine feeling the way you wish to feel. Then, when ready, count from one to five and awaken yourself.

Most hypnotherapists use a similar method to help clients establish a peaceful place. The act of taking the deep breath (or touching your thumb and finger) while imagining your peaceful place anchors a sense of inner peace to that act. Anchoring your peaceful place into your trigger during trance compares to programming a computer. Activating your trigger during the conscious state compares to pushing the "Execute" button on your PC. Your deep breath (and/or touching thumb and finger) will now become a trigger for inner peace.

Use your inner peace trigger in conjunction with your stress-coping technique, and notice an increased ability to cope with life's stresses. (You can also call this the peaceful place trigger.)

Sleeping at Night

Have you ever found yourself unable to sleep easily because of stress or worry? If you can honestly answer no to that question, count your blessings and skip down to the next chapter; otherwise, keep on reading.

Frequently I have used self-hypnosis to go to sleep at night, and have taught clients to do likewise. Most of the time the mental mini-vacation technique adequately helps people fall asleep even during stressful times; but sometimes a major stress can inhibit one's ability to respond to the techniques described thus far in this book. For the benefit of readers experiencing the same difficulty, let me share another technique that may work wonders. This unusual self-hypnosis exercise consistently proves valuable for me personally, as well as for clients.

First, be aware that some sleeping disorders may have physical causes; so please consult with your physician if you have any reason whatsoever to believe that more than just stress keeps you awake. Also, if your stress seems related to serious unresolved emotional issues and/or family problems, consider seeking the help of a competent professional. (For your own protection, similar advice appears several times throughout this book, as repetition is good emphasis.) Anyone on medication because of insomnia may also need to consult with a physician prior to using this next exercise.

One main type of trance induction employs what hypnotherapists call *mental confusion*. Mental exercises which cause the logical mind to sort through confusing input can also create a trance state. Many hypnotherapists guide their clients into trance with mental confusion techniques; and I have adapted one into a simple self-hypnosis technique for going to sleep. Causing the conscious mind to work at a time when we would prefer to rest allows some interesting things to happen at a subconscious level.

Remember when your parents told you to count sheep at night in order to fall asleep? Adding a few autosuggestions to that same child's technique can produce an alpha state that soon turns into theta and delta . . . resulting in sound sleep. My variation involves counting backwards rather than forwards, and you may imagine the numbers any way you wish. These numbers may appear on sheep (or other animals) passing by, jumping over a fence, and so on; or the numbers may be on signposts (or any other visual image) or simply whispered by the wind.

When you notice that your mind wants to wander away from the technique, you should be closer to drifting off to sleep. What you say to yourself at this point can help or hinder, so learn from my experience. First, find a comfortable position and then take three very deep breaths. Continue breathing slowly and deeply. Say to yourself words similar to those in the following script.

> As I count backwards from 100, one number per breath, my mind just wishes to drift off to sleep . . . 100. *[Inhale.]*
>
> I can imagine seeing or hearing each number just before I say it to myself . . . 99. *[Inhale.]*
>
> As I imagine my peaceful place, with pleasant sights, sounds, and feelings, the numbers start getting farther away . . . 98. *[Inhale.]*
>
> As the numbers get smaller and smaller, I get sleepier and sleepier, wanting to wander asleep . . . 97. *[Inhale.]*

Exercises to Manage Stress

My mind starts wandering as I wander closer to the realm of deep sleep, getting sleepy . . . 96. *[Inhale.]*

The more my mind wanders, the sleepier I get . . . and my mind wanders away from remembering the numbers . . . 95. *[Inhale.]*

The numbers get easier to forget, or difficult to remember, and I get sleepier and sleepier . . . 94. *[Inhale.]*

When I forget the last number, or skip the next number, or repeat a number, it DOUBLES my drowsiness . . . *[Next number; inhale.]*

If I take two breaths between numbers, or remember to forget, or forget to remember, my mind just wants to sleep . . . *[Next number; inhale.]*

The more I try to remember to forget, or skip or repeat, the last number or the next one, the sleepier I get . . . *[Next number; inhale.]*

As it becomes easier to fantasize my peaceful place, I soon find myself dreaming of my peaceful place . . . *[Next number; inhale.]*

The numbers are getting farther and farther, smaller and smaller, deeper and deeper, into sleep . . . *[Next number; inhale.]*

I TRY to stay with the numbers, but my mind wants to wander . . . or drift . . . and wander . . . to sleep . . . *[Next number; inhale.]*

As I skip numbers, repeat numbers, or forget numbers, I go deeper and deeper into sleep . . . *[Next number; inhale.]*

If you are still awake at this point, take two breaths between numbers and imagine that the numbers (or sheep) gradually move farther and farther away.

Now I take two breaths between each number, and it gives my mind more time to wander to sleep . . . *[Inhale.]*

The more I try to remember the script, the easier it is for my mind to wander, or the sleepier I get . . . *[Next number; inhale.]*

If I think of two numbers in a breath, or breathe three times between numbers, I get MUCH sleepier . . . *[Inhale.]*

It would be SO much easier to simply forget about the numbers and just let myself go to sleep . . . *[Next number; inhale.]*

As I try to remember to forget the numbers or the script, my mind simply finds it easier to doze off, or sleep . . . *[Inhale.]*

As the numbers start jumping around now, I get sleepier and sleepier, or drowsy and sleepy . . . *[Next number; inhale.]*

I don't know if I forgot the last number, or the next number, or both, because my mind wanders more . . . *[Inhale.]*

It's SO much easier to simply imagine a pleasant place, until what I imagine becomes a dream . . . *[Inhale.]*

The numbers are fading farther away, allowing my mind to wander and dream . . . or dream and wander . . . *[Inhale.]*

If you still find yourself awake, simply continue counting backwards while whispering words similar to those contained in the script. Be sure your breathing remains slow and easy. Most people using this technique properly will rarely get clear down to the last number before falling asleep, although I have been the exception twice in ten years. On one of those occasions, I remember whispering to God, "Well, God, I got clear down to number one. It didn't work this time . . ." and that was the last thing I remembered before waking up the next morning.

Other People's Successes

How effective are these empowerment exercises? I can best answer that question by providing some case summaries from satisfied clients.

Roger (name changed) devoted himself to his family, his church, and his career. In spite of unexpected financial setbacks and professional frustrations, he continued to put forth quality work for his employer. Within a few short months, he found himself in such an emotional mess that he worked more hours weekly to accomplish less than when he worked normal hours. The cycle of stress resulted in lost sleep, increasing anxieties, and marital problems. While I could not advise him regarding the marital stress, he strongly desired to learn how to simply respond more maturely whenever somebody pushed his buttons. Although he originally saw me for habit control, he told me that the benefits derived from learning the stress-coping technique proved to be worth the entire investment in a series of sessions. The stress-coper enabled him to pause just long enough to make better responses, thus increasing his sense of empowerment as well as building his self-esteem. The majority of clients practicing the stress management meditation have reported benefits over the years, ranging from slight to profound. The degree of help depends on both the need and the commitment of the person utilizing this technique.

Many clients have thanked me for teaching them the peaceful place meditation or the mental mini-vacation. Often just ten minutes in a self-hypnotic trance can provide as much benefit as a one-hour nap.

While the exercise to sleep at night benefits many patients, I find one fact quite interesting. Very few clients have ever seen me for insomnia; and the majority of those who have seen me for (non-medical) sleeping disorders have often encountered subconscious resistance. On the other hand, hundreds of clients over the years seeing me for habit control have reported sleeping better than in years simply after mastering the art of self-hypnosis.

Subconscious Programming

Become proficient in at least one of the empowerment exercises above to help you manage stress. Then, when you feel ready to learn more, go on to Part III and prepare your journey for successful goal achievement.

Part III
Planning the Journey

Chapter 9

Clearing Obstacles

After seeing how the subconscious mind can be programmed, let us consider life's journey itself. We cannot reach a chosen destination without choosing the right road or path; and we must also either clear any obstacles or find a way around them. How do we clear the obstacles? How do we find the best path toward our goals? This chapter answers the first question; the next three chapters will answer the second question.

Obstacles and negative thinking seem to attract each other; so take a look inward at any habits or repetitious negative thought patterns you may wish to change. You may recognize the influence of one or more of the methods of subconscious programming. For example, most smokers started because of the desire to identify with peers or adults; but they often feel a desire to light up whenever someone tells them to quit. Overeating sometimes relates to low self-esteem, which can often be traced to past failures and/or negative emotional experiences; stuffing food into the body seems to help stuff negative feelings deeper into the subconscious. Usually we need to release the past in order to change negative thinking and clear the obstacles.

Unfortunately, many people have been told by practitioners that they should blame their parents (and/or other people) for their "dysfunctional" backgrounds. This type of counseling makes clients feel disempowered because of being victimized by other people. While it is a fact that friends or family with selfish motives can often cause hurt, it is important to overcome this by learning from past events and then releasing the feelings without condoning the actions of others.

The consequences of hanging on to the past (such as old grudges) can compound upon themselves, putting more obstacles in our path and trapping us into negative thinking. This chapter explains why. I'll discuss some common (and similar) traps and attitudes caused by various failures and hurts, and how to release them. Notice how some of these traps overlap with others.

The Failure Trap

Have you ever felt ensnared by a series of relentless disappointments and setbacks? We attract what we imagine, and this is why failure often attracts more failure. Indulging in self-pity creates an accompanying negative emotion, opening wide the subconscious gateways. The danger occurs when we relive mistakes in the imagination and replay them over and over again. Some people refer to this as "playing old tapes." The more you imagine failure, the more likely your chances of falling short again. This principle applies whether your goal involves sports, business, or simply overcoming an undesired habit. The cycle may continue until both the imagination and the feelings change.

An athlete could find a slump persisting, compounding the negative feelings in a manner that sends him/her into a downward spiral of doubt. If the athlete believes in the collapse and replays recent failures, the subconscious receives negative suggestions through the language of imagination. Normally the cycle will continue until broken by a good performance.

For a salesperson experiencing a self-perpetuating sales slump, it becomes all too easy to imagine the dreaded objection. Fantasizing customer refusals will actually influence the subconscious to construct the presentation in a negative manner. The emotion and fall-off may change with a big sale; but that deal normally requires imagining the desired success first.

The smoker who feels guilty for always backsliding often puts energy into the fear of lighting up. Replaying past failures in the imagination sends a message to the inner mind, and past relapses attract yet another disappointment.

The frequent dieter often remembers indulging in the goodies and blowing past diets; and if he/she believes that another diet will fail, guess what happens?

One difficulty impacting our ability to overcome failure, even when we consciously desire to do so, is that acceptance of non-achievement tends to attract more disappointment because we keep on imagining it. We must break this cycle by training ourselves to imagine success, or to replace a negative fantasy with a positive one. We will lose in the land of logic, so we must win in the field of daydreams. Trying to use logic alone to overcome a painful setback can be ineffective, because negative daydreaming leads to justification of failure, resulting in the subconscious persisting in pessimistic beliefs. When we are ready to analyze a setback, we must keep our emotions in check and avoid replaying the failures in our imagination; otherwise we can easily fall victim to the justification trap.

The Justification Trap

Have you found yourself among the ranks of those so involved with analyzing reasons for blocking success that you find the achievement you seek slips farther away? As long as you search for reasons to justify your disappointment, you will continue to fail.

It seems that our society invests considerable time, money, and effort into studying reasons for failure. Hindsight may bring insight; but in order to find success, we need to devote more of our time and resources to where we are going instead of where we have been. By spending your energy searching for roadblocks in your path, your subconscious mind may very well be creating new obstacles, keeping you locked inside the justification trap.

I know some people who have gone to counselors or hypnotherapists for several years looking for causes of problems without seeking release, only to end up finding more real or imagined obstacles from the past to justify keeping their problems. Some search their childhood diligently for reasons to blame a third party for negative programming. Unless we explore the past with the intention of releasing it and learning from our mistakes, we could fall into the self-pity pit.

Wallowing in shame and/or prolonged anger over past hurts usually leads to further justification of failure by blaming others, thus creating greater difficulty in our efforts to change negative feelings. The self-pity pit permits more failure because our behavior now becomes easier to justify, and our obstacles appear bigger.

"If Only . . ."

This commonly heard phrase haunts many of us. Can you think of times where a goal might have been realized if only circumstances had been just a little different?

- A smoker says: "If only my friend hadn't pushed my buttons."
- A dieter says: "If only my spouse hadn't eaten dessert in front of me."
- A salesperson says: "If only the competition had called one day later."
- A student says: "If only I had one more day to study."
- An athlete says: "If only the umpire hadn't made that bad call, we would have won the game."

This phrase makes it easy to continue justifying the problem and its apparent cause(s). We can easily defeat ourselves by getting emotionally involved with reasons for failure. It is too simple for us to get caught saying "If only . . ." and then justifying the reasons for non-achievement. I know, because I have been there and done that. If this phrase becomes a habit, we can start feeling like we are in a victim trap; and success will have a way of eluding us until we get out of this way of thinking. Taken to an extreme, some people might engage in anti-social behavior by saying, "If only I wasn't abused, I could live a normal life," because it is easier to blame others for their unacceptable conduct rather than accepting responsibility for their own actions.

Does the phrase "If only . . ." sound familiar to you? If so, perhaps it is time to forgive those who have hurt you so that you can get on with life. While it is true that any of us can sometimes be surprised by the unexpected negative actions of others, we need to get up as quickly as possible and keep walking on our own path. If you find this difficult, consider investing in some sessions with a hypnosis professional.

Forgiveness and Responsibility

So what should we do when someone blindsides us because of greed or dishonesty? I often tell my hypnotherapy students that there is no magic in hypnosis, but there is often magic in the power of forgiveness. Often, this is the most controversial topic of my entire nine-month hypnotherapy course.

Forgiving others does *not* mean condoning their actions, nor do you have to forget how others might have hurt you; but you do have to let go of your own anger toward others for those past hurts. Why do I say this? Forgiveness provides a powerful key to escaping from the traps described in this chapter; but it is human nature to keep our anger against those who have harmed us until they pay for their mistakes. We might wisely choose to separate ourselves from a bad situation for our own protection (or to put a criminal behind bars for the good of society), but we must escape from our own grudges in order to be free.

I believe that we are the ones who remain in bondage to grudges . . . not the people who hurt us. In my opinion, until we learn to let go of anger over past harms, it may be virtually impossible to clear the obstacles in our path and make the changes we desire. Some people believe that they might be more "functional" today *if only* someone else had not been responsible for causing harm or abuse. Some counselors claim that we can gain back our power only by confronting the perpetrator. In my own opinion, forgiveness outshines blame, and is absolutely essential for our complete healing. At the very least, we must release the other person to his/her higher power (or karmic fate) and forgive ourselves for carrying the hurt.

One of my clients (in her forties) told me that another counselor had instructed her to confront her father for alleged childhood abuse as a condition of her healing. Since she stood to inherit a substantial fortune, she was not willing to pay millions of dollars as a condition of the "healing" that the counselor discussed. If something similar happens to you, my opinion is that you might benefit by looking for another therapist. You do *not* need to hear someone say that you would be normal "if only" you had never been abused.

I personally know the healing power of forgiveness, because of abuse received from a cousin during childhood. Forgiving and releasing resulted in my ability to heal and get on with life; and contrary to the opinion of a psychotherapist, I have not been scarred for life. My choice was to heal through forgiveness (rather than saying "If only he hadn't hurt me, I could be normal"). I am grateful that I chose the path of forgiveness; that decision cleared many obstacles from my path, making my life's journey more enjoyable.

Regardless of our past, we can change our present response to it. Don't stay in the victim trap. In spite of the pain and stress others might inflict upon us, we must all accept responsibility for our reactions to other people, places, and things. (If you feel like you are currently trapped in stressful family problems, a bad job, and so on, seek competent professional help from an appropriate source.)

At the opposite extreme we find people whose idea of "accepting responsibility" means that *you* are somehow responsible for the actions of people who hurt you. Accepting your own responsibility does not mean taking the blame for the actions of others; but rather, only for your own actions. Let us find a balance here. When you determine your share of the responsibility, learn from it and forgive yourself also, because self-forgiveness is equally as important as forgiveness of others.

Dealing with Criticism

Unexpected criticism often challenges our ability to forgive both self and others. While I will avoid commenting on how to handle the particulars of any specific caustic remarks, I must address the importance of our subconscious reaction to negative putdowns or character slams. How we handle criticism determines whether we can remove obstacles or suffer more impediments as a result of the censure. An entire book could easily be written concerning how to give and receive criticism, so I will make only a few important comments here.

Our response might be influenced by a combination of our own feelings at the time, the attitude and motives of the critic, the relevancy of the criticism, and whether or not we asked for it. We may expect constructive critique from an employer or supervisor, but a variety of factors may influence its impact on the subconscious. However, we might not be as willing to receive criticism from a friend, unless given positively and with a motive to help.

While attending a convention in 1997, I heard an interesting presentation on dealing with negative criticism from a very successful Australian businessman (Peter J. Daniels). He said that negative criticism binds the receiver while giving a sense of power to the sender, and he encouraged us to avoid buying into it. When someone puts me down with negative criticism, I whisper to myself "Cancel, cancel."

Many of us have experienced less-than-satisfying encounters with self-appointed teachers who try to convince us to accept responsibility for "creating the reality" of attracting manipulators or abusers into our lives. My conclusion is that some people would rather blame someone else for "creating a poverty consciousness" as an excuse to justify their own greed; and I have personally known people who take unfair advantage of another person's time and talents in self-serving ways, under the guise of "spirituality." Then, when the victim tries to assert himself/herself, the user proceeds to give the victim a lecture about accepting responsibility and/or "manifesting a prosperity consciousness." When you recognize such selfishness for what it is, you are wise to remove yourself from such influence. You can forgive them; but you do not have to allow them to convince you that you are the one with the problem. Some years ago I came right out and told a negative critic, "I reject what you said, and cancel it," and turned around and walked away.

We do not have to accept responsibility for the actions of others; rather, we are accountable only for how we respond to others. Sometimes our best response is to separate ourselves from someone who hurts us repeatedly or tries to take advantage of us. Give your time and talents to people who recognize you and appreciate you. Success comes more easily to those who are free of incessant denigration. Just maintain enough internal integrity to determine whether there is any validity to the comments, regardless of the motive and manner of the sender. If in doubt, seek counsel from a trusted friend or professional.

Suppose the criticism you receive is valid . . . now what?

Self-Criticism

Upon recognizing any truth in the criticism of others, we need to look for solutions rather than putting energy into the problems. If your critic genuinely wants to help, ask him/her to offer resolutions. A person with a genuine desire to help should critique your performance rather than criticizing you personally; but sometimes even the best of intentions can come out wrong and cause pain.

If he/she tried to hurt you, but gave valid criticism in the process, then seek counsel elsewhere in your quest for a solution; but don't come down too hard on yourself. Indulging in excessive self-criticism can send us right back into the self-pity pit. If we wait until we find perfection, success may elude us. Simply being your best is easier than trying to be perfect.

Success does not mean doing things flawlessly, nor does it mean having a fat bank account. Many people don't realize this, and often disparage themselves for either not having enough money and/or for being less than perfect. By now it should be obvious that looking back excessively and replaying perceived failures in the mind's eye can disable us.

Even minor self-criticism can hurt when accompanied with negative emotions, because we end up energizing the problem rather than the solution. A semi-professional bowler seeing me for sports improvement demonstrated the power of self-criticism. He said, "Whenever I leave the 10-pin by itself I always get nervous and blow the spare." His self-criticism reinforced the failure, which he imagined every time he left the 10-pin standing, making the problem worse. After some private sessions to help him focus on the desired result, his self-criticism stopped and his average improved by 17 pins.

Indulging in self-criticism creates guilt, destroys motivation, and compounds problems. Many people literally stress themselves into illness through constant self-criticism. Looking for better ways of doing things can be constructive if done without putting yourself down; however, throwing mud at yourself for mistakes or financial setbacks damages your self-esteem. Furthermore, nagging at yourself for failures will attract more failures. While a brief moment of guilt might guide us to change our actions or minimize anti-social behavior, indulging in prolonged guilt can cripple us. In other words, criticizing yourself for real or imagined underachievement is hazardous to your health and wealth. We need to learn from our mistakes as well as from the mistakes of others. Then let us release the disappointment and get on with life.

Techniques for Releasing

So how do we release? The person with a painful past may need far more help than I can provide here; but let me offer some techniques that might help, beginning with past hurts.

Past Hurts

When negative feelings arise because of past hurts, go into a meditative state with your chosen technique (such as those described in Chapter 4), and fantasize being in your peaceful place. When you feel sufficiently mellow, say or whisper the person's name and say, *"I forgive you and release you to your highest good."* Another affirmation is: *"I release all people, places and things that must be released for my highest good."*

In case you need more releasing than provided by the above affirmations, I'll share another releasing technique that requires some time and conscious effort. I call this the Letter to God. (If you do not believe in God, you can consider it to be a letter to your higher power, or to the earth.) Write a letter that nobody else will read, and irrevocably dispose of it in a meditative or prayerful state. You may either use a writing tablet, typewriter, or computer. Begin the letter by telling the person(s) who have hurt you anything you wish to say regarding your feelings and how their actions damaged you, without mincing your words. If you believe in God or a higher power, express your frustration over the concerns. Release the other person(s) to God (or fate), with forgiveness of any apologies owed to you. Absolve yourself for carrying the hurt, and release it to divinity. State your desired resolution with apology and/or recompense from the person who harmed you, and state your best possible resolution without such recompense. Affirm release of the obstacle and hurt regardless of the outcome, and ask for your highest and best good. Date it and sign it. (If you use a computer, print one copy and then delete the file from your computer.) Decide whether to burn it, shred it in a paper shredder, or tear it up into small pieces and dispose of it. Go into a light meditative state; pray if you wish, and say something such as, *"I release these concerns to the universe."* (You may release them to God, to Jesus, to a higher spiritual power, to your guardian angel or spiritual guide, or to the earth, to fate, and so on.) Remember that forgiving does not mean condoning.

Intense past hurts may require hypnotic regression from a hypnosis professional for full release. If you believe this to be appropriate for you refer to Appendix 2 for guidelines on how to choose a competent hypnotherapist trained in hypnotic regression. Anyone facilitating hypnotic regression must be objective and offer sessions without any preconceived opinions; otherwise he/she can taint the trance and leave you with false memories. False or distorted memories are often mistaken for "repressed" memories, so be careful.

Some hurts that seem to be in the past might actually be current unresolved issues that require resolution. If you require conscious resolution of a present conflict, refer to the exercises in Chapter 8 to keep your anxiety levels under control when you attempt this. Seek outside help if necessary. Several years ago a male client saw me for professional confidence. While practicing his releasing technique, he suddenly emerged from trance in tears. During his meditation he had relived several intense fights with his former wife. She was abusive both to him and to their children, and he was suing for custody. This example provides two lessons: (1) Just as a weightlifter starts working out with lighter weights instead of heavy ones, we need to begin releasing smaller past pains before attempting larger ones; and (2) some situations require professional help. I referred this man for traditional counseling.

Present Hurts

If another person says or does something that causes us to indulge in negative thinking, we can apply the stress-coping technique (from Chapter 8) and deal with the issue at hand. If we sink into negative thinking simply because of circumstances, or if we allow bad feelings to persist after using the stress-coping trigger, we need to do more releasing.

Stopping negative thoughts is easier said than done, so I am including two mental exercises that may help to release negative thoughts at the moment they occur.

Remember the discussion of anchoring and triggers from Chapter 5? We can train the subconscious to respond to a signal that triggers our freedom of thought. Both of the following releasing techniques enable you to replace a negative thought with a positive one simply by giving yourself a signal. Let me emphasize that replacing is easier than erasing, especially when thoughts or feelings dominate our minds.

The first technique involves the simple use of the trigger established with the mental mini-vacation described in Chapter 8. Whenever you feel negative thoughts taking root, it is time to activate your inner peace trigger and immediately fantasize your peaceful place. If necessary, practice the mini-vacation exercise several times to increase the power of this trigger. Also remember that the imagination is the rehearsal room of your mind. Fantasize the ability to go from a stressful situation immediately to your peaceful place, and then to return to the present with a feeling of calm.

The second technique expands on the first. Practice the stress-coping exercise along with your mental mini-vacation exercise. Then, either before or during your trance, say the following two affirmations:

1. *Whenever I use my peaceful place trigger, I immediately imagine anything I choose.*
2. *My peaceful place trigger instantly empowers me to use my best wisdom, knowledge, understanding, training, and experience to make wise decisions.*

In real life, the peaceful place trigger now serves two functions: (1) As previously practiced, we can send a message of inner peace to the subconscious, providing at least some sense of calm; and (2) the trigger reminds us to make wise decisions. Perhaps we could fantasize the solution of the presenting problem. If that seems too difficult, then visualize something totally different instead, and address the problem later.

Remember that any self-hypnosis empowerment exercise compares to the rehearsal before the performance. When negative thoughts try to invade the mind, it is performance time! Several rehearsals improve the performance. Once you master the rehearsal, remember to use your peaceful place trigger. If neither of these provides sufficient empowerment, you may also write the Letter to God as described above.

Additional Thoughts

If you only succeed in releasing a portion of the negative feelings, more work might be necessary. If past or present hurts squash your self-esteem, then seek counseling and/or hypnotherapy from a competent therapist. While you may listen to the advice or opinions of friends or counselors, however, retain the power of choice for yourself. You must live with the benefits and consequences of your decisions, so do *not* give your power away (not even to a therapist). The ethical practitioner will help you gain more empowerment through problem resolution and healthy releasing.

The importance of releasing cannot be emphasized enough. Without release, the subconscious will remain trapped among the obstacles. I believe that is one reason why the world is filled with so much negativity and distrust.

Let me conclude this chapter by reiterating that we must stop energizing problems, and instead start energizing solutions and their benefits. Instead of constantly looking back, we must frequently look ahead, planning our journey toward our goals. The chapters that follow will help you do just that.

Chapter 10

Define and Celebrate Your Success

Are you ready to continue the journey? We must keep our eyes on the road ahead as we continue moving forward. How far do you think you would get driving down a highway with your eyes glued to the rear-view mirror 75% of the time? In this example, we easily accept the importance of looking ahead at the road in front and following the signs. Unfortunately, we don't find the journey toward our goals mapped as clearly; nor does the direction make itself obvious. It is easy to either get on a detour or go off the road entirely when driving toward success, especially when different people have different definitions of success.

The subconscious can follow our directions more efficiently when we establish a course of action; therefore each of us must determine our own definition of success, whether you desire achievement in business or in other areas of your life. Contrary to the opinions of some, who put money ahead of happiness, success cannot be measured solely by the size of a bank account. In other words, choose the right road!

What Is Your Definition of Success?

To many people, success means simply doing what we enjoy doing and doing it well. To some, achievement describes an ongoing journey through life filled with academic, artistic, social, personal, religious, and recreational goals and accomplishments.

Others measure their success by the size of their bank account; but I have known some wealthy individuals whose financial attainments resulted in sadness because of the personal price paid for acquiring money. Some self-centered achievers discover that their financial success comes at the cost of failure in love and happiness. Those who obtain success by forfeiting friends and family may risk bankruptcy in the happiness department. Some roads to wealth might glitter brightly at first; but they may end in darkness.

Most certainly we can welcome financial successes; but I believe other goals are worth our efforts also. Choose your accomplishments wisely, because the benefits of any success will normally come at a cost; and you must accept responsibility for deciding whether or not you wish to pay the price.

The first vital step toward reaching a goal successfully is to become results-oriented. Choose the road you wish to travel; but first learn what awaits at the end of that path. Determine the results you desire and identify your personal benefits for enjoying this outcome. Imagine them often. This helps sell your own subconscious on following your directions. (This is detailed in Chapter 13, along with an empowerment exercise.)

Next, determine the best method(s) of reaching your objective. Whatever you have to do to manifest your desire into reality represents the price you pay for successfully attaining your goal. Some people prefer to call the cost of success an action plan. Regardless of your preference, life is full of tradeoffs. Very seldom will we find a goal simply handed to us without any effort on our part. We need to define both the objective and the action plan. In other words, decide what you want and then go for it.

Once you determine that a goal merits your time and energy, then work toward manifesting it into reality. As you progress toward that target, realize that you deserve to enjoy your accomplishments, no matter how small they may seem. Look for them. Recognize them. Honor them.

Now we come to an important metaphor, leading into a very valuable empowerment exercise. Just as the driver will occasionally glance in the rear-view mirror, looking back at our past successes can be constructive.

Love Yourself: Celebrate Your Success!

Many clients from all walks of life give me good feedback regarding the benefits of the next self-hypnosis exercise; but let me provide some important preliminary information first.

Just as we have the ability to replay old tapes of failures, we also have the opportunity to rerun our success tapes. Remembering past accomplishments reinforces both personal and professional confidence. Also, enjoying happy memories helps build self-esteem and self-love. Some people might ask: "Why should we learn to love ourselves?" If you really love or like somebody, you'll find yourself much more prone to do something good for them, even if that person is you! I realize, however, that our present day culture presents a real challenge for us to find the proper balance in loving ourselves. How can we love others fully unless or until we love ourselves? Many people put so much energy into being good husbands, wives, parents, employees (or employers), citizens, Christians, and so on, that they get wrapped up in others and forget to love themselves too. Jesus instructed us to love our neighbor as we love ourselves, which also includes *loving ourselves*. I call this the forgotten half of the golden rule.

If someone you love gets discouraged, would you criticize and make him/her feel worse, or would you say something kind and encouraging instead? Then next time you feel discouraged, be kind to yourself! We can show kindness to ourselves by remembering our successes. Since 1991 I have emphasized the importance of taking time to simply journey through memories of our own past accomplishments: remembering, reliving, and celebrating them. Clients from all walks of life enjoy profound benefits from the next empowerment exercise.

Empowerment for Peak Performance

I guide my client (or audience) through an empowerment meditation process, which I call "Celebrate Your Success!" Clients enjoy this variation of a technique used and taught very effectively by

Richard Zarro, who owned Futureshaping Technologies prior to his passing. The process involves establishing your own success trigger or "power point" for success. We can benefit more by experiencing this personally rather than simply reading about it in a book; so pay close attention to both the instructions and the script. (I also refer to this empowerment exercise as the peak performance meditation.)

First, choose a personal gesture that will become your peak performance trigger. Some clients touch two fingers together; others squeeze their wrist. Touching my thumb to the palm of the other hand serves as my power point. A computer technician chose to pinch her earlobe. A professional singer decided to touch the back of his tongue to the roof of his mouth, as he could activate this trigger without anyone else knowing.

Choose a peak performance trigger that feels comfortable to you. During the meditation, you will make a decision the first time the script says, "Activate your power point . . ." At this moment, you may either accept the trigger you consciously chose, or you may choose a different trigger instead.

Next, choose an induction from Chapter 4. During trance, after counting down to your desired depth, imagine yourself in a safe place. The script will guide you on a series of short journeys back in time to various past successes: academic, artistic (including performing arts), athletic (such as a game-winning hit), professional, social, spiritual, and so on. With each journey, replay the success in your imagination with as many of your five senses as possible. Remember any and all of the good emotional feelings you felt, and feel them again. Ignore any criticism received later from people trying to deflate the experience; think only on the positive.

Now activate your power point (or success trigger) and imagine yourself in a special area for winners. This action anchors confidence and self-esteem into your peak performance trigger. Your winner's area can be a "winner's circle" or anything you wish to fantasize for achievers, such as an Olympic awards stand for medalists. Years ago a banker fantasized her winner's area to be a temple with an angel awarding her a medal. It is your mind, so choose what you wish.

When the script projects you into a desired future success, activate your trigger again and imagine the same feeling along with the desired success. Remember that the imagination is the rehearsal room of your mind (or your own personal holodeck). Fantasize yourself at peak performance!

Notice that I have written the empowerment exercise for peak performance in the second person. For best results, I recommend that you either have someone else read the script to you, or record it onto tape or CD and use it for your own personal use. (Note that comments in italics are instructions, and should not be read out loud.) If you wish to practice this exercise without hearing a recorded voice, become familiar with the wording. Use a 3 x 5 inch card or sheet of paper and write down a key word for each journey that you wish to take.

Are you ready to begin? Choose your desired induction from Chapter 4. Once you enter the trance state, enjoy.

> Now imagine yourself in your own safe place . . . You may come here in your mind whenever you wish to experience peace within . . .
>
> Imagine beautiful sights, sounds, and feelings, which make you feel at one with nature. This is a journey of imagination. In the rehearsal room of your mind, you may rehearse or relive anything you choose. You may travel through time or space simply by imagining. In an instant you may imagine yourself in your favorite vacation spot . . . You may now return just as quickly to your own safe place . . . and as you imagine that inner peace, it becomes real . . .
>
> In the storehouse of your mind is a record of everything you've ever experienced, including your successes and your triumphs . . . And as you allow my voice to be your guide, your inner creative mind will find that it is easy to recreate your accomplishments as you go deeper and deeper into the soothing state of hypnotic relaxation . . .

Planning the Journey

Now go back in time to an academic accomplishment and relive it in your imagination . . . Enjoy the accomplishment and appreciate the recognition . . . Activate your power point as you feel the feelings . . . *[Pause several seconds.]*

Go to your winner's area . . . *[Brief pause during each visit to winner's area.]*

Now come back to your place of peace, and take a deep breath, and go deeper . . . deeper and deeper. You are responding very well as you allow my voice to be your guide . . .

For your next journey you may choose a time when you enjoyed either an athletic or artistic accomplishment . . . a sports success or an artistic success . . . RELIVE the experience with as many of your five senses as possible . . . Activate your power point as you feel the sensations of satisfaction and you create an attitude of gratitude . . . *[Pause several seconds.]*

Go to your winner's area . . .

Now come back to your place of peace, and enjoy the increasing awareness that you may recall and relive your successes whenever you choose . . .

Now go back to a social success . . . a time when other people appreciated you . . . Activate your power point as you feel the appreciation . . . go deeper into the feelings of appreciation and into the awareness that it is good for you also to appreciate yourself . . . *[Pause several seconds.]*

Go to your winner's area . . . *[Pause several seconds.]*

Now come back to your safe place once again, and take a deep breath and go deeper . . . deeper and deeper . . .

Now take a journey to a success involving a job or career . . . Just BE THERE and relive the time of triumph . . . Activate your power point . . . *[Pause several seconds.]*

Define and Celebrate Your Success

Now go to your winner's area as you feel your increasing confidence . . . *[Pause several seconds.]*

This VICTORY is ALSO a part of who you are, and you may remember your time of triumph whenever you choose . . . *[Brief pause.]*

As you come back to your place of peace once again, you realize that we all appreciate a moment of special love or friendship from a friend or loved one. I want you now to go back to a totally pleasant experience when you appreciated an act of love . . . As you relive this experience, activate your power point and realize that you are worthy of love . . . *[Pause several seconds.]*

We are asked to love our neighbor as we love ourselves, and that means it is good for us to love ourselves too . . . As you come back to your safe place of peace, go deeper into the realization that you deserve to love yourself . . . Feel the wonderful power of love transforming you into the best that you can be . . .

Now project yourself into whatever success you choose to imagine, and activate your power point . . . and imagine MAXIMUM SUCCESS! *[Pause several seconds.]*

Feel the power of love, as you know that through the power of love you are free to celebrate your success! By loving yourself more, you love others more . . . and you find your life filled with greater love. By loving yourself more, you find yourself becoming more and more aware of your successes, both big ones and little ones . . . And all these suggestions are going into the storehouse of your mind, as you remember to remember your successes.

[Say the following with feeling and conviction.] You have the freedom to enjoy even more successes. You have the freedom to love yourself enough to celebrate your successes . . . freedom to love yourself enough to be the person you choose to be. *[Pause briefly.]*

The power of choice is yours, and like a muscle that is used becomes stronger with use, your power of choice becomes stronger with use . . . know it . . . feel it . . . OWN it! You love your power of choice, and this gives you greater confidence as you become more empowered to be the person you choose to be . . . free to be the best you can be . . . free to love yourself as you love others!

. . . And so it is.

Now, I am going to count from one up to five and then I am going to say "fully aware." At the count of five, let your eyelids open and you are calm, refreshed, relaxed, fully aware, and normal in every way.

One . . . Slowly, calmly, easily, and gently you are returning to your full awareness once again.

Two . . . Each muscle and nerve in your body is loose, limp, and relaxed, and you feel wonderfully good.

Three . . . From head to toe you are feeling perfect in every way . . . physically perfect, mentally alert, and emotionally serene . . . and whenever you get behind the wheel of a motor vehicle, you are totally alert in every way, responding appropriately to any and all traffic and road situations.

Number four . . . Your eyes begin to feel sparkling clear, just as though they were bathed in fresh spring water. On the next number now, let your eyelids open and you are then calm, rested, refreshed, fully aware, and feeling good in every way.

Number five . . . Eyelids open now. You are fully aware once again. Take a deep breath; fill up your lungs, and stretch.

Note: This script also appears in Chapter 14 of *The Art of Hypnotherapy* (4th edn, Crown House Publishing, 2010).

Chapter 11

Choosing Goals

Would you consider getting in a car without a road map, and then driving into an area where you had never traveled before? Would you drive from New York to Los Angeles without choosing a route first? Choosing goals compares to mapping your route through life's journey.

Numerous books emphasize the importance of setting and defining goals and objectives, and then writing them down. While targets provide us with an easy way of measuring success on life's journey, few people actually follow the advice of experts regarding this topic.

Some people believe that it is a waste of time to write down their goals; but if you consider an objective worthy of your effort, doesn't it deserve a few minutes of your time to write it down? I recommend that you do so whether your goal is personal or professional. One person told me, "I don't need to write down my goals, because I already know what I want in life." If we find reasons to avoid putting our aims into writing, we may also find reasons to fail.

Let us return to the metaphoric car trip to Los Angeles. First you imagine being there, and then you decide on a route. You may take a northern or a southern route, or you might take the shortest course. Once you choose your route, there may be unexpected roadblocks and detours. You may encounter traffic delays along the way, but you keep heading toward your destination. Additionally, you may take planned side trips and enjoy the scenery. Attainment of a goal may involve several methods to help you along the way, with one or more enjoyable (or not-so-enjoyable) activities or detours before arrival at the final destination. You might choose interim objectives while heading toward your primary goal.

Planning the Journey

The rest of this chapter presents simple guidelines to help you list goals according to types and categories, whether you define them as personal or business ambitions, and to help you arrange them in order of importance to your happiness.

Goal Types

There are several main types of goal: short-term, intermediate, long-term, and life.

Short-term goals are realistic aims attainable within the near future, such as up to six months or a year from now. Examples of short-term goals might be to quit smoking, take off ten pounds, close an important business transaction, paint the kitchen, reach a monthly sales quota, or buy a new car.

Intermediate goals normally can be attained within one to five years. Examples of intermediate goals might include a trip to Europe, buying a new home, or changing careers. Some of you reading this might already be in a position to take a trip to Europe on one week's notice (or less); so what might be an intermediate goal to one person could simply be a routine business trip to another. Also, buying a new car could be an intermediate goal to many people rather than a short-term goal. Opinions and personal preferences vary. It is your life, so you decide.

Long-term goals and life goals may be considered as major life-changing successes for you that normally take longer than five years to accomplish. Typical examples of long-term goals include: setting up retirement plans, putting your children through college, building a new home, and starting a new business. (Many people define goals of between two to five years as long-term, and beyond five years as life goals. They consider intermediate goals to be attainable within two years. Again, you decide.)

Goal Categories

Now you have considered types of goals, so let us look at some categories to help trigger your choices. My partial list of main categories includes achievements, possessions, characteristics, projects, and changes. More than one type of goal can fall within any category.

Achievements are personal or business accomplishments you would like to enjoy. A personal achievement might be to put a child through college, to master an art or sport, or to sing solo for a church choir. A business achievement might be to reach a sales quota, to attain recognition for expertise in your field, or to become a published author.

Possessions represent those things you wish to own, such as a new car. Setting up your own business could be a short-term, intermediate, or long-term goal. Financial rewards could be either the results of achievements, or they might be considered goals of and by themselves. You could put a financial ambition either in this category or the first one.

Characteristics are personality traits you wish to incorporate, or professional titles you wish others to recognize. You might want to be mellower, more confident, more outgoing, and so on. The characteristic might be a position or professional title. Of course, these could overlap with achievements, as most positions or titles (such as Ph.D., etc.) require certain qualifications, which include prerequisite achievements.

Projects could be something you wish to start, or a scheme already started but not yet complete. Perhaps you began a book last year, and wish to complete and edit your manuscript for possible publication. Perhaps you wish to assist with a church project or get involved with the Chamber of Commerce. Maybe you would like to remodel the basement and create a spare bedroom.

Changes normally involve habits, attitudes, or ways of thinking. Quitting smoking and/or reducing requires a change of habit.

Again, remember that once you learn something subconsciously, you cannot simply erase it; but you can replace the habit with a positive one, such as taking one deep breath of air every time an old light-up trigger occurs. When dealing with the subconscious, replacing unwanted habits is easier than removing them.

Improving your golf game also involves changes of both habit and attitude at the time you address the ball. If you imagine your ball going into the water hazard, guess where the ball will land! Instead, change the negative image into a positive one by imagining where you do want the ball to go. I often tell clients that golf is really mind over matter – matter that happens to be the size of a golf ball! Many sports activities involve more mental imaging than most people realize. (Chapter 14 contains some exercises for sports enhancement.)

Some changes can overlap with characteristics. For example, learning to like yourself changes your attitude about yourself and others while giving you more positive personality characteristics.

List your goals on a separate sheet of paper, using the above guidelines to trigger ideas. You may wish to use separate sheets for each type (short-term, intermediate, and long-term). Some people like to separate personal or family goals from career goals; but I prefer simply to mix them. Anything important to me in my career is also important to me personally.

If your first listing of goals produces a total of fifteen or less for all types, then you should combine them all before doing the exercise in the next chapter. If you have a substantial quantity, you may wish to do the exercise once for each goal type.

Since most of the information presented in this book relates to subconscious programming, some people might ask why I have devoted space to an exercise primarily completed by the conscious mind. Often we can best determine our priority goals by accessing the subconscious rather than by trying to decide through logic alone. Nonetheless, before using the subconscious to determine our priority goals, we must do the preparation with the logic of the conscious intellect.

After completing your list of goals, you may wish to repeat a self-hypnosis exercise from Chapter 4. Simply go in and out of trance somewhat quickly. Then immediately after returning from the alpha state to full beta consciousness, look over your list and add anything new that comes to mind. You might be surprised at what you add! Once you have established and defined your goals, you are ready for the exercise in the next chapter.

Chapter 12

Prioritizing Goals

I designed this exercise to combine logic with feelings to help you establish a priority for your goals. Please read this chapter thoroughly before you begin the exercise, and make certain that you understand the instructions. Also, you have the author's permission to photocopy the chart rather than writing in this book.

Make sure you stay fully alert while reading and comprehending the instructions. While these instructions may seem straightforward, numerous clients have failed to complete the chart correctly. When you actually complete the chart, you should be in a light alpha state (or just returned from one), but you will have an easier time completing the exercise properly if you understand exactly what to do before entering a state of self-hypnosis.

The concept is really quite simple: you will be comparing every goal you establish with every other goal, but *only once*. Ask yourself this question: *"If I could have only one of these two goals, which one would I choose?"* Indicate your preference by writing the number of the preferred goal in the box where the two goals intersect. For example, if Goal 7 is more important than Goal 9, write "7" in row 7 under column 9. If Goal 9 is more important, then you would write "9" there instead. Note that I have marked some boxes with an "X" to prevent comparing the same goals twice. The results determine which goals are most important to your happiness.

Step 1: Numbering the Goals

Number all of your goals in the order listed, without regard to type or category. If you have over twelve goals, then you may wish to segregate by type (and renumber the segregated goals). If you still have over twelve goals in a goal type, you may do one of two things: (1) Extend the chart with additional numbers up

Goal Prioritizing

Number your goals. In a meditative state, choose between each goal where the number on the left side intersects with the numbers across the top. Indicate your choice by writing the appropriate number where the two goals intersect. Afterwards, count the number of times you chose each numbered goal, and indicate in the space provided under the "Score" column. (*Photocopy for your own personal use.*)

Goal	2	3	4	5	6	7	8	9	10	11	12	Score
1												
2	x											
3	x	x										
4	x	x	x									
5	x	x	x	x								
6	x	x	x	x	x							
7	x	x	x	x	x	x						
8	x	x	x	x	x	x	x					
9	x	x	x	x	x	x	x	x				
10	x	x	x	x	x	x	x	x	x			
11	x	x	x	x	x	x	x	x	x	x		
12	x	x	x	x	x	x	x	x	x	x	x	

Complete this exercise while in a relaxed state of mind. However, you can only follow the instructions in an alpha state if you understand them while in a beta state, so be certain that you grasp the purpose of this exercise before proceeding.

Scoring: Count one point for each time you have written a preference for each goal. Note that I have simplified the scoring by allowing numbers to only appear in their respective row or column. The goal with the highest score is your priority goal, and so on.

to the total number of goals you wish to analyze, or (2) combine two similar goals ("trip to Greece" and "trip to Australia" could become "take a trip abroad").

Step 2: Entering Self-Hypnosis

Get comfortable, and have the following items: your list of goals, a copy of the chart, and a pen or pencil at hand. Enter self-hypnosis as you've previously practiced, but *go only part way*. When you feel more relaxed, open your eyes and proceed with this exercise. You should be feeling somewhat mellow, though consciously aware. If you go deep, then bring yourself up into a lighter state. I actually recommend the latter if you feel stress for any reason. You might benefit by giving yourself a chance to unwind before beginning this exercise. Some people discover that simply listening to soft music helps them to feel calm.

Step 3: Using the Chart

On the following pages you will find a sample set of goals and a completed goal chart. Using my example, follow the instructions until you understand them.

Place your numbered goals next to a photocopy of the blank chart. Notice the row of numbers going down the left side of the chart. Find 1 in the left-hand vertical column, which will be your starting point. Read your own Goal 1 and compare it with Goal 2. Choose the more important between the two goals, and mark your choice by writing "1" or "2" in the box in the row to the right of Goal 1 and below column 2. (My sample chart indicates that Goal 2 had more importance than Goal 1.) Now compare Goal 1 with Goal 3 and mark your choice in the box below column 3, and so on. Compare your first goal with every other goal in this manner. After comparing Goal 1 with each other goal, only the top line of the chart will be completed.

Now go on to Goal 2, comparing this goal with each other remaining goal in the same manner, as in my sample list. Do likewise until each of your goals is compared once with every other one, and you will be ready to score the results.

Sample Goal List

1. Buy new home
2. Revise book
3. Take trip to Greece
4. Enjoy abundant cash flow
5. Establish more branch offices
6. Establish average work week of less than 50 hours
7. Pay off all debts
8. Take trip to Australia
9. Buy new computer system
10. Own a new car free and clear

Step 4: Making the Choice

There are two ways to choose between two goals, happiness and chronology. The happiness method (previously mentioned) requires that you ask the question: *"If I could have only one of these two goals, which one would I choose?"* This gets into your gut feelings to help you determine the importance of your goals. I personally use and recommend this method most of the time.

The chronology method involves asking yourself: *"Which of these two goals must come first?"* This more intellectual approach might be useful for deciding what you should work on chronologically; but it does not lend itself for use with goals of mixed types, as short-term goals would normally come chronologically before intermediate ones, and so on. There may be a time and a place for this method, so I include it here.

Once you choose which method to use, be consistent throughout the entire exercise. The only exception is that if you find yourself totally undecided between two goals, you may break the tie by using the alternate method; but remember to return to your original method for the next goal choice.

Prioritizing Goals

You may find it interesting to note how different the results can be after using both methods with the same goals.

Step 5: Scoring

Once you have completed the chart, come back up to total conscious awareness by counting from one to five. Stand up and stretch to be sure you remain fully alert.

Now, count the number of times the number "1" appears in any box, and indicate the score in the column to the left of the chart. (Note: In my example on the next page, 1 appeared four times.) Now count all your 2's and do the same.

Continue until you have counted all the occurrences of each number. Remember to check both the rows and columns. If you have completed the chart properly, each goal number selected should appear either in the column below its number, or in the row to the right of the same number on the chart.

Step 6: Assigning Priorities

Note the goal with the highest score. The goal chosen the most is your priority goal, and should be listed as Goal 1 on a new sheet of paper. Renumber and list the rest of your goals according to priority by listing those with the highest scores first. Continue down to the lowest score, your least important goal.

Break a two-way tie by reviewing the chart to see which of the two goals you chose during the exercise. For example, my Goals 3 and 7 tied with a score of 6. Since I selected Goal 7 when comparing these goals against each other, Goal 7 is more important. If you have a three-way tie, select either the most important or the least important of the three, then use the above method to determine the order of the other two.

Goal Prioritizing

This is my completed sample goal list. The goals were set in 1997; and I accomplished seven of them, including three of the top four goals.

Goal	2	3	4	5	6	7	8	9	10	11	12	Score
1	2	3	4	1	1	7	1	9	1			4
2	x	2	4	2	2	2	2	2	2			8
3	x	x	4	3	3	7	3	3	3			6
4	x	x	x	4	4	4	4	4	4			9
5	x	x	x	x	6	7	8	9	10			0
6	x	x	x	x	x	7	8	9	10			1
7	x	x	x	x	x	x	7	9	7			6
8	x	x	x	x	x	x	x	9	10			2
9	x	x	x	x	x	x	x	x	10			5
10	x	x	x	x	x	x	x	x	x			4
11	x	x	x	x	x	x	x	x	x	x		
12	x	x	x	x	x	x	x	x	x	x	x	

Sample Prioritized Goal List

1. Enjoy abundant cash flow
2. Revise book
3. Pay off all debts
4. Take trip to Greece
5. Buy new computer system
6. Buy new home
7. Own a new car free and clear
8. Take trip to Australia
9. Establish average work week of less than 50 hours
10. Establish more branch offices

Step 7: Evaluating the Results

Note my sample goal list in its new order of priority. Your goals should now be listed legibly on a fresh sheet of paper so that your priorities will stand out clearly.

Review your prioritized list of goals. You may discover a surprise or two. Often a goal that you consider important comes out low on the list, and a seemingly unimportant one comes out high. Frequently clients discover that a goal previously considered vital comes out below several others, and vice versa. Such surprises prove the validity of the exercise. I personally prioritize my own goals in this manner several times yearly, and I am sometimes astonished at the results. Our goals change with time. You may find yourself updating old goals, adding new goals and, hopefully, deleting the ones that you have reached.

In Conclusion

Why would we invest our time and energies into goals that do not contribute to our happiness and well-being? Remember that the results may reflect your true desires if you use the happiness method. Also, entering an alpha state (or at least being mellow) will facilitate your ability to get in touch with your feelings. I believe that the comparisons carry greater meaning when our feelings are involved instead of logic alone. Knowing which goals provide the greatest happiness has almost as much importance as having those goals defined in the first place.

Investing time and energy into goals that have little importance to your own happiness (just because your conscious mind, your boss, or a loved one tells you which target to work toward) can cause frustration. You can still choose to work toward that less important goal, but by putting equal or greater energy into your own higher priority objectives, you can be happy as well as successful.

Accept your own right to change your mind. Feelings can change with circumstances. If you repeat this session in six months with your exact same goals, you may notice differences in the order of your goals; because factors in your life influencing your state of happiness might have changed. I accomplished most of the goals on my list; the ones not important for my happiness dropped off later lists.

Many people consider happiness to be a state of mind. One may attain intellectual, professional, and/or financial success while failing emotionally after fulfilling the wrong goals. In light of this, I highly recommend that you analyze both your intermediate and your long-term goals with the happiness method.

Also, remember that success is doing what you enjoy doing, and doing it well. People who live in their own egos might try to judge your success only by financial results. Do you live to please them, or to discover your own full potential and happiness? A person earning an average income but totally enjoying life will attain far more success in the pursuit of happiness than a millionaire living in slavery to the demands and stresses of uncontrolled ego.

Know which goals are important for your happiness. Once you use this chapter to help you do that, plan your course and go for it!

Part IV
Creative Daydreaming

Chapter 13

Preparation

Once you have identified your priority goal, it is time to prepare for subconscious acceptance of both your goal and your method(s) of goal achievement. Simply knowing where you want to go fails to get you there without action.

People sometimes come to my office wanting a magic hypnotic wand to suddenly make them thirty pounds lighter without any effort or planning on their part. Hypnosis is not magic, nor will a trance replace the use of a proven method for obtaining successful results; but hypnosis can motivate a willing mind to accept a proven action plan. Self-hypnosis primarily benefits us by helping the subconscious mind to accept what the conscious has already decided to do. Without that acceptance, the inner mind may defeat us before we ever begin. Once we have that subconscious acceptance, we still must invest our time and energy and pay the price of success, because the universal law of cause and effect influences us all.

Cause and Effect

Every action causes a reaction. Put in different words, in order to achieve a desired goal, an *action* must cause that goal to manifest in our lives. The action plan (such as changing eating habits) causes the *reaction*, or manifestation of the chosen goal. We cannot simply sit back and hope to "attract" our desires without taking any other action.

Personally and professionally, I refer to all necessary actions for goal achievement as the *price of success* because of my sales background; and most clients respond quite favorably to this metaphor. Although some readers might consider the word "price" to be negative, we willingly spend money almost on a daily basis for goods and services desired. In my opinion, the word price becomes negative only when the cost is too high. Most of us willingly engage in the action of paying a fair value in order to obtain a desirable product or service. Ownership of the product (or benefit of the service) now becomes the effect caused by paying the price.

Now let us explore further how the law of cause and effect applies to goal achievement. Once we decide which goal to work toward, we should logically use the left brain to determine what will cause our chosen aim to become reality, and establish an action plan for successful goal achievement. Remember that your action plan will cause a reaction that will help manifest your goal into reality. If the price is too high (or the required action is too difficult), we might not wish to spend the effort necessary to manifest the desired reaction. You have the responsibility of determining the value; then you must decide whether or not you choose to pay the price that buys your benefits. Do you wish to motivate yourself to create the actions that cause the reactions?

Numerous books describe ways of establishing your action plan for various objectives: effective weight control programs, methods of minimizing stress, sales techniques, study habits, body building, proper ways to hold a golf club, and so on. It is wise to use any valid source available to help you determine the best course of action most likely to achieve your goal.

Similarly, excellence in music comes neither by wishful thinking nor by self-hypnosis alone. Proficiency comes through paying the price of lots of practice; although self-hypnosis can reduce the amount of training that might otherwise be required. The same rule of practice applies to any art, from dancing to painting.

Likewise, reducing thirty pounds does not come only by daily daydreaming in an alpha state. You must consciously choose whatever eating and/or exercise habits you desire in order to program them into your subconscious. The same holds true for any type of motivation or goal achievement. A salesperson cannot achieve high sales quota by simply sitting in the office in an alpha state all day waiting for the telephone to ring. He/she must actively do something to generate leads.

These examples demonstrate the law of cause and effect. Since the action plan (or price of success) must be determined with your conscious mind, this book provides no specific advice regarding nutrition, salesmanship, tobacco withdrawal, and so on. Instead, I specialize in teaching people how to get the subconscious to buy their conscious decisions and manifest their goals into reality.

Once you determine your best course of action, and choose to follow it, you have your road map to success. Your next step is to convince your subconscious to accept the next part of your journey. Be prepared to *persuade* your subconscious to cooperate, otherwise you might run into resistance from your inner mind. Get your imagination involved with the benefits of achieving your goal by fantasizing them during self-hypnosis. I call this process selling success to your subconscious.

Selling Success to Your Subconscious

We tend to resist a salesperson trying to force us into buying something before we have made a decision. This metaphor also applies to selling motivation (or any habit change requiring motivation) to the subconscious. Why do I use the analogy of selling? Let me respond by stating that mentally we have all tuned into the mind station WII-FM. These letters stand for: **What's In It For Me?** Answering this important question will enable you to sell motivation to the inner mind.

The subconscious tends to resist being forced into changing a habit just because the conscious mind makes a decision. Until the subconscious bonds with the emotional desire to achieve a goal, motivation is difficult at best. Our inner child might rebel against pressure, but will respond to persuasion if the benefits are appealing. Likewise, we may refuse to buy a high priced product when pressured; yet how often have we paid more than we thought we wanted to pay for a product or service simply because we fell in love with it?

The subconscious resists giving up dessert, but will be comfortable (and happier) imagining the benefits of trying on an ideal clothing size. So, in a sense, the conscious mind must promote success to the subconscious by using the language of imagination.

Once you fall in love with the benefits of your goal, this action causes the effect of greater motivation to follow the action plan. So the key to overcoming subconscious resistance to change lies in persuading the subconscious to buy the *benefits* of change before trying to sell the *price* of change. In order to accomplish this important step, we must identify the specific benefits of the desired change.

Before proceeding to Chapter 14, take out a sheet of paper and list the main benefits you will enjoy upon fulfillment of your priority goal. Your subconscious responds better when you choose your own benefits rather than simply accepting someone else's. Nonetheless, if your priority goal fits into one of the common exercises described in the next chapter, you may wish to add more benefits to your list after reviewing some common ones chosen by my clients.

When you complete your list of benefits, you can marry two powerful methods of subconscious programming: *hypnosis* and *emotion*. Now you are ready to sell success to your subconscious; and the next chapter will show you how!

Chapter 14

Creative Daydreaming Exercises

The alpha state opens a wide gateway to the subconscious, enhancing the imagination and our creativity. Furthermore, since imagination is the language of the subconscious, why not use the state of mind that increases our ability to daydream?

Emotion opens an even wider gateway to the subconscious. Remember that emotion is the motivating power of the mind. You become a servant to your uncontrolled feelings; but controlled emotion actually becomes your servant instead of vice versa. Someone who gets emotionally excited about reaching a goal seems to have the energy or drive to get there faster, such as an athlete spending many hours practicing in preparation for possible Olympic competition. Emotional excitement generates energy to motivate the subconscious into action. With that fact in mind, I have designed empowerment exercises to help increase your emotional desire to attain a priority goal.

I am not talking about artificial emotional hype; rather, we will use positive controlled emotion added to constructive fantasizing. I call this process *creative daydreaming*. You now combine two powerful methods of subconscious programming with more than double the impact. The effectiveness of creative daydreaming surpasses that of simply visualizing the goal; it is like putting a high-energy fuel into your car and driving on a superhighway.

General Guidelines

This chapter serves both as a reference and as an introduction to a more powerful self-hypnosis exercise for empowerment. As such,

I encourage you to experiment with creative daydreaming at least once before finishing this book. You can add your key word and affirmations later.

Before you begin, choose the goal you wish to work on and identify its benefits. This chapter contains numerous common goals, making it a lengthy section; so feel free to select only the particular goal you choose for now if preferred.

List your desired benefits on a sheet of paper and keep it handy. (Refer to the last section of Chapter 13: "Selling Success to Your Subconscious.") Amend your list of benefits as desired. Common benefits chosen by clients appear in the creative daydreaming exercises for popular goals described below.

Remember that every invention and innovation must first originate in someone's mind. When we enter the alpha state, we access greater creative energies as well as enhanced imagination. New ideas originate from the subconscious; these ideas can flow into the conscious mind, and may contribute to success. In light of this, creative daydreaming may help you discover new methods of goal achievement that you have never thought of before. Your subconscious may supply you with new ideas to simplify your action plan, facilitating your ability to succeed. After emerging from trance, determine with your logical mind whether to use, modify, or discard any specific new idea.

If you are practicing creative daydreaming for the first time, proceed as explained here as well as is described in the appropriate section related to your goal. Review your list of benefits, making any desired amendments. Memorize them, or at least become familiar with the main ones.

Note: If you are using this chapter as reference upon completion of the book, then you may now include your properly constructed personal affirmations in accordance with the instructions contained in Part V. Once you understand those instructions, read your affirmations out loud *before* practicing HypnoCise. Enjoy fantasizing your benefits, using creative daydreaming to make them personal. (Review the other guidelines in this section if necessary.)

Incorporate your key word several times throughout your trance, especially during times when you feel positive emotions. The energy of emotion helps to anchor your key word, thus adding strength to its use as your empowerment trigger. During your creative daydreaming exercise, remember to fantasize successful use of your key word; and then use it in real life. This will maximize your benefits from HypnoCise.

Now that you are ready, find a comfortable place and enter the alpha state according to the instructions in the self-hypnosis exercises described in Chapter 4.

Once you enter the trance state, imagine that you have already reached your goal. Experience fulfillment of your goal inside the rehearsal room of your mind. Imagine yourself seeing, hearing, and feeling your personal benefits as well as successful achievement of your goal. Daydream your benefits as *present reality*. Fantasize engaging in activities that become more enjoyable because of your benefits. You may either open your eyes to review your personal benefits if necessary, or memorize them before entering the alpha state.

Get all of your five senses involved in what you imagine. Feel that sense of emotional satisfaction as you allow yourself to enjoy the fantasy. Imagine your appreciation of the benefits. As you visualize your success in the rehearsal room of your imagination, fantasize that you absolutely have the ability to do what it takes to realize this ambition. Imagine successfully doing what it takes to manifest this goal into reality.

As you begin to feel the positive emotions increase, fantasize that the course of action you have planned becomes easy, and daydream yourself doing whatever is necessary to bring the desired results into reality.

Construct your meditation along guidelines similar to those described for one of the popular goals presented below. The common benefits presented for each motivational goal represent the ones frequently identified by my clients over the years, and may help you to amend your own list of benefits. Choose only those that *you* consider important, and include any additional benefits you might enjoy even if not listed in the sample exercises.

Let me add some important advice. While creative daydreaming enhances the subconscious desire to achieve a goal, some people might encounter unexpected subconscious resistance caused by "old tapes" or old subconscious programs. A competently trained hypnotherapist can help you discover the source of such resistance. (Refer to Appendix 2 if you desire some guidelines on how to choose a competent hypnotherapist.) This book is not intended to be a substitute for hypnotherapy or other professional help; but rather, my goal is to assist you on your path of empowerment. Nonetheless, the proper use of creative daydreaming may facilitate your ability to respond to other professional help.

Now you can choose the exercise that best fits your priority goal, and enjoy.

Smoking Cessation/Reduction

Common benefits for smokers wishing to quit or cut down are:

- better health
- longer winded
- more energy
- more stamina
- more money
- greater social acceptance
- better self-image
- better professional image
- personal pride
- better complexion
- sense of accomplishment
- more freedom
- good parental example
- cleaner environment (car, home, clothes, etc.)
- whiter teeth
- clean breath
- better sense of taste and smell

Amend your list of personal benefits if desired. Put the benefits into a positive format. For example, "I won't have smoker's cough" is better stated as: "clear throat and lungs."

Once you are satisfied with your benefits, enter self-hypnosis using your chosen induction. Imagine yourself in better health. Your lungs reward you with more stamina and/or energy as you imagine enjoying your favorite recreational activity. If you enjoy swimming, see the water. Hear the splashing, and feel your body gliding smoothly as you swim. If you enjoy hiking, then see the surroundings. Hear the sounds of the great outdoors, and/or the sound of laughter of your child or friend with you. Feel the warmth or coolness of the clean air. Imagine taking some of the money that formerly went up in smoke, and create the fantasy of spending it as fun money, because you deserve it! Daydream yourself in a social setting or a professional situation. Imagine your other benefits with as many of your five senses as possible.

Choose rewards for your personal success with this goal, and imagine enjoying those rewards. Take a deep breath and think the word "relax" (and/or another key word) for quitting or cutting down. Since replacing a habit is easier than erasing it, fantasize that one deep breath satisfies you more than an old light-up. Imagine enjoying your new self-image as a non-smoker (or occasional smoker). Fantasize your feeling of pride or satisfaction with this personal success.

In real life, make a conscious effort to take one deep breath whenever any situation occurs that previously triggered a light-up or an urge. Be especially careful about the times when you might enter spontaneous trance, such as while watching television. The subconscious forms an emotional bond with the cigarette as a fair-weather friend; so I believe strongly in the importance of bonding emotionally with your personal benefits in order to break the bond. People who quit cold turkey (without selling the subconscious totally) could end up grieving for the loss of the fair-weather friend for months or years. You will make quitting (or cutting down) much less difficult by doing everything possible to make your decision enjoyable. Also, remember that quitting smoking is not an easy task for most people, even with hypnosis.

You must make a total commitment to give up the habit. Note the absence of affirmations in Appendix 7; instead, I have decided to include a full script for your use. If you have subconscious resistance, seek additional help.

Client Successes

Perhaps the most profound success I know of happened in the late 1980s in my hypnotherapy college class. I simply discussed the "benefits approach" (which I also call "Selling Success to the Subconscious"); and one of my students went home and listed his benefits. After using self-hypnosis several times to visualize his benefits, incorporating the techniques in this book, he quit totally without any additional help.

Another success that taught me something important occurred in 1986. A professional woman initially indicating a desire to quit kept seeing me for a number of weeks because she could not let go of smoking one cigarette after each meal. She decided to stop seeing me, and waited almost a year before calling up again. When I received her phone call, she said, "I hope you don't think I'm a failure. When I first saw you, I had it in my head that I had to either not smoke at all, or be totally out of control. You taught me to take one deep breath for most of my smokes; but I *enjoy* having one cigarette for dessert after each meal. After ten months, I'm still at only four cigarettes daily . . . one after each meal, and one before bed at night. Thank you for helping me to control my habit." This businesswoman taught me how to facilitate smoking reduction programs for smokers who do not wish to quit. Note the script in Appendix 7 for smoking reduction.

Weight Reduction

Common benefits for weight reduction are:

- better health
- more energy

- more attractive
- greater freedom with clothes
- lighter on feet
- easier mobility (or freedom of movement)
- better self-image (social and/or professional)
- personal pride
- sense of accomplishment
- more sex appeal
- more money

Note: People whose income depends on commissions and/or making a good impression on people often list this last benefit.

When you feel satisfied with your list of benefits, choose your induction (from Chapter 4) and enter self-hypnosis. Remember to put your benefits into the desired result rather than avoidance of the problem. For example, "I won't get tired going up stairs" can be translated as "more energy" or "more stamina."

If you desire to take off thirty pounds, imagine yourself standing in front of a mirror looking at a reflection of yourself at your desired weight. Imagine yourself enjoying your favorite activity while being at your ideal weight. Picture yourself wearing the sizes and styles of clothing you desire at your ideal body weight, and feel these clothes fitting comfortably. Visualize yourself enjoying the company of friends or loved ones while enjoying your ideal body. Feel that sense of satisfaction as you imagine doing things you enjoy at this ideal weight. Imagine having more energy and being lighter on your feet. In your mind's eye, *be* on the dance floor, at the beach, and so on. Whisper your key word at appropriate times throughout your meditation (unless doing this exercise for the first time).

Now imagine you have already been at your ideal weight for a year. Picture yourself buying that new outfit in a smaller size, and imagine this clothing fitting you well. Continue this fantasy in your mind until you actually begin to feel a little excitement about the possibility of being there. Feel an improved sense of pride or satisfaction with your new image. Clients have informed me that the reality surpasses the fantasy!

In real life, remember to replace snack urges with a few sips of water; trying to ignore snack urges could result in major backsliding. Additionally, take enough time to eat slowly, paying attention to each and every bite. Awareness of the taste of each mouthful of food will increase the emotional satisfaction derived from what you eat, giving you more pleasure from fewer calories. Also, get into the habit of leaving food on your plate. Would you rather have your food go to waste, or waist? As with any goal, you must make a commitment to control your eating habits; however, remember that diets work on the body, but not the mind.

Client Successes

A professional consultant saw me for weight reduction, as she felt that her image might influence her income. I saw her only three times, emphasizing primarily self-hypnosis techniques because of her apparent inability to get past a light state of trance. At the third session, I spent most of the time discussing with her on how to maximize her self-hypnosis; and I gave her a hypnosis tape on empowerment for weight management, along with the recommendation that she listen to it frequently. She was accustomed to leading rather than following, so I encountered considerable analytical resistance to trance.

One year later, an attractive and slender woman approached me in a restaurant. At first I failed to recognize her; but she took my hand and introduced me to her husband. He said, "So this is the man you take to bed every night!" After my face turned several shades of red, the three of us laughed loudly. Since I can't help all the people all the time, I must admit that her profound success surprised me pleasantly. She later saw me for help with another goal.

A devout Christian decided to try hypnosis as a last resort. Unfortunately, she consumed over a quarter-pound of chocolate nightly. She taught me that it is not what we eat; rather it is how much and how often. This client needed to take off about thirty pounds; but she refused to give up her chocolate. She cut down to only two pieces of candy nightly, and made minor modifications in her other eating habits. Although she spent seven months reducing, she minimized subconscious resistance by avoiding diets and simply changing her eating habits. As far as I know, her success remained permanent.

Several years ago a hypnotherapist asked me to work with her in front of a group of professionals during a workshop. She had a number of sessions over a period of several years trying to deal with her weight; but an advanced hypnotic technique helped her to discover the subconscious cause and attain the breakthrough that had previously eluded her. She followed up that session using self-hypnosis to stay on track.

Sales/Business Motivation

Identifying business benefits can sometimes be a two-step process. The first step is to identify your direct benefits. My professional clients often select these common direct benefits:

- more money (higher income, etc.)
- security
- promotion
- recognition
- performance award(s)
- greater prestige
- pride of success

The second step involves identifying those benefits related to financial success. Most people wishing greater success in business are strongly motivated to earn a greater income, and need to list the benefits related to a higher salary and/or commissions. Complete the second step by identifying what money can buy that will improve your life. Clients most frequently choose from the following:

- new home
- new car
- new furniture

- new boat
- put child through college
- get advanced degree
- freedom to travel more
- vacation to (destination)
- be debt-free
- more free time
- new (desired item)

First, after entering self-hypnosis, imagine your direct benefits. Fantasize yourself receiving a promotion and/or a professional award. Imagine the feeling of security in ways that you consider important. Since money itself is a direct benefit, imagine holding a large check in your hands, payable to you! Imagine depositing this money into your account. Fantasize the deposit slip, and/or the bank balance. Whisper your key word (unless doing this exercise for the first time).

Next, imagine your related benefits of a greater income in vivid detail. Be personal, with as many of your five senses as possible. For example, don't just think of a new car as two words. Instead, imagine yourself in the driver's seat. See both interior and exterior. Hear the purr of the engine or sound of the stereo. Feel the wheel and the comfort of the seat. Smell the new upholstery. Imagine yourself putting the pink slip in a safe place, indicating to your subconscious that you own the car. (One of my clients simply imagined driving a new car; and he rented a new vehicle while his older car visited the repair shop. That was not what he had hoped for!)

If you desire a new home, see it in your mind's eye (both inside and outside). See the living room. Feel the carpet. Imagine hearing the voices of loved ones inside this house. Imagine eating and relaxing here, and so on.

Does a luxury cruise appeal to you? Imagine yourself sipping champagne or tropical juice on the deck of a ship while you smell the salty sea air. See the sea and hear the sounds. See, hear, and feel anything pleasant that you anticipate from this experience.

Creative Daydreaming Exercises

If you strongly desire more money, imagine yourself holding a wad of crisp, new $100 bills (or the currency of your country). What would you do? What would you buy? How would you feel? Let your imagination run free. (One of my clients got a wad of one-dollar bills and put a $100 bill on top and bottom. He felt the money while doing his self-hypnosis, imagining all as $100 bills. This helped renew his motivation for sales.)

Finally, fantasize your feeling of dignity gained as a result of your success.

Client Successes

The most surprising success in this department occurred when a successful salesman came to me when he was already earning a six-digit income. (I did not reveal to him that I envied his income!) Naturally, I taught him the techniques presented in this book. One year later, he informed me that he had almost doubled his income by utilizing my techniques.

My most encouraging business success brought tears of joy to my eyes. A physician referred a patient to me for stress management; and the patient worked for a company that took unfair advantage of its sales force. (Having gone through a similar experience, I had great empathy with him.) After using creative daydreaming with his benefits, he realized that he needed to change employer. Although I explained that he might benefit from talking with a vocational counselor, he chose to work on confidence and self-esteem first. He also mastered the stress-coping technique presented in Chapter 8. Two months later he accepted a position with another company at a salary of double his previous income, plus commission.

Job Performance

Self-hypnosis to improve your job performance compares to the exercise described above for business motivation. Identify your direct benefits (similar to business motivation benefits) as well as the related benefits if your income will improve as a result of better job performance. Enter trance, using your chosen induction. Fantasize your personal benefits with as many of your five senses as possible. Include your related benefits. If you simply wish to feel good about your current job, consider all the things your paycheck allows you to buy, and identify the benefits of receiving regular paychecks. During trance, fantasize those benefits even if you already experience them. With either situation, imagine yourself performing well at your job. Rehearse it in your mind, with as much detail as possible. Remember to use your key word (unless doing this exercise for the first time).

Those who wish to change careers may need more help than this book can provide. Seek appropriate professional help if necessary.

Client Successes

A self-employed woman moved across the country to the Pacific Northwest, selling her old business. Even after consulting with a vocational counselor, she could not decide whether to start a new business or seek employment. She listed a dozen prospective new careers as goals, and used the goal prioritizing exercise detailed in Chapter 12. Her "priority goal" became the career of choice; and she became successful and happy.

An experienced hypnotherapist from another state saw me for confidence and personal instruction in advanced techniques, and became a professional hypnosis instructor.

A successful businessman took a credible hypnosis course and experienced inner conflicts over whether to stay in his career or become a full-time hypnosis practitioner. By using an advanced technique to help him resolve his inner conflicts, that part of his subconscious wanting to stay in sales made an agreement with the part wanting to change careers. The result was that he remained involved in his career part time while also practicing professional hypnosis, using self-hypnosis to do well in both.

Memory and Study Habits

If improving study habits involves motivation to complete your assignments, identify and list your own specific benefits for keeping pace with your academic goals and objectives. Common benefits are:

- better grades
- graduation
- promotion
- better job
- degree

Fantasize those benefits during the trance state. Imagine holding a good grade report in your hand. Visualize receiving your award, certificate of completion, or diploma. Feel the handshake. Hear any associated sounds, such as "Pomp and Circumstance." Imagine any opportunities for career advancement made possible by your accomplishment. Make the benefits real in your imagination. Selling your inner mind on the benefits of successful studies will increase the motivation needed to do your homework. Remember to use your key word (unless doing this exercise for the first time).

For test anxiety, master the mental mini-vacation exercise described in Chapter 8. Your peaceful place trigger will help calm pre-test anxiety. During your creative daydreaming, imagine yourself *successfully* using that trigger just before an exam; and imagine a high score! Next time you find yourself taking a test, remember to use your peaceful place trigger.

If your concern involves the ability to concentrate during your scheduled study time, you might need to seek help beyond this book.

Client Successes

My most profound success resulted from a simple hypnosis demonstration at a high school psychology class. The teacher asked me to demonstrate hypnosis in the classroom; and after she produced signed parental consent slips, I agreed. During the presentation, I gave affirmations for memory and study habits. One year later the same teacher invited me back, and told me a success story. Apparently one of my earlier volunteers was a "D" student. The following semester this student got a 4.0 Grade Point Average (GPA), and obtained the highest score of any other student in all the psychology classes taught by this teacher. Faith at a subconscious level gets results.

Miscellaneous Habits

To overcome undesired habits, identify and list your own personal benefits as previously instructed. Enter trance, using your chosen induction. As in the above examples, fantasize vividly your benefits, using as many of your five senses as possible. Create scenarios in your mind where you enjoy your benefits. Whisper your key word at appropriate times (unless doing this exercise for the first time).

Note: If you have a difficult habit to break, seek other professional help. Even with traditional therapy, however, you might find creative daydreaming helpful in maintaining the motivation to put into practice any advice given by another professional. If in doubt, show him/her this book, so that any self-hypnosis exercises can be individualized to your specific needs.

Client Successes

In 1990 a client entered my office and said, "I want you to help me overcome the Coke habit." As I started to refer him to a substance abuse counselor, he interrupted me rather quickly. He apologized and explained that he meant Coca-Cola. Simple use of the benefits approach helped him sell success to his subconscious. He substituted water part of the time, two cups daily of regular coffee, and several cups of de-caffeinated coffee part of the time, while gradually reducing his daily Coca-Cola intake.

Note: If you are cutting down on excessive caffeine consumption, it may be wiser to gradually taper off rather than quitting cold. (Consult your physician or health care practitioner before withdrawing caffeine abruptly.)

Motivational Goals

Motivational goals can fall into any of the goal categories mentioned in Chapter 11: achievements, possessions, characteristics, projects, or changes. If your priority goal requires motivation and does not appear elsewhere in this chapter, then identify and list your personal benefits. This applies whether your aim is to achieve political office, remodel the kitchen, write a book, participate in a church project, or go into business for yourself. Ask yourself the question: "What do I get from this goal?" (Remember WII-FM from Chapter 13.)

Client Successes

A career woman asked me to help her increase her motivation to keep her house clean, as she wished to set a good example for her children. Although I asked her to list her personal benefits, the subconscious can often be quite creative. Her new way of solving her concerns surprised both of us. She decided to hire a housekeeper to do the major portion of the housework, and pay for this from the income earned by working overtime. She decided that paying someone else to have the work done was far more important than trying to do it herself. Although she could have reached this decision consciously without ever seeing me, the idea came instantly during trance. Sometimes the obvious comes much more readily from the subconscious than from the conscious mind.

Confidence/Self-Esteem

I believe you will find that using the peak performance meditation may prove to be the best starting point for improved confidence or self-esteem (see "Love Yourself: Celebrate Your Success!" in Chapter 10). My opinion comes from the experience of clients. You may also incorporate affirmations for confidence, and fantasize yourself being the person you choose to be. Depending on your circumstances, you may need outside help for confidence and/or self-esteem.

Note: If you have not yet finished this book, choose a motivational goal for your first creative daydreaming exercise.

Client Successes

A professional speaker whom I respect greatly emerged from trance giving me a strong emotional appeal. I facilitated an earlier version of the peak performance meditation for her. She looked at me as though she could see right into my soul, and said, "This is too good to keep hidden in this office. You must get this out into the business world!" While I respect her confidentiality, I am grateful for her encouragement. She told me that numerous successful people need more confidence and self-esteem.

Sports Enhancement

Unlike habits and professional goals, sports enhancement frequently does not involve motivation. Usually we simply wish to improve our skills and/or our consistency. Where improvement requires increased motivation to practice, creative daydreaming helps whether the sport is primarily physical or mental.

Some sports involve principally physical fitness and endurance, such as running and swimming. The athlete wins chiefly through endurance and fitness or strength rather than mental skills, although the mind must focus on victory. Other activities seem far less physical, such as golf; but all sports involve the mind far more than many athletes realize. Even basketball, which requires great physical stamina, could be classified as a mental sport as well as a physical one. Baseball players most certainly recognize the importance of keeping your eye on the ball! Just ask a pitcher whether or not confidence and concentration can influence pitching skills. Football players, who must be very fit physically, quickly discover how attitude can influence their game.

General Guidelines

Motivation frequently becomes necessary only for the person who finds it difficult to practice often enough to attain his/her athletic goals, regardless of whether the sport is primarily physical or mental. If you fit this category, then list your benefits of staying motivated. Do this in a manner similar to the previous exercises in this chapter, selling your subconscious on the benefits of staying motivated. Schedule regular practice time for yourself, and stick to it. During your creative daydreaming exercise, fantasize the benefits of mastering the sport, as well as the pride of accomplishment. If your goal involves becoming (or remaining) professional, visualize the desired championship and/or the benefits of compensation. You may also imagine successful participation in the activity itself. Blend in your key word as appropriate, and say it to yourself at the times you set aside to practice your athletic activity. Your word to trigger motivation will be different than the performance trigger used to enhance skills and actual performance.

Enhancing sports skills can best be accomplished through understanding and using triggers for peak performance. (Refer to Chapter 5 to review the section on anchoring and triggers if necessary.) Practice the exercise for peak performance described in Chapter 10 again, exclusively remembering past successes involving sports. One deep breath accompanied by thinking the word "focus" will generally be your best trigger for enhancing peak performance in sports; but you may also add your other peak performance trigger (power point) for extra empowerment if you wish, making it an alternate sports trigger. Anchor your past athletic successes into your sports trigger. During your activity, you may use either the word "focus" or your power point (or both) as a sports trigger for peak performance.

Regardless of which sport you wish to improve, remember that imagination is the language of the subconscious. It is better to imagine the desired result rather than the problem you wish to avoid.

For more specific guidelines for some common sports, refer to the appropriate subsection below. If you already participate in professional sports, you may find it a very worthwhile investment to spend a few private sessions with a hypnotherapist for sports enhancement. A properly trained therapist can help you work through any specific weak areas that might be influenced by your subconscious mind. (If choosing a hypnotherapist, remember that experience in the use of hypnosis for sports enhancement is more important than a background in psychology, unless you also have psychological problems to resolve.)

Archery/Darts

Determine those specific areas where you desire improvement in skills and confidence. Upon entering trance, take a deep breath and think the word "focus" and then fantasize successful application of the desired skill. Feel yourself holding the bow and arrow (or dart). See the target. Imagine hitting the bull's eye. Next time you engage in this activity, use your key word (or sports trigger) at each turn just before launching the arrow or dart.

Baseball

Determine those specific areas (batting, fielding, pitching, or catching) where you desire improvement in skills and confidence. Upon entering trance, imagine yourself in those precise situations. Take a deep breath and think the word "focus" and/or activate your power point; then fantasize successful application of the desired skill.

Batting: Fantasize several times at bat. Imagine hitting the ball squarely for a single, or for a double down the line (or in the gap). See the pitcher. Feel the bat in your hands. Hear the sound of bat meeting ball as you swing it. If you need to improve your bunting skills, do so in your mind's eye. Make it vivid! Now imagine hitting a home run. Remember to use your trigger before each exercise in your mind. In the real game, use your sports trigger when you step up to the plate. Do *not* imagine striking out or hitting into a double play, otherwise you increase the risk of doing so.

Fielding: Regardless of the position you play, fantasize yourself fielding the ball to the best of your ability. Remember to use your sports trigger as you practice creative daydreaming. In real life, use your trigger as each new batter steps up to the home plate. Do *not* think of possible errors; instead, imagine making the best play possible.

Pitching/catching: Just before each pitch, fantasize exactly where you wish the pitch to go. If catching, practice moving the mitt as needed to catch each pitch. In your mind, practice throwing out a runner trying to steal second base. If pitching, think the word "focus" and visualize all the right motions. See the ball going precisely where you wish.

Basketball

Determine those specific areas (free throws, lay-ups, jump shots, 3-pointers) where you desire improvement in skills and confidence. Upon entering trance, imagine yourself in those precise situations. Take a deep breath and think the word "focus" and/or activate your power point; and then fantasize successful application of the desired skill. Imagine the sounds of the crowd and/or the ball bouncing on the court. In the actual game, you will be able to use your key word before making free throws; but you might be too busy running up and down the court at other times to think of it. Use your sports trigger with each time out, before each jump ball, and before each free throw (regardless of who makes the shot). Should you feel yourself losing concentration at any time during the game, use your sports trigger during a momentary pause.

Bowling

Determine those specific areas (first ball, single-pin leaves, 7-10 splits, etc.) where you desire improvement in skills and confidence. Upon entering trance, imagine yourself in those precise situations. Take a deep breath, think the word "focus" and/or activate your power point; and then visualize rolling the ball appropriately. Feel the follow-through. Hear the ball land. See it hit the pin(s). Next time you bowl, remember to use your sports trigger just before each frame and/or second ball. Take a quick moment to fantasize your desired outcome just before you roll the ball.

Football

Determine those specific areas (offense, defense, special teams, passing, receiving, etc.) where you desire improvement in skills and confidence. Upon entering trance, imagine yourself in those precise situations. Take a deep breath and think the word "focus" and/or activate your power point; and then visualize successful application of the desired skill. Imagine yourself catching the pass, making a touchdown, breaking a tackle, making the tackle, and so on. Fantasize all the sounds and feelings as well as what you can see in your mind's eye. During the game, use your sports trigger just before lining up prior to each play. If you need help in specific areas for confidence or attitude, invest in private sessions.

Golf

Prior to entering trance, identify the specific skills you wish to improve. During your creative daydreaming exercise, fantasize successful application of these skills. Just before each imagined application, activate your sports trigger; and then visualize success.

Tee/fairway: Do you wish more distance, more accuracy, or both? In your imagination, *be* at the fourth hole (or seventh hole) of your favorite golf course. Fantasize reaching for your driver or desired iron. Imagine details! Now use your sports trigger, and then visualize properly addressing the ball. In your mind, swing the club. See and hear the club connect with the ball. Feel the follow-through. Imagine the ball flying perfectly through the air, touching the fairway, rolling and landing exactly where desired. During a real game, use your sports trigger and take a brief moment to fantasize making a perfect drive.

Chipping/putting: Imagine yourself chipping onto the green in the same manner as the above examples, and/or putting. Use your sports trigger and imagine the ball landing exactly where desired. Imagine the ball rolling perfectly and dropping into the cup. See and hear the ball drop. Do this exercise several times with the ball at various distances from the cup.

The occasional bad lay: So you find yourself in a sand trap or the rough? Remember to use your sports trigger before addressing the ball, and momentarily fantasize making the perfect shot to get your ball in good position.

Gymnastics

Determine those specific areas (parallel bars, rings, etc.) where you desire improvement in skills and confidence. Upon entering trance, imagine yourself in those precise situations. Take a deep breath and think the word "focus" and/or activate your power point; and then fantasize successful application of the desired skill. Go through the entire routine in your mind, from start to finish. During actual practice or performance, whisper or think the word "focus" just before beginning your routine and/or activate your power point.

Physical Sports (Swimming, Track, etc.)

Determine those specific areas where you desire improvement in skills and confidence. Upon entering trance, imagine yourself in those precise situations. Take a deep breath and think the word "focus" and/or activate your power point; and then fantasize successful application of the desired skill. If you need more motivation to practice, list your benefits as described previously. Visualize victory. During the actual competition, use your sports trigger while approaching the starting line.

Skiing

Fantasize yourself getting ready to go down the slope. Take a deep breath and think the word "focus" and/or activate your power point; and then visualize beginning your downhill run. If you know the particular slope you wish to master, go through it from start to finish in your mind. See the snow in front of you. Feel yourself making the appropriate movements as you glide downhill. Hear the sounds in your mind's ear. Make it real. If you wish to prepare for a competition, use creative daydreaming at least once daily for at least one month before the competition. During the actual competition, take one deep breath and think the word "focus" (and/or activate your power point) just before beginning your run.

Soccer/Hockey

Determine those specific areas (defense, offense, goal tending, etc.) where you desire improvement in skills and confidence. Upon entering trance, imagine yourself in those precise situations. Take a deep breath and think the word "focus" and/or activate your power point; and then visualize successful application of the desired skill. Imagine making a goal. If you tend the goal, fantasize various blocks.

Other Sports

Determine those specific areas where you desire improvement in skills and confidence. Upon entering trance, imagine yourself in those precise situations. Take a deep breath and think the word "focus" and/or activate your power point; and then fantasize successful application of the desired skill. For example, if you engage in competitive diving, visualize the entire dive from start to finish. See it in your mind. Feel your body making the desired moves. Hear the sounds as you hit the water. During the actual dive, take one deep breath and whisper or think the word "focus" (and/or activate your power point) just before diving. For skating, fantasize your entire routine in your mind, from start to finish. Use these same guidelines for other competitive sports.

Client Successes

A semi-professional golfer invested in four sessions before a tournament. In the first two sessions, I used the techniques presented in this book. During the third and fourth sessions, I took him through the entire course in his mind, having him rehearse every stroke. He placed among the top five in the tournament.

A swimmer wanted to place in the top ten, and saw me primarily for motivation to maintain his practice schedule. I also taught him to use the peak performance trigger as his sports trigger, and he won bronze in an international competition.

If Your Goal Isn't Included Above . . .

Read the rest of this book and apply whatever you consider useful. Practice self-hypnosis, incorporating creative daydreaming along with your affirmations and key word. Fantasize total achievement of your desires. Seek professional help if needed.

When to Consider Hypnotherapy

You may wish to consider hypnotherapy if you still need help after completing the exercises in this book. Certain problems usually require outside assistance, whether from a hypnotherapist and/or from another professional. Among these are: phobias, unresolved grief, serious self-esteem issues, post-traumatic stress disorder, health problems (illness or injury), alcoholism or substance abuse, obsessive eating disorders, obesity, chain smoking, depression and other serious mental problems, family or relationship problems, vocational problems, and so on.

Be sure to read the discussion of this issue in Appendix 1, while Appendix 2 provides some guidelines for choosing a competent hypnosis professional.

Part V

Adding Words of Power

Chapter 15

How Words Impact the Mind

Effective self-hypnosis requires a basic understanding of how words impact the mind, especially when one or more of the subconscious gateways may be open. Additionally, good affirmations (positive statements of belief) can enhance the trance, adding more power to your experience.

Remember Emile Coué from Chapter 3? He taught autosuggestion to all who would listen. Just as many hypnotherapists refer to Mesmer as the grandfather of hypnosis, we may consider Coué as the grandfather of self-hypnosis.

While most researchers of hypnosis took the role of hypnotist who tried put subjects "under their power," Coué sought to help people become self-empowered through autosuggestion. I believe that he was a man before his time. Autosuggestions gave birth to affirmations, which remained in an embryonic stage for decades. Though both forms of suggestion are similar, autosuggestion is normally only used during a trance state; while affirmations may be used at any time of day, whether or not you believe in the benefits of trance. This entire chapter revolves around one very important similarity between affirmations and hypnotic suggestions: they enter the subconscious.

Numerous religious books written throughout the twentieth century recommend the use of affirmations. Just check the bookstore in any Unity Church or Church of Religious Science and you can easily find books with affirmations. In spite of this fact, however, some churches consider affirmations to be "bootstrap" methods. They may use the sarcastic metaphor: "Try to pick yourself up by pulling on your own bootstraps." The church I formerly attended used this trope frequently to discourage the use of both affirmations and autosuggestions. During the 1960s, I saw very little material recommending affirmations, and my friends and work associates shunned autosuggestion in any form.

Affirmations finally became more popular in the 1970s and 1980s; but even now too few seem to know how to properly structure and use them. Used wisely, words are powerful tools to help us create motivation and success attitudes in the subconscious mind. If misconstructed or misused, however, autosuggestions and affirmations can actually move our goals farther from reach. We must use caution when using affirmations.

Sticks and Stones

Remember the old saying: Sticks and stones may break my bones, but words will never hurt me? It is my professional opinion that inappropriate words *can* and *do* hurt us when a subconscious gateway is open. Allow me to illustrate from my own personal experience.

When my first marriage broke up, my sales hit rock bottom even though I had previously enjoyed success in the insurance industry. While I was experiencing a multitude of mixed emotions, an insurance executive told me, "Nobody does well in sales for two years after a divorce!" This negative idea entered my mind like a powerful hypnotic suggestion, jetting through the subconscious gateway of emotion. Afterwards, I found myself still doing the same actions as in previous years, but without the successful results of the 1970s. My financial strength vanished quickly enough to send me into a near panic. My income dropped to a fraction of its previous level, leading me into overwhelming debt. Self-help books no longer worked, and I kept wondering why.

Today I know what happened. During the crisis of divorce, my subconscious believed what this insurance authority had told me; and that belief remained stuck in my subconscious. My mind replayed that executive's statement like a broken record; and it became a negative affirmation, in spite of my best efforts to get around it. I received a double whammy, because this statement originated from a professional authority figure and entered my subconscious through the gateway of authority as well as the gateway of emotion.

Now let me share some other examples that many people relate to.

A mother exclaims loudly to her child, "Don't spill the milk!" The glass often gets tipped over within seconds, because the child's mind immediately creates the image of spilling the milk.

Parents often tell their children, "Don't forget your coat!" Need I explain what happens? Next time, simply tell your child: "Remember your coat."

A golfer says, "I'm not going into the water," and where does the ball land? This same concept applies to other sports as well. For example, during an important at-bat in a baseball game with runners on base, a teammate says, "Don't strike out!" How often does the feared strikeout manifest?

A dieter says to a friend (or self), "I'm not eating any dessert at this party!" Many clients have reported either eating dessert at the party or eating dessert at home after the party. Someone I know personally attempted to control her eating habits with affirmations such as, "I don't like sweets anymore." Doesn't that statement make you imagine something sweet? Her subconscious responded by increasing her consumption of chocolate.

A well-known corporation encouraged salespeople to tape a 3 x 5 inch card to the dashboard of their car with the following statement: "I don't quit until it hurts!" Upper management expected that affirmation to remind each representative to make one last call at the end of each day. In reality, however, the statement gives the subconscious two very negative messages: (1) Prospecting hurts, and (2) when it does, you can quit! Indeed, one of my clients resigned a good sales position after the damage done by this affirmation. By the time he saw me, he earned a lower income in a less desirable company.

During my successful years in the insurance industry, management told me: "Everyone has call reluctance; it comes with the territory." Even now, many salespeople accept this as their reality. Sales management school taught me that nobody likes to make prospecting calls, but prospecting is the cause producing the effect of secured appointments and new clients.

Many firms create a "success formula" which can also serve as an affirmation. Here's the one that I taught my agents: "Thirty calls daily equals ten interviews weekly equals three sales per week." I personally used this prospecting formula (and its affirmation) consistently to generate a good income for almost a decade. Reflecting back on my sales career, however, one consistency jumps out at me. Whenever I expected a sale, I usually got it; if I expected to lose the sale, the result met my expectation.

The Law of Expectancy

This subheading could also just as easily be called: *The Principle of the Self-Fulfilling Prophecy*. This basic natural law means that we tend to get whatever we believe or expect at a subconscious level. My late mentor, Charles Tebbetts, taught that we can help to empower our clients by helping them change what the subconscious expects; and many years of professional experience validate this opinion.

Affirmations, hypnotic suggestions, and/or autosuggestions should be constructed to convince the subconscious mind of the possibility of what the conscious mind already accepts. I recommend that we choose affirmations that take advantage of the law of expectancy, and avoid making statements to ourselves that create negative expectancy; otherwise they can actually become counterproductive. Choose your words wisely.

While I am not a family counselor, I would recommend that parents heed this advice when giving parental commands to their children. Frequently we tend to emphasize the unacceptable behavior rather than the desired result, such as: "Don't talk back to me!" What usually happens? This leads me to a discussion of another important law of the mind.

The Law of Reversed Effect

For some strange reason, the subconscious tends to ignore negative statements, causing the imagination to focus on the reverse. In my profession we call this the law of reversed effect. To illustrate this law, ask a friend or relative to read the next paragraph to you:

> Take a deep breath. Close your eyes and relax. Now, you MUST NOT think of a dog!

How did you respond? In your imagination, did you see, hear, or pet a dog? Most people almost immediately imagine one. When you tell the mind *not* to do something, it creates the fantasy of what is to be avoided.

A smoker wishing to quit usually thinks, "I can't have a cigarette; I don't want one anymore." This self-talk usually results in a nagging desire to imagine how good one would taste or smell, and the craving increases until he/she either lights up or replaces the fantasy of a cigarette with a totally different desire. Untrained hypnotists often tell people, "You don't like chocolate now. Sweets and junk food simply don't appeal to you anymore." Doesn't this make you imagine chocolate or some other junk food? You must *replace* the undesired fantasy with a *different* fantasy.

A client who had been through a quick-fix stop-smoking program listened to the audiotape she purchased, and then wondered why she gained 40 pounds in nine months. At her request, I listened to the hypnosis tape. One of the hypnotic affirmations was: "You do not need food as a substitute for smoking." You guessed it! She wanted hypnosis to stop her from substituting snacks for her cigarettes.

The Law of Awareness

Another law of the mind is called the law of awareness. In simple terms, this law means that you tend to attract whatever dominates your mind. Joe Vitale calls it *The Attractor Factor*, and wrote a book by the same name.

As you put mental energy into the problem, you tend to magnify its effect at a subconscious level, attracting circumstances that could intensify the very problem you wish to overcome. In light of this, I consider it imperative for us to use affirmations that focus the subconscious on the desired results rather than on avoidance of the problems. This law goes hand in hand with the law of reversed effect.

Many of our state governments promote the statement: "Don't drink and drive." Have you wondered why so many drivers ignore that statement? The subconscious hears (or reads) those words without the negative. Furthermore, this authoritative statement puts one's awareness on the problem rather than the solution, thus creating the image of drinking and driving. This happens even more frequently when television opens the hypnosis gateway to the subconscious. I believe a better message would be: "Drive sober." The best advertisement that I ever saw regarding alcohol and drinking focused on the solution. The narrator said, "The man in this car is too drunk to drive . . ." The scene hovered above a car, showing headlights on a foggy night, with the car parking and depositing a passenger. The next statement was: "That's why he took a cab home."

Remember that any statement designed to enter one of the subconscious gateways serves like an affirmation or hypnotic suggestion, whether spoken by you about yourself, or spoken by somebody else when your subconscious is receptive.

Be Careful What You Say

During my time of trial, I read a self-help book that gave numerous examples of affirmations about avoiding fear and eliminating poverty. The basic concepts and ideas seemed logical to my conscious mind, but negative results cropped up like weeds in a field. The author of the book had used faulty wording; so the more I used the affirmations, the more they hurt me. At the time, I did not know why. Many of my clients have also learned the hard way to avoid common negative statements. Wise King Solomon said "death and life are in the power of the tongue," so we must choose our words wisely. Careless use of negative statements just might enter one of the subconscious gateways with adverse results. Consider the risks of commonly used statements such as:

- That makes me sick.
- That gives me a pain in my . . .
- That job was a major headache.
- I am going to finish this if it kills me.
- That almost gave me a heart attack.
- That will be the death of me.
- No pain, no gain.
- Fear is a mind killer.
- That was a back-breaking job.
- That tears me up inside.
- That burns me up/makes my blood boil.
- He/she is driving me crazy.
- How can I be so stupid/dumb/ignorant?

Have you found yourself using any of these negative statements? Only time will tell whether or not these (or similar) assertions will influence the subconscious to cause negative things to happen to us.

A competently trained hypnosis professional understands the importance of semantics when dealing with the subconscious. Affirmations are like hypnotic suggestions (because they enter the subconscious) and must be constructed similarly, but stated in the first person format. Remember this fact as you read the next chapter.

Chapter 16

Choosing Your Affirmations

Using the guidelines presented throughout this chapter, you may choose several affirmations relating to your number one priority goal. Some people prefer to write their own affirmations; others would rather find some that appear in a book. Either choice is acceptable, so long as the statements contribute to the desired results.

Affirm the Desired Result

Remember the law of reversed effect? Positive statements motivate the subconscious much more effectively than negative ones. For example, if you say, "I am not afraid to speak in public," your subconscious mind ignores the negative, and you still claim the fear. A better way of stating this is: "I am a confident public speaker."

Amazingly, numerous professionals both inside and outside the hypnosis profession focus on the problem to be avoided rather than focusing on the solution. Some hypnosis scripts on sale contain numerous negative suggestions, which often result in causing the subconscious to fantasize the problem.

Examine the statement: *"I am in control of my temper."* This simple sentence sounds harmless enough, but what awareness does it create? Does this remind you of a time when you got angry? Rather than claiming ownership of a temper, why not claim a calm disposition instead? A better way of saying this would be: *"I am a calm person."*

On rare occasions you may need to state a problem in order to affirm the solution in the same statement. Should this become necessary, state the problem in the past tense and put the solution in the present tense. Remember to put your awareness into solutions as well, as in the following example: *"Whenever something occurs that used to push my stress buttons, I take one deep breath and remain calm, totally in control of my feelings."*

You can affirm your desired results in three areas: *journey, destination,* and *attitudes.*

- Journey: *I am a person who exercises daily.*
- Destination: *Exercise keeps me energetic and physically fit.*
- Attitude: *I enjoy exercise and appreciate its benefits.*

The journey serves as a metaphor of your course or action plan. The destination is your goal fulfillment, including the benefits. You may also affirm positive attitudes about both the benefits and the price of success, such as with an attitude of gratitude. Now let us discuss some other important guidelines to consider in choosing (or writing) your affirmations.

Present Tense vs. Future Tense

Human nature tends to procrastinate, and an open-ended future allows the subconscious to escape by dragging its feet. If you give your subconscious an escape hatch, it usually takes advantage of the opportunity.

Examine the following statement: *"I will control my eating habits."* This assertion contains no trigger to activate the action; it is open-ended. We all know that tomorrow never comes. The subconscious, however, might get worried and say, "Eat, drink, and be merry, for tomorrow we diet!" The statement could be rephrased: *"I make wise choices regarding my eating habits."*

Sometimes doubts prevent a present-tense statement from obtaining subconscious belief. For example, an obese client might not comfortably say, *"I am slender and attractive,"* because the subconscious knows otherwise. We can effectively bypass this problem by making a slight modification: *"Each day I am becoming more slender and attractive."* Even though the conscious mind recognizes this as a future possibility, present improvement is implied; and this becomes more comfortable to the subconscious mind.

For many years I avoided all other uses of the future tense, until I learned about some research done by Arthur Winkler, Ph.D., who hypnotized over 34,000 people during his lifetime. He used the future tense with many hypnotic suggestions, without subconscious resistance, by linking them to triggers. He associated the suggestions to a specific time or event as the trigger for the action; and this makes a difference to the subconscious.

Use Active Words

I can sing. Does that tell you that I actually *do* sing? I can also cook, when I get around to it. (God bless microwaves!) "Can" is a passive word. If you desire to affirm ability, then you may use "can" in your affirmation; however, active statements carry more power than passive ones.

For example, *"I can improve my memory"* does not carry nearly the strength as: *"I am improving my memory each time I use it."*

Many hypnotherapists (including me) use more permissive suggestions with "can" while working with clients, simply because the subconscious often accepts indirect suggestions more readily than direct suggestions from an external source. My own experience, however, indicates that the direct approach normally works best when we are stating our own affirmations. Rather than trying to be fancy, just be direct and specific.

Be Specific

The subconscious knows no jokes; so we can leave no room for error. We must state our desires with simple, clear, and specific words. For example, examine the next statement: *"I am losing my excess weight."* Can you find the subconscious escape hatch here?

During childhood, others programmed us to find what we lose. How many people keep losing weight, only to find it again? One client told me that he had "lost and found" over 1,000 pounds during a ten-year period! We can reduce, take-off, release, discard, get rid of, give away, throw away, eliminate, or donate excess pounds; but using the word "lost" sends a message to the subconscious to try to find it again. Say instead: *"I am reducing regularly, until I reach my ideal weight."*

Also, my mentor encouraged all his students to keep their language simple enough for a child to understand. Since the subconscious responds much better to plain language, I agree totally. Some people seem to thrive on long, ambiguous affirmations with big words; but if the conscious mind has difficulty understanding the statement, it is almost a sure bet that the subconscious will also be confused.

Now let us examine two powerful words.

I Am . . .

These two words contribute toward self-empowerment; so use them often in a positive way. Affirm how you think, act, and feel about the reality of your goal as well as your method(s) of goal attainment; and also affirm your benefits. For example:

- I am a non-smoker now.
- I am enjoying the right amounts of the right foods.
- I am more energetic at my ideal weight.
- I am self-motivated.
- I am thankful for my increasing success.
- I am more confident with each passing day.

Bear in mind that goals must be believable to the subconscious in order for "I am" statements to be effective. If you don't believe in your ability to reach your goal, then choose some affirmations that will contribute toward that belief.

If you wish to write your own affirmations, remember to be specific, keeping all your statements in the present tense ("I *am* becoming more confident every day" rather than "I *will be* confident"). Remember the important laws of the mind discussed in Chapter 15 as well as the guidelines presented above. Review them as often as necessary. Please understand the importance of this advice before attempting the final empowerment exercise, as your goal may depend upon it.

If you prefer, you may import affirmations written by others. For your convenience, Appendix 7 contains affirmations for various goals. Please feel free to use whichever ones you wish, making changes as desired.

Why Use Affirmations?

Proper affirmations help convince your subconscious to believe in your ability to reach your goals, as well as to pay the price of success. Simply using creative daydreaming of your benefits would be like finding that car you wish to buy, only to discover that nobody is willing to tell you how to buy it!

Also, frequent positive statements can help you become self-motivated, since motivation and subconscious beliefs frequently become closely related. Your affirmations represent the post-hypnotic autosuggestions you will be programming into your own subconscious; and that is why I place so much importance on their structure. Remember that you may affirm your benefits, your journey (or action plan), and your attitudes about your goal.

Are you ready to move on now? If so, you may either choose existing affirmations, or you may write your own in accordance with the above guidelines. In either case, pay close attention to the rest of this chapter.

Edit Your Affirmations

Once you feel satisfied with the affirmations you have written and/or chosen, I recommend that you edit them before use. Here are some examples of improperly written affirmations, all of which other professionals have recommended either publicly or in writing. Notice how and why I edit them. The better way of making each statement follows, along with the reason(s) for the changes.

By avoiding sweets and junk food, I am losing weight.

This statement violates the law of reversed effect. Furthermore, it put awareness into sweets and junk food. Personally, it makes me imagine potato chips. Perhaps you might think of pizza, pie, or candy. Next, this statement reminds me of the old saying, "Finders keepers, losers weepers!" That sends a message to the subconscious to go looking for what was lost. Let us simply say: *"My good eating habits help me attain and maintain my ideal weight."*

I hate smoking, because it harms my health.

This statement affirms the problem rather than the solution. Worse yet, it also affirms health problems. I can't help but wonder how many people may actually develop health problems because of the excessive attention given to the hazards of smoking. Even those who do manage to quit smoking might easily find themselves feeling very uncomfortable in the presence of people who still smoke. Let us state the desired solution: *"My lungs reward me for the fresh air I give them. I am a tolerant non-smoker."*

I easily forgive people who hurt me, understanding their weakness.

I have used this as a poor example of an affirmation numerous times over the years, because it contains hidden negative messages. If you decided to use this, you would affirm that other people hurt you; but that's okay, because other people are weak and don't measure up to your standards. This statement could easily become a path to self-righteousness. A much more positive statement is: *"I am a forgiving and understanding person,"* or *"I am tolerant of other people's opinions."*

I love objections, and each NO gets me closer to the next sale.

Are you a professional salesperson? If so, avoid this statement like the plague. The problem is simple: if you love objections, you will most certainly get them! Furthermore, you'll think of them as a customer's objections to buying rather than concerns of ownership. Many sales organizations, including the one that formerly employed me, teach their sales force to use this statement. The logic is to help salespeople put a value on each interview, since no salesperson bats a thousand; but the subconscious receives negative messages. If you use this statement as an affirmation, your subconscious might alter your presentation to attract objections. I have advised many salespeople to rephrase this as follows: *"I give wise responses to customer (or client) concerns because they move us closer to the best decision. I accept that each interview has value regardless of the final decision."*

I will be out of debt by XX/XX (month and year).

This statement is personal, because I discovered its flaws the hard way. First, unexpected setbacks (such as car repairs, illness, etc.) may delay the target date. Second, if the target date approaches without the goal coming into sight, it becomes more difficult to believe, resulting in increasing stress. Worse yet, this statement leaves the method of debt clearing totally open. In my case, I made the mistake of using this exact affirmation (lifted from a self-help book) and specified January 1984 as the date for being out of debt. Bankruptcy was not what I had in mind! I learned the hard way to use the following: *"My increasing money supply replaces past debts. I am grateful to God for my increasing abundance, and I am becoming more confident with each passing day."*

I'll share another mistake from my past . . .

I always have enough money to pay my bills.

Where's the extra money left over to pay you? Some of you probably play "credit card bingo" by transferring balances from one credit card to another. I know what it is like to borrow from Visa to pay MasterCard, and so on; and the results can be very costly and depressing. This is better: *"My income continues to surpass my expenses."*

Financial concerns plague many millions of people worldwide, so I'll include one more example of a dangerous affirmation regarding money.

I see myself depositing $XX,000 into my bank account.

One of my clients followed the advice of a seminar leader, who recommended making out a deposit slip for $10,000. The facilitator instructed him to visualize putting that deposit into the bank and repeat the above statement every day for thirty days. Within one month after following that advice, a lawsuit settlement required him to liquidate some real estate in a forced sale, netting just over a third of the actual equity. You guessed it; he got just over ten thousand dollars, when he should have netted almost $30,000! It is better to affirm something like: *"I have $XX,000 in divine ways which are good for all concerned."*

I am not afraid of speaking in public.

Before reading further, try your own hand:

_____

_____

_____

Which two laws of the mind did this statement violate? How close did you come to my sample change: "*I am becoming a more confident public speaker every time I speak in public*"?

If you are still unclear, then I suggest you reread both Chapter 15 and this chapter. Now let us take a look at one of the most confusing examples of ambiguity that I have ever seen in all my years of practice.

I realize that we are NOT our body, actions or awareness, and that blame and guilt are NEVER valid because any fault in what we do lies NOT in us but in our faulty awareness.

Can you believe that I lifted the above statement verbatim? Use your new skills to decide what to change:

_____

_____

_____

These few examples represent only a very small fraction of poorly written affirmations recommended by alleged experts. We must remember that whenever the subconscious gateways are open, it accepts statements literally. Subtle wording, often overlooked by the conscious mind, can alter or reverse the objective of an affirmation. Choose your affirmations carefully, whether you import them or write them. Use the guideline that imagination is the language of the subconscious, so ask yourself what the prospective affirmation will cause you to imagine. Then, before using them, edit them carefully. Once you believe that your affirmations are ready, I recommend two more important steps.

First, review your personal affirmations slowly and carefully while feeling mellow, or while in a relaxed state of mind. Add any new ones flowing through your thoughts at the time. Delete or change

Adding Words of Power

any existing ones unless they feel comfortable to you. Second, edit them according to the guidelines presented in this chapter to be sure they are worded properly. (If you need assistance, I am available for coaching or consulting for a fee – go to <http://www.royhunter.com/consulting.htm>.)

Last but not least, add your key word as described in the next chapter.

Chapter 17

Adding a Key Word

Many professionals recommend that we should read or say our affirmations many times daily in order to gain the benefit of repetition, but I prefer to use a subconscious trigger. Rather than trying to pick one or two affirmations to say over 100 times daily (as one self-help book advocates), you can simply choose one word or phrase that represents an entire group of affirmations to your subconscious mind. You will therefore only have to spend time with your affirmations at the time that you do your self-hypnosis. Your chosen word can work for you the rest of the time, serving as a subconscious trigger for all of your affirmations.

I call this a *key word*, because it acts like a key to the subconscious. I recommend that you choose a key word for your priority goal, and add it to your list of affirmations:

> My key word is _____. Whenever I say, see, think or hear the word _____, it automatically reinforces all of these affirmations.

Let us explore some reasons for this recommendation. Many people involved in network marketing practice what is commonly called "treasure mapping" for success. The treasure mapper places a picture that symbolizes the desired goal in a handy place (like the refrigerator door). This could be an old photo of one's self at an ideal weight, or a picture of a tropical beach, a new car, and so on. The picture then becomes an automatic subconscious symbol to follow the action plan required for goal achievement. This incorporates the anchoring and trigger concept discussed in Chapter 5. Key words work in much the same way, only better with some people (especially those who do not visualize well). Furthermore, you can have several key words, with each word representing a different goal.

We all carry a set of keys to unlock doors. I have a set of key words that unlock certain doors of my subconscious mind. For example, the word "relax" means that I am calm, confident, and in control of my feelings. The word "money" reminds me that money is a tool empowering me to express greater love, and to enjoy greater freedom. The word "love" serves as a master key, linking all of my business, personal, and spiritual affairs to the win-win attitude.

Start by selecting a key word for your priority goal.

Choosing the Best Word

Your key word should feel good emotionally as well as make sense intellectually. Smokers wishing to quit or reduce smoking normally choose the word "relax" as their key word. One deep breath usually accompanies this key word, as replacing an undesired habit with a new habit facilitates the change of habit. If you prefer, you may use the word "free" (or "occasional" if you choose to smoke occasionally rather than frequently).

The following list shows typical key words chosen by clients for weight management:

- slender
- slim
- attractive
- satisfy
- shape
- sexy
- healthy

One man tried "self-discipline" for his key word, but his subconscious rejected it. The subconscious hides the "child inside" and does not like discipline, which explains why my client chose a new word. Another client chose "get buffed" and found his mind quickly rejecting it, because the phrase brought back painful memories. Make certain your key word *feels* good.

For sports enhancement, I normally recommend "focus" as the best key word.

Typical key words chosen by clients for confidence, success, or sales motivation are:

- confidence
- success
- client
- money
- abundance

Clients wishing to improve memory and/or study habits frequently choose:

- remember
- memory
- grades
- mind

The sample words shown above should help you to choose one that suits you, even if neither your goal nor the prospective word appears in this chapter. Select a positive word, related to your goal. Then sit back, relax, and take a deep breath. Close your eyes and ask yourself, "Do I like this word for my key word?" You should have a feeling of either yes or no. Once you feel satisfied with your word, write it down.

How to Use Your Key Word

Although your last affirmation should define your key word, you may find it helpful to include this key word with several other affirmations. For example, if you choose "satisfy" as a key word for weight reduction, you might say: *"Nutritious foods satisfy me physically, mentally, and emotionally."*

The final empowerment exercise describes how to incorporate the key word into the subconscious and enjoy its maximum benefit.

Adding Words of Power

Each of us must then accept responsibility for using the chosen word frequently. Obviously, you may prefer a common word instead of one rarely used. You may find yourself using and hearing the key word many times daily in conversation, with that word acting like a trigger at a subconscious level.

If desired, you may put a 3×5 inch card with an affirmation containing your key word on your refrigerator, vanity mirror, desk, or dashboard – anywhere that causes you to see it frequently. You can also make a point of saying or thinking your word often, until you are well on the road to reaching your goal.

Now that you have your list of benefits together with your affirmations and key word, are you ready to attain your ideal self-empowerment? Continue on with Chapter 18 on HypnoCise and put it to use in your life.

Chapter 18

HypnoCise

Are you ready to magnify the effectiveness of your empowerment exercises? Let us blend self-hypnosis together with key words, affirmations, creative daydreaming, and positive emotion. I call this HypnoCise. To the best of my knowledge and experience, this is the most powerful technique of creative self-hypnosis available for motivation. Get your completed list of affirmations ready for use, as well as your list of personal benefits.

Review

In Part I we explored the purpose of this book, the various states of the mind, what happens when we enter the alpha state, and how to prepare for altered states. We dug a little deeper into the past and present of hypnosis. Practicing the simple relaxation techniques described in Chapter 4 will give you at least some exposure to self-induced hypnosis, even if you attain only a light state. By becoming familiar with the feeling, you increase your awareness of other trances during the day, such as simply staring out the window and daydreaming.

Part II discussed subconscious programming: why we need to program the subconscious and how to reprogram the mind. We traveled through the five subconscious gateways in order to understand how the subconscious is influenced. We can avoid possible traps by understanding these gateways, or subconscious motivators, and increase the probability of success. Emotion is the motivating power of the mind, so it behooves us to remain in control of our emotions; so the stress reduction exercises are important. The mental mini-vacation meditation provides an inner peace trigger; and the technique for falling asleep is a godsend to some of my clients. Remember to use your stress-coping technique when someone pushes your buttons. Whether or not you feel on top of the circumstances surrounding your life, you can at least choose your response to those circumstances. Practice the stress management exercises often until you feel you have a better handle on things. This can benefit you in both your business and personal life.

Part III presented some help in clearing obstacles from the road on the journey toward our goals. We often need to release negative attitudes and become aware of past successes in order to empower us to work more easily toward a future goal. Caution is necessary whenever analyzing past mistakes, because of the power of imagination. We must learn from our mistakes without dwelling on them. You also learned how (and why) to list your goals, and discovered an effective way to establish goal priorities by using an exercise that combines logic with feelings. This facilitates choosing the right road to success, so that your efforts work toward goals that are important to your happiness.

Part IV discussed the important law of cause and effect. We must decide upon a course of action so that we know where we are going. Following this action plan is like paying the price of success; but first, the subconscious wants to know what we are trying to sell to ourselves. We need to identify and list the benefits of achieving our priority goal in order to add the power of emotion in a positive way. We can greatly increase subconscious acceptance by getting our emotions involved with the benefits of success before trying to cram the price of success down the throat of the inner child. For this reason, you need to fantasize your sense of emotional satisfaction at achieving your goal when doing creative daydreaming. Chapter 14 contains empowerment exercises for various common goals. Refer to these exercises as needed.

So far in Part V we have discussed the power of words, and why we must structure affirmations properly. Self-hypnosis works as quickly and easily as your ability to daydream, especially when combined with positive emotion. Together, imagination and emotion make a good marriage for motivating the subconscious. Combine these two methods of programming with the use of your affirmations, and find out how much faster you can make affirmations work for you. Unless you have decided to read this book through once before doing any of the empowerment exercises, you should already have a key word chosen for your priority goal. If not, then go back and review Chapter 17 on key words and make a temporary selection before proceeding.

Now let us put everything together and master HypnoCise.

Doing It!

As with each empowerment exercise in this book, you should read the instructions through more than once – enough to become familiar with what to do when you put the book down. Follow the steps outlined below.

1. *Get comfortable* as in previous exercises, with your own affirmations on hand as well as your list of benefits. If you find your priority goal among those exercises described in Chapter 14, you may expand upon those instructions by including all the steps described in this chapter. If you choose, you may use mellow background music (although avoid music with lyrics, as your mind may wander too far into the song).

2. *Review your benefits list and memorize them.* Although you may open your eyes to refer to your benefits during trance, if necessary, reading and/or thinking with the logical mind during trance may bring you partially up out of the hypnotic state. I also recommend memorizing your benefits so that they become a part of you.

3. *Read your affirmations slowly.* When linked to your key word, your affirmations become your autosuggestions. Even if your mind tends to wander, you should still keep reading your autosuggestions one word at a time. Reading out loud helps to slow you down, because it is important to read each word. You may also wish to fantasize the reality of each affirmation as you read it, provided only good feelings emerge. If any subconscious resistance surfaces as you read your autosuggestions,

Adding Words of Power

then practice the creative daydreaming exercise several times *without* reading your affirmations. Selling success to your subconscious will cause your inner mind to become more receptive to your affirmations later.

Should you choose to use one of the scripts provided in the Appendices, include your affirmations at the appropriate place designated in the script.

4. *Read the affirmation designating your key word three times.* This will help to anchor your key word and affirmations together in your mind, so that your key word becomes a trigger for your goal.

5. *Remove glasses, contact lenses, and so on, and enter the alpha state using one of the inductions learned previously.* Takes steps to minimize any possible distractions (from pets, ringing phone, etc.). Ask family members to avoid disturbing you for a few minutes. When you feel mellow and easily able to fantasize, continue with the next step.

6. *Daydream your benefits* using as many of the five senses as possible (as in the creative daydreaming exercise). Make your daydream vivid.

7. *Once you feel yourself becoming emotionally involved in your benefits, think of your key word.* You may say it several times in your mind, or even say it out loud if desired. You do not need to open your eyes to review your affirmations, because your key word now represents all the affirmations at a subconscious level. Your key word triggers subconscious recall of your affirmations, transforming them into autosuggestions. This is the next best thing to actually hearing someone else give you the affirmations as hypnotic suggestions. (If you wish, you may record your affirmations in the second-person format, playing them back at this time. See my comments below on "Tips for Success.")

8. *Imagine that you have already achieved your goal.* Review your benefits again. Imagine doing things you enjoy with this goal

a present reality. Be there within your imagination. Fantasize your appreciation of the reality of your goal, and allow yourself to be open for any new ideas flowing into your conscious awareness from the creative part of your mind to help you succeed. Remember that the alpha state helps you become more creative as well as imaginative; but keep it positive. Keep a note pad handy to record any new ideas you create. If negative thoughts creep in, replace them. Remember that you cannot delete negativity simply by "trying not to think of it." The subconscious would rather allow us to replace a negative thought instead of trying to erase it; so substitute the problem with the solution.

9. *Establish a method of waking up.* You may lose track of time. The alpha state is so pleasant that time can easily expand or contract, depending on your own perception and thoughts. Losing track of time is what professionals call time distortion, which can also happen when we get engrossed in an intense movie. Your mind may also have a tendency to wander, causing your perception of time to change; so, as with each empowerment exercise, you might wish to set an alarm. Some clients also tend to drift on into the theta state while doing their self-hypnosis exercises. If you feel yourself drifting close to sleep, you might actually wish to open your eyes and read your affirmations a second time. Then close them again and daydream your goal as explained above.

10. *Bring yourself back to full conscious awareness* when ready by slowly counting from one to five and opening your eyes. If you use a CD or MP3 for background music, you may wish to give yourself the autosuggestion of awakening when the music ends.

    Note: If you attempt to awaken yourself too quickly, you could find yourself feeling the same way you might feel if suddenly woken from a nap.

11. *Now that you have a key word, use it!* Put a 3 × 5 inch card with your key word on it in a location where you will see it several

times daily. Find other ways to see, hear, or say your key word frequently.

After understanding the above instructions, you may refer back to Chapter 14 if desired; the empowerment exercises there will take on new meaning now. Remember that HypnoCise includes (but is not limited to) creative daydreaming.

Tips for Success

Practice HypnoCise regularly until you find yourself more automatically motivated to reach your goal; then use the same tools to help yourself reach other important goals. You will find that your ability improves with practice, just as your muscles strengthen with physical exercise. Nonetheless, just as a couch moves more easily with someone at the other end helping you lift it, you might find some goals come faster with the help of a hypnotherapist.

As mentioned earlier, you may wish to record your affirmations with your own voice for playback during your HypnoCise sessions. If so, you should state them clearly and slowly into the recorder in the second-person format so that your subconscious hears them during playback as though you were hearing hypnotic suggestions. For example, "I am" statements become "you are" statements. You may wish to include your benefits in the recording as well (e.g. imagine having more energy while you enjoy your favorite activity). You can even include your own induction and wake-up instructions if desired, as long as you record them in the second-person format. (Note: If you use any of the scripts provided in the Appendices, they already appear in the second-person format.)

During day-to-day living, remember the five subconscious gateways. Far less effort will be spent in avoiding motivation pitfalls than would be required in getting out of the pit afterwards. We can also look for possible ways to incorporate all five subconscious motivators into additional tools for motivation, including the quintuple whammy discussed in Chapter 7.

While using any subconscious programming tool, make certain you monitor what enters your mind. You must guard your thoughts when the subconscious gateways are open, and especially protect your imagination. If you do not filter out the garbage, you may find yourself more easily manipulated by others. Also, by being aware of when your subconscious is open and vulnerable, you retain a much greater opportunity to really take control of your life.

Allow me to review and emphasize two very important concepts that I teach to both clients and hypnosis students: *imagination is the language of the subconscious* and *emotion is the motivating power of the mind*. Keep your focus on the desired results, and imagine the emotions you will enjoy upon attaining your goal. Rather than worrying about the price of change, fall in love with the benefits of success. Then use your key word often as a subconscious trigger for success. If you follow this advice consistently, I believe that you will achieve and maintain greater self-empowerment than ever before. So where do we go from here?

Before storing this book in your personal library, please read my closing comments in the last chapter and take them to heart.

Chapter 19

Where Do We Go from Here?

I can best answer this question by repeating what I say to clients: these techniques only work when you choose to use them.

For example, people have pushed my buttons many times over the years, and whenever I forget to use my peaceful place trigger, I can get just as stressed as anyone else. I have also endured painful setbacks at times, and have sought hypnotherapy from one of my peers to help me get back on track. At such times, motivation might have been almost impossible without utilizing what I teach. It seems as though an unseen hand often forces me to walk my talk, so that I can more effectively teach these powerful techniques. The empowerment exercises are a blessing to anyone who masters them, so I wish to teach them to all who are willing to learn and apply them. Some of you may also wish to help others.

Helping Friends and Loved Ones

Human nature does have some good qualities. We often like to help friends and loved ones by sharing valuable ideas; I sincerely hope you have learned something worthy of sharing with your friends and family. While I also hope that you will encourage others to buy this book, I must ask that you consider some important thoughts before giving advice to those who need help, so let me speak from my heart.

Over the years, numerous clients seeing me for various goals have endured the added burden of unnecessary guilt, often compounded with negative criticism from friends, relatives, or loved ones. Criticism from others frequently contributes to an individual's difficulty in overcoming a problem.

Adding Words of Power

Putdowns reported to me by both clients and friends include: (1) Don't you know smoking will kill you? (2) Fat people are out of control. (3) You have a poverty consciousness. (4) Get out of the victim trap. (5) Why did you create this problem? (6) Why did you make yourself sick? (7) What is God punishing you for? (8) You must have a karmic lesson to learn. (9) You need to learn how to manifest abundance (or good health). (10) If "The Secret" is not working for you, then you must be doing something wrong. (11) Why are you attracting such negativity into your life?

These types of remarks, even if spoken with good intentions, often cause further damage to one's self-esteem. Such negative criticism disempowers the recipient, often inhibiting his/her ability to overcome negative subconscious programming, regardless of whether such negativity is self-created or planted by other people. Furthermore, when the problem is serious, these comments hurt even more; and they could tarnish a friendship. If you must say something negative, criticize the performance but *not* the person.

A personal friend received hurtful putdowns while trying to escape from an abusive relationship. Prior to marriage, she had no clue whatsoever that the man she loved would become an abusive controller who manipulated with guilt and threats. She needed professional help, not more criticism and guilt; but instead, her life was shattered. Unfortunately, the first two counselors she saw asked her what she had done to attract an abuser into her life in the first place. The added stress of that unexpected criticism literally made her physically ill.

Another friend who was devoted to a spiritual path got cancer, and lost several alleged friends after she lost her health. They criticized her for having a "disease consciousness" and attracting the cancer. (In my opinion, her acquaintances were bankrupt in the compassion department.) Although she was very saddened by what she perceived as betrayal by some of her former friends, she was at peace before her passing; so let anyone who would dare judge her for having a "disease consciousness" consider their own possible reactions in similar circumstances.

When unexpected events knock you down, you quickly discover who your true friends are. One of my most profound demonstrations of this fact occurred in 1981 after the stress of divorce hurt my ability to sell. I prayed for money just to buy food. The very next day a close friend took me to lunch, and handed me a $100 bill. He said, "God directed me to give you my tithe, because you deserve it!" He told me that he derived greater satisfaction from giving to people personally than giving to a church or charity just to get the tax deduction. Shortly before that experience, a millionaire who pretended to be my friend criticized me when I asked him for help in finding a decent-paying job. He told me to learn how to "manifest abundance" and get into a "prosperity consciousness"; so I totally understand the difference between being helped or getting kicked when I am down. It should be obvious which action helped me the most!

If you are blessed with the ability to help a friend in need, either respond with compassion and generosity, or simply say "no" kindly. Your friend (or relative) may not yet understand the role of the subconscious. He/she may have suffered financial setbacks resulting from the greed of others. He/she may still live in slavery to past subconscious programming, or developed illness after repeated setbacks in life. The "tough love" approach just might be the final blow crushing that person's spirit. While a harsh approach *might* be necessary for someone who is unwilling to change, a more gentle approach is far better for an individual who has already made a commitment to change.

Even when people successfully alter their subconscious programming, they might need just a little outside help to change external circumstances. The motivation may be genuine, but an obstacle can still look quite large if you have to lift it by yourself. Do we move a heavy piece of furniture alone, or do we get someone to help us lift it?

If your friend (or relative) needs help, make a few phone calls. Lend a helping hand. Exchange services if possible and help each other. Hire him/her to do a job for you. Give a gift or loan if you are blessed and so inclined. You could simply say, "Pay it forward"; sometimes it is more rewarding to give to someone in need rather than to a charity, and then you can ask the recipient to do something kind for someone else later on. Either be supportive, or just say no.

You can also refer your friend to someone else who can help if you are either unable or unwilling to do so. Admit that you are too busy if that is the case. You can offer to pray, but don't say something offensive such as, "I'm being hard on you because I care about you." I won't put into print what that sounds like to someone who is down!

Instead of criticizing the person, analyze the performance and offer solutions. Help empower him or her to obtain the desired results. Share what you have learned from this book (consider giving him/her a copy if you wish). Additionally, encourage your friend to seek professional and/or spiritual help when appropriate.

Conclusion

Self-hypnosis helps us make desired changes at a subconscious level; but it should be clear by now that hypnosis is not a panacea to all of life's problems. Wise King Solomon said that there is a time and season for all things. There is a time and a place for self-hypnosis. There is a time and place for traditional therapy and hypnotherapy. Yet even when seeking professional help, the proper use of self-hypnosis can still provide many benefits to enhance the journey to greater empowerment. (It is also my personal opinion that both self-hypnosis and hypnotherapy can provide valuable keys to greater spiritual awareness.)

I am totally convinced that trance has a valid place in the world today for all who desire to improve themselves, whether personally, professionally, or spiritually. In my opinion, trance is the key to helping us attain our ideal self-empowerment.

We must train ourselves to imagine good things. Lots of people believe in positive thinking yet indulge in negative daydreaming, and then wonder why they get negative results. Remember, it is not what we think; it is what we *imagine* that usually influences our behavior. Consider those who tell themselves not to eat candy while they imagine how good it would taste, as this demonstrates what imagination can do to the subconscious. Imagination can make or break your success in goal achievement.

In closing, let me repeat that you cannot *force* your subconscious to accept anything, any more than a high pressure salesman can force you to buy; and that is why willpower has such a low track record for success. You must allow your subconscious mind to be *persuaded* to accept the desired changes by getting involved in the benefits.

Additionally, I believe we must learn how to make our subconscious minds become our servants rather than our slave masters. Claim your God-given power of choice. Be the captain of your subconscious programming and send your mind-ship at warp speed toward your dreams. Now you have the tools; the rest is up to you. The journey continues . . . You may now master the power of self-hypnosis in order to empower yourself to make your best dreams in life come true. Now go, and make it so!

Thank you for reading *Mastering the Power of Self-Hypnosis*; I sincerely hope that this book helps you make beneficial changes in your life. Be sure to browse through the Appendices, especially if you desire help from a hypnosis professional.

Appendices

Appendix 1
When Might Hypnotherapy Be Needed?

This book has several recommendations to seek outside help when necessary, yet some readers might wonder: When do I seek a hypnosis professional?

Using self-hypnosis is like using mental muscles. Some changes require only easy "lifting" that you can make without any help. Other changes require removing a mental "block" (subconscious resistance to change) and can be more easily facilitated by someone else guiding or assisting you. Before I answer the question posed in the first paragraph, I'll mention those areas where this book may prove to be valuable.

Self-hypnosis can empower you to greater or lesser degrees primarily in the common goals presented in this book. Even if you consult with a hypnotherapist for one of these goals, you may derive sufficient benefit from the empowerment exercises to help you go the full distance. When motivation alone is the primary need, this book will pay for itself many times over, provided you practice self-hypnosis often and make full use of the empowerment exercises.

Give yourself several weeks to work on a specific habit or motivational goal, utilizing all the relevant exercises explained in this book. Within a month or less, it should become quite clear whether the subconscious wishes to cooperate or resist. If the subconscious indicates only minor resistance to change, you should be rewarded for your patience. If the resistance persists, the need for outside help should become obvious as time moves on. You might be your own best judge of knowing whether you need a hypnotherapist for the common goals presented below; nonetheless I will provide some indicators that might signal the need for outside help. (If in doubt, you may wish to refer to Chapters 5 and 6 and estimate how many subconscious motivators oppose your goal.)

Smoking Cessation/Reduction

Within two or three weeks of quitting, you should notice at least a 50% reduction in both the frequency and severity of urges. Complete the motivation map for smokers provided in Appendix 4.

Half of the smokers contemplating giving up might need more help than this book provides. Remember that the subconscious accepts a new response to an old trigger much more readily than any efforts to erase the trigger. One deep breath has no calories and no side effects. Additionally, you may wish to do some of your own research into other related concerns, such as physical withdrawals from nicotine. Seeking hypnotherapy might make your struggle easier; but the choice is yours. Even if you seek outside help, the empowerment exercises in this book should provide valuable assistance.

Weight Management

Your attitude toward food should change within a few days, although your body might wait longer to reflect the changes in your weight and figure. You should feel more motivated to reduce. Strong inner conflicts would indicate a probable need for outside help. Lack of satisfying progress would be another clue that you need additional help. Whether or not you seek professional support, I strongly urge *you* to accept responsibility for doing your own research into proper nutrition.

No hypnotherapist (or counselor) should consult with you on nutrition unless he/she can document specialized training in nutrition. With questions or concerns regarding nutrition and/or physical exercise that might be appropriate for you, consider consulting with a licensed health care professional trained to help you in those specific areas. Even where exercise is concerned, some physical exercises may be good for some people while dangerous for others.

One of my clients saw me for weight management because her physician recommended hypnosis to help her become motivated to follow appropriate medical advice. Her physician also recommended *against* all exercises except walking because of her heart condition. Use wisdom when you plan your course of action. If you have any concerns about nutrition or exercise, please consult with the appropriate licensed health care professional first; then use self-hypnosis and/or hypnotherapy as an adjunct to your weight-reduction program.

Note: If you believe that you are overeating because of stress at home, you might need to consider family or marriage counseling rather than hypnosis or hypnotherapy.

Business Motivation/Job Performance

Your attitude should improve within days after practicing the creative daydreaming exercises, especially when you enjoy your work. If your job fails to provide satisfaction, consider talking with a vocational counselor. Hypnosis will not make you like a job that you hate; but it will help you become more willing to do the undesirable tasks that provide benefits that you deem important (such as a weekly paycheck).

Memory and Study Habits

Some of my clients have enjoyed profound improvement simply by using HypnoCise. Depending on the cause, self-hypnosis may provide help ranging from almost total success to no noticeable improvement. If the memory problems are related to physical health or serious emotional problems, even hypnotherapy may not be sufficient. Other professional help will be needed from either a mental health professional or licensed physician, depending on the cause of the memory problems. If you feel that there is any possibility of a physiological cause, consult with your physician. If you have major unresolved stress (family, marital, etc.), your memory problems might be a symptom of those unresolved issues. You may need to consult with a professional for assistance. If memory problems are primarily related to lack of motivation and/or test anxiety, a hypnotherapist may be the best answer.

Sports Enhancement and More

Self-hypnosis really shines here! Unless an athlete suffers a serious confidence problem, mental imagery can help greatly to improve existing abilities, especially when combined with the sports trigger. You would most likely only require professional hypnosis if you desire more intensive help, or if the subconscious wants to hang on to stubborn resistance.

Self-hypnosis can also help in varying degrees with the other goals mentioned here. I recommend that you remain aware of your progress in order to determine whether or not you need extra help. The primary question to ask yourself with any goal is: Am I making progress, or does my subconscious block most of my efforts? If you believe the latter to be true, seek outside help.

While you might still derive benefit from some of the empowerment exercises in this book (such as the ones for reducing stress), releasing heavy subconscious resistance normally requires assistance from someone competently trained. I believe in both self-hypnosis and professional hypnosis; but the ethical hypnotherapist also knows when to refer a client to another health specialist.

Certain problems usually require outside assistance, whether from a hypnotherapist and/or from another professional. Among these are: phobias, unresolved grief, serious self-esteem issues, post-traumatic stress disorder, health problems (illness or injury), alcoholism or substance abuse, obsessive eating disorders, obesity, chain smoking, depression and other serious mental problems, family or relationship problems, vocational problems, and so on.

When Might Hypnotherapy Be Needed?

Normally an ethical hypnotherapist will only help you with pain management upon medical referral. Some of the other issues mentioned above may frequently require help beyond the qualifications of a hypnotherapist. When the problem has possible physical causes, seek a licensed health care professional. When serious emotional trauma or ongoing abuse contributes to your problem, seek traditional mental health care (or traditional therapy). When the problem can be resolved with simple subconscious programming, you may choose either self-hypnosis or professional hypnosis (or both). See Appendix 2 to find guidelines for choosing a competent hypnosis professional.

Appendix 2

Choosing a Competent Hypnotherapist

Most proficient hypnotherapists have completed formal training in hypnotherapy, such as courses of 120 hours or more as recommended by several professional hypnosis associations. This is true even in those states that prohibit hypnotists without a graduate degree in medicine or mental health from using the title of "hypnotherapist". In these states, they might be called a hypnocounselor, consulting hypnotist, and so on.

Hypnotherapy is an art or skill best learned from those who actually have done considerable hypnotherapy. Ask where your prospective hypnosis professional received training, how many hours of schooling he/she took specifically for hypnosis, and whether or not he/she works full time or part time with hypnosis. (One who works full time is more likely to master the art faster than someone who only practices occasionally, although some excellent hypnotherapists have to work a second job just to pay the bills.) However, remember that all of us were just starting out at one time, so please do not disqualify someone simply because he/she is new to the profession.

Additionally, any ethical hypnotherapist should be a member of at least one professional hypnosis association. If he/she does not belong to a professional association that has either the word hypnosis or hypnotherapy in its name, consider it a yellow light and proceed with caution.

If you choose a physician or Ph.D., you still have the right to ask where he or she received *specific* training in hypnotherapy. Be aware that someone specially trained in hypnotherapy may quite possibly be far more competent with hypnosis for motivation than a physician (or Ph.D.) who only occasionally practices hypnosis. Having a degree in medicine or psychology does not of and by itself guarantee proficiency with hypnosis even though there may be competence in the primary field of expertise. Seeking out a physician or psychologist to hypnotize you may result in going to someone who has only had a weekend course in hypnosis (or worse, who is self-taught). Would you ask your family doctor to work on your teeth?

Anyone practicing hypnotherapy should, in my opinion, have *at least* a minimum of 100 hours (preferably 150 or more) in specialized training in the applications of hypnosis, regardless of other qualifications. In spite of my opinion regarding training, however, ethics are more important than training or education. Given the choice, I would rather see a new yet ethical hypnotherapist with 100 hours of training than to go to a well-educated individual working from ego or greed.

Sometimes the initial phone call might leave you in doubt. If your discussion does not provide adequate information to make a decision, you may ask your prospective therapist for a short personal consultation to help you decide. Most ethical hypnotherapists are willing to offer a free session of 20 to 30 minutes to meet with a prospective client.

For some links to hypnosis professionals, visit: <http://www.hypnotherapylist.com>. But please do your own homework – these links are not an endorsement of the hypnosis professional who requested to trade links with me.

Appendix 3

Questions and Answers about Self-Hypnosis

This was a popular section of the Appendices in the 1998 version of this book, and I eventually included these questions on the official hypnosis FAQ posted at <http://www.royhunter.com>. The questions and answers here differ somewhat from those that appear on my website and there are references here to other sections of the book. The most frequently asked questions regarding self-hypnosis appear first.

Q. What technique works best?

A. Each of us is unique in the universe. I often tell clients, "God didn't make a bunch of yellow pencils." This metaphor serves to illustrate the fact that no one technique will work for all the people all the time; so this book presents a variety of methods.

I recommend that you attempt each basic technique at least once (except for those designed for specific goals that may be unimportant to you, such as those described in Chapter 14). The basic induction techniques are covered in Chapter 4.

If you reflect back on the book as a complete presentation, consider that I have given you a foundation to construct your own specific HypnoCise program for empowerment. Within that foundation, you may choose your own preferred induction, a unique set of benefits ideally suited to your desires, specific affirmations more suitable to you than to anyone else, and a key word to trigger your new subconscious program. Your personal HypnoCise program should be uniquely suited to you.

Q. What if I am unsure about visual imagery techniques?

A. If you are unsure, here is a little self-test. Imagine you are near a waterfall on a perfect day with a blue sky, with trees nearby. You sit on a log or big rock, and you reach down and pick up a small rock and hold it in your hand. Put your hand in the water. Now go through the exercise with your eyes closed. Afterwards, answer these questions: Was it easier to *see* the waterfall, or *hear* it? Did you *see* the blue sky, or did you *feel* warmth (or a gentle breeze)? Did you *feel* the small rock (smooth or rough), or did you *see* it? When you put your hand in the water, did you *see* yourself do so, or *hear* the sound of the water, or *feel* whether the water was warm or cool?

Most people will be able to easily imagine vivid use of at least one of the three senses mentioned above. If you get nothing, then you most likely will need professional assistance.

Q. What is the best time of day for self-hypnosis?

A. This varies from person to person. I personally prefer the afternoon. Some people obtain maximum benefit in the early morning, while others find the evening better. Experiment with various times until you determine the best one for you.

Q. Should I turn out the lights when I do self-hypnosis?

A. The answer to this question depends on your personal preference. Some people quickly become distracted by light (particularly bright light), which can sometimes penetrate closed eyelids. Other people prefer total darkness. I personally prefer soft lighting. Again, experiment until you determine what works best for you.

Q. What about background music?

A. Decide according to your desires. Some clients, including many who visualize quite well, prefer total silence. Others enjoy background music. My preference is to use background music whenever possible, as I prefer to focus on music rather than on other distracting sounds such as traffic, barking dogs, and so on. I can also meditate quite easily out in nature with only natural sounds around me. Those of you who love the sounds of the natural world might find certain "nature" CDs or MP3s helpful. Again, experiment until you discover what works best for you.

Q. How did you get interested in hypnosis?

A. When I worked as a highly stressed out sales manager for a major corporation, I went to a hypnotherapist for stress management. I learned the peaceful place meditation and a simple stress-coping technique, and found my life forever changed. The coping technique has prevented me from buying into stress levels that could have jeopardized my health and possibly even my life; and the peaceful place meditation (or mental mini-vacation) keeps me calm and centered.

The benefits gained personally from my sessions, as well as learning self-hypnosis, made me appreciate the value of hypnosis. Through the encouragement of friends and family, I studied at the Tebbetts Hypnotism Training Institute in Washington and started full-time hypnotherapy in 1983. Four years later I started teaching a hypnosis course at a college. My course is based on the teachings of the late Charles Tebbetts, updated through many years of experience.

Q. Can you quit smoking in one session?

A. In this fast food society, we want everything now, and yesterday isn't soon enough! Many people have been disillusioned with hypnosis after failing in the "quick-fix" programs that appeal to those who want something fast and cheap. Although these quickie programs may work for someone who simply needs one extra push to get over the hump, those people who do succeed may put on thirty pounds of weight as a substitute for the discarded smoking habit.

There are three kinds of people who used to smoke.

1. *The smoker who does not smoke today* could easily backslide, as he/she fantasizes smoking, often looking longingly at second-hand cigarette smoke. Some people can go for months or years in this category, backsliding instantly during a moment of stress simply because they are still subconsciously programmed as smokers.

2. *The ex-smoker* gets a divorce from the smoking habit, and turns the love of the fair-weather friend into hate. These people are usually very uncomfortable around others who smoke. While some are considerate of those who still exercise their freedom to smoke, others try to convert the entire world by becoming very actively negative toward anyone who smokes.

3. *The tolerant non-smoker* totally changes their subconscious programming so that he or she can actually be in the presence of a smoker and forget to notice when the other person lights up. This is the ultimate success.

If you want to become a tolerant non-smoker, go to someone who requires three or four visits minimum. Most of my clients do manage to quit smoking at the first session; but a second session devoted to learning self-hypnosis for stress management increases the long-term probability of success. I include a third session for confidence-building and/or to help with trouble spots, as I believe in a professional approach. Sometimes advanced techniques must be used to enable the subconscious to reveal the cause of strong subconscious resistance to quitting.

The one-session quick-fix plans fail frequently because they rely on suggestion alone. With many smokers, I complete a motivation map involving the five subconscious motivators presented in Chapter 6. If you wish, use the self-directed motivation mapping exercise in Appendix 4, and then seek professional help if you need it.

If you consider attending any of the hotel seminars, remember that you get what you pay for. If you have smoked for 29 years, you cannot expect to feel like a non-smoker in 29 minutes. You may indeed stop lighting a match to your money, but you might feel grief for the loss of your "friend" for many years to come. Furthermore, you especially want to avoid those smoking cessation programs which employ gross aversion techniques. The use of fear motivation pushes the "rebel" button in many people, causing a high backslide rate even with those programs that misrepresent their success rate as 97%. If the success rate sounds too good to be true, it probably is. (See my comments below about aversion therapy and the potential dangers of hypnosis.)

Q. Why wasn't self-hypnosis taught during the 1800s?

A. I can only provide a speculative answer to this question: human nature. One who masters self-hypnosis gains greater self-empowerment. Some people derive a certain sort of ego satisfaction by subjugating another person; and it seems that only a very few in the nineteenth century medical community wanted to help empower people to help themselves. Instead, they treated the individuals they hypnotized as subjects.

Considering the fact that early researchers of hypnosis believed that the hypnotist had power over the subject, perhaps you might arrive at the same conclusion as mine. My opposition to the old "mind control" philosophy is why I object to the use of the word "subject" to describe those experiencing hypnosis. That being said, I must also admit that some of the early researchers sincerely did not know that any of us could learn how to enter trance without help.

Q. Does hypnosis open up your mind to demonic influence?

A. Some religions frequently make this claim in order to discourage their members from using hypnosis. If entering the alpha state opens up the mind to demonic influence, then we had better avoid movies, TV, speeches or sermons at church which cause us to use the imagination, daydreaming, going to sleep, and so on. And, I guess that means we can't tell our children bedtime stories anymore, as their little imaginations may run free! Pardon the sarcasm; but I need to illustrate my point.

Hypnosis of and by itself is neither good nor bad; rather, the specific application of hypnosis (and motives of the hypnotist) will determine whether we can justify its use in any particular situation. Let us use our own intelligence to consider the facts; and hopefully we can ensure that trance emerges totally out of the Dark Ages once and for all. In my opinion, we must shine the light of truth on hypnosis so that it remains in a state of enlightenment.

Q. Can you share some success stories?

A. Although I can share many success stories, I'll choose one example for each of several common goals.

A smoker taking my hypnotherapy course decided to use self-hypnosis alone to quit, incorporating the benefits approach ("Selling Success to the Subconscious") along with affirmations and key words. He gave up totally, and was still a non-smoker when I last spoke with him (years after he quit).

A slender middle-aged woman once claimed that she attended a self-hypnosis class over ten years earlier taught by Pat Collins in southern California. Before taking that class, she weighed over 200 pounds. Through self-hypnosis learned in class, she took off over seventy pounds. Furthermore, she told me that she expects to remain slender for the rest of her life, and doesn't even think about the fact that she used to be heavy. This woman's success was profound. While many of my own clients have successfully reduced, people needing to lose more than thirty to forty pounds frequently need private sessions as well as self-hypnosis.

A salesman saw me for stress management after being referred by his physician. Although I also worked with him for self-confidence, I taught him the stress-coping technique presented in Chapter 8. Mastering self-hypnosis to reduce stress resulted in a significant improvement in his health. Several years later I ran into him at a trade show, and he still used my techniques regularly.

A business owner saw me for professional confidence. I taught him the techniques presented in this book; and three months later he wrote me an excellent letter. Within the first month after completing my program, he closed more business transactions than he normally closed in six months.

A military officer needed to keep calm before taking an exam. Previous failures resulted in his having only one final opportunity to pass, or be retired. He mastered the peaceful place meditation ("Mental Mini-Vacation") and the stress-coping technique. Additionally, he practiced HypnoCise. He passed the test and got his promotion.

A black belt in the martial arts mastered self-hypnosis and used the peak performance trigger, along with "focus" as his key word. He blended frequent visualization along with his sports trigger. He placed in a regional competition.

A realtor increased his income from $28,000 to $130,000 in only one year.

Will self-hypnosis work for you? Master the art and find out for yourself!

Q. If I learn self-hypnosis, when and why would I ever need a hypnotherapist?

A. Refer to the last section of Chapter 14 for this answer.

Q. Is there any danger in learning self-hypnosis?

A. In almost three decades of practice, not one of my clients has ever reported any harm resulting from learning self-hypnosis; yet I cannot guarantee that any skill has no potential drawbacks. Driving can be dangerous, but we choose to drive because of the benefits of getting where we need to go. Self-hypnosis can help us get where we need to go mentally. Just as driving is faster than walking, self-hypnosis is faster than willpower.

I believe in balance (or moderation) in all things. Naturally, if someone spent most of their waking hours in a trance, life would simply pass on by with few accomplishments. Also, it would be inadvisable to attempt self-hypnosis while driving or operating any type of heavy machinery. There is a time and place for all things.

Q. What if self-hypnosis doesn't work?

A. Some people can enter a light state of trance and be unaware of the fact that they have achieved that state. During light states, our sensory perception intensifies. We have an increasing ability to perceive sounds, feelings, and so on, and this often distracts the conscious mind. We can easily convince ourselves that something isn't working by using our awareness of the distraction as "proof" that we are still awake. (The mind can think many times faster than the spoken voice.)

Remember that imagination is the language of the subconscious. Go into your fantasized peaceful place. Try several different inductions if you don't respond to the first one. If necessary, see a hypnotherapist. Since I could not find a good set of instructions, I experienced great difficulty in learning self-hypnosis at first. Finally, a hypnotherapist guided me into a trance and gave me post-hypnotic suggestions to enable me to take myself into a trance. Hopefully this book will help you avoid the difficulty I experienced; but if you need help, seek it. For me, the help was worth the price.

Q. How can I learn more about professional hypnosis?

A. I am the author of the official hypnosis FAQs, which have evolved gradually since posting my first version in 1994 at the alt.hypnosis internet newsgroup. Years ago this was a vibrant newsgroup, but numerous negative postings over the years drove most hypnosis professionals to moderated groups elsewhere. Nonetheless, as of the revision of this book in 2010 I still post the FAQ files monthly. The hypnosis FAQ is too long to include here but you may view it at <http://www.royhunter.com/hypnofaq.htm>.

Q. Do you give presentations or workshops on hypnosis or self-hypnosis?

A. I am very happy to teach these important techniques to a live audience. Self-hypnosis helped me conquer my own fear of speaking in public, so it is personal! Several major hypnosis associations regularly invite me to present workshops at their annual conventions; but it also gives me great satisfaction to share with people who are new to the wonders of hypnosis. My topics include those that I have presented in this book, as well as professional hypnosis training where appropriate. If interested, either contact my publisher or visit my website: <http://www.royhunter.com>.

Appendix 4

Motivation Mapping for Smokers

Are you ready for one of the most unusual exercises available regarding the subconscious mind? I have devoted considerable time over the years in evolving motivation mapping. It is based on discovering your primary sources of motivation, so that you can better monitor what goes into your subconscious mind. This technique is presented in depth in Chapters 15 and 16 of my *The Art of Hypnotherapy* as well as my online *Quit Smoking for the Last Time* program workbook. Normally I facilitate this technique for a client by asking the questions myself, but I have shortened and simplified it here for your use.

As mentioned in Chapter 6, there are five gateways to the subconscious, and hypnosis is only one of them. By understanding these gateways, you can become a better gatekeeper over what goes into your own subconscious mind. Let us review them:

1. Repetition
2. Authority
3. Desire for identity (ego)
4. Hypnosis (and self-hypnosis)
5. Emotion

We can compare these gateways to file folders on a computer, or pathways into the mind. You may already recognize some of these methods as familiar ways of effecting a change. Used alone, each gateway has a chance of success, with varying degrees of effectiveness, if there is little or no opposing input. Used harmoniously, these five motivators open wide the doors of subconscious motivation to help you implement your conscious desire for change.

Before completing your motivation map, be sure to review Chapters 6 and 7.

Normally I facilitate this technique for a client by asking the questions myself, but I have shortened and simplified it here for your use.

Follow the step-by-step directions to maximize the benefit. Determining your motivation map may take up to thirty minutes or more unless you are a fast reader; so make sure you have enough time to complete it before starting. If desired, you may take a break in the middle of the exercise, or stretch this out over a couple of days.

Directions: Circle the number of any question that applies to you. If the question is divided into parts, circle the number if you answer yes to any of the parts.

Repetition

1. Old smoking triggers: Did you light up often without consciously deciding to, simply out of habit?

2. Are the "deep breath" responses to old smoking triggers a habit yet?

Authority

3. Rebel button: (circle 3 whether any apply, even if all apply)

    (a) Do you want to smoke when someone tells you not to smoke?

    (b) Do anti-smoking laws make you want to smoke more?

    (c) Do anti-smoking religious beliefs make you want to smoke more?

(d) If your health care professional has already advised you to quit smoking, did this make your desire to continue smoking get stronger?

4. Have any authority figures influenced your desire to smoke (e.g. a parent either prohibiting you, or saying you were old enough at eighteen)?

5. Have any authority figures strongly motivated you to quit (e.g. doctor, church)?

6. Are you quitting because of health benefits (whether or not by medical advice)?

Desire for Identity

7. Did you start smoking because of peer pressure, or the desire to feel more mature?

8. Do you strongly resent society's peer pressure against smokers?

9. Do you seek the company of smokers in order to feel okay about smoking?

10. Have you frequently smoked either as a reward or a way of giving yourself some attention (e.g. after completing tasks, getting off work)?

11. Have you felt a strong sense of pride with your identity as a smoker, or as a member of the remaining minority of smokers?

12. Does the anti-smoking social pressure make you want to quit? (Note: Some people answer yes to both 8 and 12.)

13. Is someone you love causing you to want to quit (e.g. parents wanting to set a good example for their children)?

14. Identity: (circle 14 whether either or both apply)

    (a) Will you have a better self-image or professional image as a non-smoker?

    (b) Will quitting give you a sense of pride, or a feeling of victory?

Hypnosis and Self-Hypnosis

15. Have you frequently smoked while watching TV, reading, or while driving?

16. Have you frequently smoked in bed, or if your sleep is interrupted?

17. Do you have a past success with hypnosis for any goal?

18. Are you listening to a hypnotic CD regularly?

19. Do you fantasize your benefits of quitting often?

Emotion

20. Do you still enjoy the smoking habit?

21. Have you used cigarettes as your usual stress-coping technique?

22. Do you feel guilt or shame regarding having smoked?

23. Are you emotionally excited about the benefits of quitting?

To score the results and determine your current motivation map, please use the next page (or a photocopy of the next page). After you score your initial results, you may wish to make a photocopy before you determine your future motivation map. Some clients prefer to use a different color pencil or pen when determining their future motivation map – this is your choice.

Your Motivation Map

Find the numbers in the frames below, and circle the same numbers circled above.

Repetition

Smoker:	Non-Smoker:
1	2

Authority

Smoker:	Non-Smoker:
3 4	5 6

Desire for Identity

Smoker:	Non-Smoker:
7 8 9 10 11	12 13 14

Hypnosis and Self-Hypnosis

Smoker:	Non-Smoker:
15 16	17 18 19

Emotion

Smoker:	Non-Smoker:
20 21 22	23

Count the number of circles in the "Smoker" category and enter "initial score": _____

Count the number of circles in the "Non-Smoker" category and enter "initial score": _____

If "Smoker" is larger than "Non-Smoker" enter the difference here: _____

If "Non-Smoker" is larger than "Smoker" enter the difference here: _____

Your future motivation map (see instructions on the following pages):

Your New "Smoker" score: _____

Your New "Non-Smoker" score: _____

Your Potential Advantage: _____

Appendices

Your Current Motivation Map

The category with the highest score indicates your dominant subconscious motivation. The greater the difference between the two categories, the stronger your motivation is to either succeed or backslide into smoking.

Difference of 0 or 1 in either category: Although you might succeed by following the information presented in this book, completing your motivation map will increase your ability to monitor what goes into your subconscious so that you may better stay on the road to success.

Advantage of 2 or 3 in Smoker category: You have a risk of backsliding, so it is important for you to use every tool at your disposal to successfully quit smoking for the last time, or remain an occasional smoker.

Advantage of 4 or more in Smoker category: Unless you can improve your future motivation map considerably, you might benefit by investing in hypnotherapy to go the full distance and stay on track.

Difference of 2 or 3 in Non-Smoker category: You should be able to succeed without ever completing this exercise, based on how well you follow the rest of the program.

Difference of 4 or more in Non-Smoker category: You should be well on the road to success. Remember to always respect the power of imagination and emotion, and guard your subconscious gateways.

If your "initial score" in the Smoker category was 9 or higher: You may be experiencing some inner conflicts regarding your decision to quit. If so, a hypnotherapist trained in a technique called parts therapy may be able to help you resolve your inner conflicts (see Chapter 7).

Note: Hidden subconscious blocks sometimes require individual hypnosis to discover the causes.

Your Future Motivation Map

In order to help you change your future motivation map, use this section as reference. Note that the numbered questions appear below as they did in the pages before your motivation map, but with comments following each question. Before proceeding, you may take a break if desired.

First: Refer to *only those questions that you circled*, and read the comments and suggestions that follow each corresponding question repeated in the following pages. You will be instructed to make changes to your motivation map, so make a photocopy of your original map. The comments teach you how to be a better gatekeeper of your gateways.

Next: After you follow the instructions contained in those comments that apply to you, follow the "Additional instructions" that appear at the end of the section of questions and comments.

Repetition

1. Old smoking triggers: Did you light up often without consciously deciding to, simply out of habit?
   COMMENTS: *Replace these triggers with the deep breath of air. Your objective is to make this a habit, so circle 2 and put an "X" over 1 on your motivation map.*

2. Are the "deep breath" responses to old smoking triggers a habit yet?
   COMMENTS: *Make the deep breath of air an automatic response to old smoking triggers (see comments for 1). It may take time and commitment, but the results are worth the effort. Circle 2 if you've not yet done so.*

Appendices

Authority

3. Rebel button: (circle 3 whether any apply, even if all apply)

    (a) Do you want to smoke when someone tells you not to smoke?

    (b) Do anti-smoking laws make you want to smoke more?

    (c) Do anti-smoking religious beliefs make you want to smoke more?

    (d) If your health care professional has already advised you to quit smoking, did this make your desire to continue smoking get stronger?

    COMMENTS: *The desire to rebel is a manifestation of a strong desire for free choice. You can rebel against the cigarette by redirecting your power of choice. Let your stress-coping technique (learned in Chapter 8) become a reminder that you have the power of choice. Your object is to gain a good level of control over your rebel button, so put an "X" over 3 on your motivation map.*

4. Have any authority figures influenced your desire to smoke (e.g. a parent either prohibiting you, or saying you were old enough at eighteen)?
    COMMENTS: *If you circled 4, this unfortunately remains on your motivation map. If you have difficulty quitting, hypnotic regression therapy may help.*

5. Have any authority figures strongly motivated you to quit (e.g. doctor, church)?
    COMMENTS: *While this may be helpful, be sure to remember your benefits.*

6. Are you quitting because of health benefits (whether or not by medical advice)?
    COMMENTS: *If health problems motivated you to quit, you may need to consult with your physician regarding any of your expected health benefits. If you are already in good health, be grateful . . . and be sure to remember your benefits.*

Desire for Identity

7. Did you start smoking because of either peer pressure, or the desire to feel more mature?
   COMMENTS: *This one fades with time, which varies from person to person. If you feel you can leave it in the past, put an "X" through 7 on your motivation map. If unsure, leave it alone; but if your original map had four or five circles in this gateway in the "Smoker" category, put an "X" through this one anyway.*

8. Do you strongly resent society's peer pressure against smokers?
   COMMENTS: *You must internalize that it is your choice to quit smoking, regardless of the anti-smoking social pressure. This can still work against you if someone catches you off guard with criticism against smokers, so 8 remains.*

9. Do you seek the company of smokers in order to feel okay about smoking?
   COMMENTS: *Choose your friends because of who they are, and not whether they smoke. Your objective is to get this handled, so put an "X" through 9. If you have trouble with this, professional hypnotherapy is an option.*

10. Have you frequently smoked either as a reward or a way of giving yourself some attention (e.g. after completing tasks, getting off work)?
    COMMENTS: *Change the reward. Remember that it is easier to replace than it is to erase, so make a conscious choice to reward yourself with something else. While the new reward may satisfy you, failure to change rewards could make you vulnerable again, so 10 remains.*

11. Have you felt a strong sense of pride with your identity as a smoker, or as a member of the remaining minority of smokers?
    COMMENTS: *Your work is cut out for you; 11 remains, and it is even more important for you to follow the program. Hypnotherapy might be needed.*

12. Does the anti-smoking social pressure make you want to quit? (Note: Some people answer yes to both 8 and 12.)
    COMMENTS: *Although this is a motivator to quit smoking, it can be a vulnerable one if you have a "rebel" button. Remember your benefits.*

13. Is someone you love causing you to want to quit (e.g. parents wanting to set a good example for their children)?
    COMMENTS: *Congratulations! This can be a strong motivator for some people.*

14. Identity: (circle 14 whether any apply, even if all apply)
    (a) Will you have a better self-image or professional image as a non-smoker?
    (b) Will quitting give you a sense of pride, or a feeling of victory?

    COMMENTS: *If you circled 14, then read my comments regarding rewarding yourself ... and you can double the effect of 14.*

Hypnosis and Self-Hypnosis

15. Have you frequently smoked while watching TV, reading, or while driving?
    COMMENTS: *The deep breath may not be enough ... so if necessary, have some water or a non-caloric beverage available to sip on as a substitute for cigarettes. Without a substitute you could be vulnerable, so this motivator remains.*

16. Have you frequently smoked in bed, or if your sleep is interrupted?
    COMMENTS: *The same comments as for 15 apply here, so 16 remains.*

17. Do you have a past success with hypnosis for any goal?
    COMMENTS: *If you have ever experienced a success with hypnosis (or a hypnosis tape or CD), then 17 belongs on your*

motivation map. Draw on that success. (Note: 17 applies to a past success with hypnosis.)

18. Are you listening to a hypnotic CD daily?
    COMMENTS: *It is difficult to overcome years of programming with only one or two sessions, so continue listening to a hypnotic CD daily for at least twenty-one days, or until the urges diminish. Circle 18 if you have not yet done so, and listen to a CD daily as instructed. If you do not have one, you may either create one using the script in this Appendix, or order one from <http: www.royhunter.com/selfhelp.htm>. If you need professional help, refer to Appendices 1 and 2.*

19. Do you fantasize your benefits of quitting often?
    COMMENTS: *You pass through hypnosis on the way to and from sleep every night. You can take advantage of some of this time by fantasizing your benefits. If you make a commitment to do this, you can circle 19 if not yet circled.*

Emotion

20. Do you still enjoy the smoking habit?
    COMMENTS: *If you circled this number, it remains on your motivation map; and it is even more important to get emotionally involved with your benefits. It is easier to fight emotion with emotion.*

21. Have you used cigarettes as your usual stress-coping technique?
    COMMENTS: *Managing stress is vital for you. Refer to the stress management exercises in Chapter 8. Unfortunately this number remains on your map, as stress could come back and haunt you if you get careless.*

22. Do you feel guilt or shame regarding having smoked?
    COMMENTS: *Forgive yourself, and put an "X" through 22.*

Appendices

23. Are you emotionally excited about the benefits of quitting?
    COMMENTS: *This could be your most important key to permanent success, especially if you circled 20. Make the commitment to get emotionally involved with your benefits, and circle 23 if it was not previously circled.*

Additional instructions: While it is not necessary to read the comments for those questions in the "Smoker" category, go back now and read all the comments for questions in the "Non-Smoker" category that you did not circle (2, 5, 6, 12, 13, 14, 17, 18, 19, and 23). Some of these comments will tell you to circle the number on your motivation map if you can make the commitment to follow the recommendations. Circle the appropriate numbers *only* when the comments instruct you to.

You may also add the power of rewards (Question 14) in the following manner if you have quit smoking totally. By planning and scheduling your rewards, you may circle 14 if not yet circled, or write another "14" on your motivation map and circle it. Here are my recommendations:

(a) One week without cigarettes (or upon completing this lesson, if you have gone more than one week without smoking).
(b) One month after your last light-up.
(c) Three months after you quit smoking for the last time.
(d) One year after you quit smoking for the last time.
(e) Optional: each anniversary as a tolerant non-smoker.

Buy something you want, or do something you enjoy . . . and spend some of the money on yourself that used to go up in smoke! Also remember that since it is your success that you are celebrating, you choose the reward.

Next comes the most interesting part.

Computing Your "Potential Advantage" Score

Now go back and count the number of remaining circled numbers in the "Smoker" category, and enter this figure on your motivation map as your new "Smoker" score.

Likewise, count the circled numbers in the "Non-Smoker" category and enter this figure on your motivation map as your new "Non-Smoker" score.

Most people who follow this program properly should have a higher new Non-Smoker score than in the new Smoker category. Record the difference as your "Potential Advantage" score.

If your Potential Advantage is 6 or more, you should be well on the way to success. Even if it seems easier than you thought possible, you must still remember the power of imagination and monitor what you imagine. Sometimes those who quit easily can also backslide easily by taking their success for granted.

If your Potential Advantage is 4 or 5, you still may be able to succeed without additional help beyond this workbook, but it becomes more important for you to be consistent and persistent.

If your Potential Advantage score is 1 to 3, your work is cut out for you. While it is possible for you to succeed on your own, you have a higher probability of needing hypnotherapy to remain a non-smoker permanently.

If your new "Smoker" score is equal to or greater than your new "Non-Smoker" score, then you are a likely candidate for private hypnotherapy to discover the causes of your subconscious blocks if you want to enjoy long-term success. This is rare, but does occasionally happen.

If your subconscious still shows a higher "Smoker" score, then it is advisable for you to see a hypnosis professional. Make certain to choose a therapist who knows how to help your subconscious "discover" the cause of the resistance, as there are many practitioners who use only suggestions and imagery. Ask whether he/she is trained in hypnotic regression and/or parts therapy or one of its variations. You may wish to read the articles on my website <http://www.royhunter.com/hypnosis_articles.htm>.

Appendix 5

Motivation Mapping for Weight Management

If necessary, refer to the opening comments in Appendix 4 regarding motivation mapping for smokers. Charles Tebbetts, a pioneer of client-centered hypnosis, was considered a master teacher during his life. According to Tebbetts, there are five basic ways to change our subconscious programming (see Chapter 6). He discussed them thoroughly in his professional hypnosis training course, and summarized them in his book, *Self-Hypnosis and Other Mind Expanding Techniques*.

Follow the step-by-step directions to maximize the benefit. Determining your motivation map may take up to thirty minutes or more unless you are a fast reader, so make sure you have enough time to complete it before starting.

Directions: Circle the number of any question that applies to you. If the question is divided into parts, circle the number if you answer yes to any of the parts.

Repetition

1. Old snack triggers: Did you snack often without consciously deciding to, simply out of habit?

2. Are the "non-caloric beverage" responses to old snacking triggers a habit yet?

3. Do you exercise as a regular habit?

Authority

4. Rebel button: (circle 4 if any apply, even if all apply)

    (a) Do you want to splurge when someone tells you to control your weight?

    (b) Do you want to rebel when people insist that you avoid certain foods, such as ice cream or potato chips?

    (c) Do religious beliefs about being healthy make you want to overeat?

    (d) If your health care professional has already advised you to reduce (or avoid certain foods), did this make your desire to overeat get stronger?

5. Have any authority figures strongly motivated you to reduce (e.g. doctor, church)?

6. Do you wish to reduce because of health benefits (whether or not by medical advice)?

Desire for Identity

7. Did you start overeating because of peer pressure, or the desire to do what your friends do?

8. Do you resent society's peer pressure against overweight people, and/or do you resent a relative or spouse who is pressuring you to reduce?

9. Do you seek the company of overweight people in order to feel okay?

10. Have you frequently snacked either as a reward or a way of giving yourself some attention (e.g. after completing tasks, getting off work)?

11. Have you felt a strong sense of pride with your identity as an overweight person?

12. Does the anti-overweight social pressure make you want to reduce? (Note: Some people answer yes to both 8 and 12.)

13. Is someone you love motivating you to reduce (e.g. parents wanting to set a good example for their children)?

14. Will you have a better self-image or professional image at your ideal weight, and/or a sense of pride, or a feeling of victory?

Hypnosis and Self-Hypnosis

15. Have you frequently snacked while watching TV, reading, or driving?

16. Have you frequently snacked in bed, or if your sleep is interrupted?

17. Do you have a past success with hypnosis for any goal?

18. Are you listening to a hypnotic CD, tape, or MP3 regularly?

19. Do you fantasize your benefits often?

Emotion

20. Everyone enjoys the taste of food . . . so circle this number.

21. Have you used food or beverages as a stress-coping technique?

22. Do you feel guilt or shame regarding your weight?

23. Are you emotionally excited about the benefits of reaching your ideal weight?

To score the results and determine your current motivation map, please use the next page (or a photocopy of the next page). After you score your initial results, you may wish to make a photocopy

Your Motivation Map

Find the numbers in the frames below, and circle the same numbers circled above.

Repetition

Old You:	New You:
1	2 3

Authority

Old You:	New You:
4	5 6

Desire for Identity

Old You:	New You:
7 8 9 10 11	12 13 14

Hypnosis and Self-Hypnosis

Old You:	New You:
15 16	17 18 19

Emotion

Old You:	New You:
20 21 22	23

Count the number of circles in the "Old You" category and enter "initial score": _____

Count the number of circles in the "New You" category and enter "initial score": _____

If "Old You" is larger than "New You" enter the difference here: _____

If "New You" is larger than "Old You" enter the difference here: _____

Your future motivation map (see instructions on the following pages):

Your New "Old You" score: _____

Your New "New You" score: _____

Your Potential Advantage: _____

before you determine your future motivation map. Some clients prefer to use a different color of pencil or pen when determining their future motivation map – this is your choice.

Your Current Motivation Map

The category with the highest score indicates your dominant subconscious motivation. The greater the difference between the two categories, the stronger your motivation is to either succeed or backslide.

Difference of 0 or 1 in either category: Although you might succeed by following the information presented in this book, completing your motivation map will increase your ability to monitor what goes into your subconscious so that you may better stay on the road to success.

Advantage of 2 or 3 in "Old You" category: You have a risk of backsliding, so it is important for you to use every tool at your disposal to successfully control your weight.

Advantage of 4 or more in "Old You" category: Unless you can improve your future motivation map considerably, you might benefit by investing in hypnotherapy to go the full distance and stay on track.

Difference of 2 or 3 in "New You" category: You should be able to succeed without ever completing this exercise, based on how well you follow the rest of the program.

Difference of 4 or more in "New You" category: You should be well on the road to success. Remember to always respect the power of imagination and emotion, and guard your subconscious gateways.

If your "initial score" in the "Old You" category was 9 or higher: You may be experiencing some inner conflicts regarding your decision to control your eating habits and manage your weight. If so, a hypnotherapist trained in a technique called parts therapy may be able to help you resolve your inner conflicts (see Chapter 7).

Note: Hidden subconscious blocks sometimes require individual hypnosis sessions to discover the subconscious causes.

Your Future Motivation Map

In order to help you change your future motivation map, use this section as reference. Note that the numbered questions appear below as they did in the pages before your motivation map, but with comments following each question. Before proceeding, you may take a break if desired.

First: Refer to *only the numbers for those questions that you circled*, and read the comments and suggestions that follow each corresponding question repeated in the following pages. You will be instructed to make changes on your motivation map, so make a photocopy of your original map. The comments teach you how to be a better gatekeeper of your gateways.

Next: After you follow the instructions contained in those comments that apply to you, follow the "Additional instructions" that appear at the end of the section of questions and comments.

Repetition

1. Old snack triggers: Did you snack often without consciously deciding to, simply out of habit?
   COMMENTS: *Replace the former snack triggers with several sips of water or a non-caloric beverage of choice. Your objective is to make this a habit, so circle 2 and put an "X" over 1 on your motivation map.*

2. Are the "non-caloric beverage" responses to old snacking triggers a habit yet?

COMMENTS: *Make the ability to take a few sips of water an automatic response to old snack triggers (see comments for 1). It may take time and commitment, but the results are worth the effort. Circle 2 if you've not yet done so, and make a commitment to make this a habit.*

3. Do you exercise as a regular habit?

    COMMENTS: *My clients must accept responsibility for their own decisions regarding exercise, especially since what might be appropriate for one person could actually be a health risk to someone else. If (and only if) you are exercising regularly, then circle 3 on your motivation map. If you are not yet exercising regularly, then be sure to consult with a licensed health care professional regarding exercises that are appropriate for you. That being said, it is easier to stay motivated with an exercise that you like instead of choosing one that is not enjoyable.*

Authority

4. Rebel button: (circle 4 if any apply, even if all apply)

    (a) Do you want to splurge when someone tells you to control your weight?

    (b) Do you want to rebel when people insist that you avoid certain foods, such as ice cream or potato chips?

    (c) Do religious beliefs about being healthy make you want to overeat?

    (d) If your health care professional has already advised you to reduce (or avoid certain foods), did this make your desire to overeat get stronger?

    COMMENTS: *The desire to rebel is a manifestation of a strong desire for free choice. You can rebel against meddlers by redirecting your power of choice. Let your stress-coping technique (learned in Chapter 8) become a reminder that you have the power of choice. Your object is to gain a good level of control over your rebel button, so put an "X" over 4 on your motivation map.*

Appendices

5. Have any authority figures strongly motivated you to reduce (e.g. doctor, church)?
   COMMENTS: *While this may be helpful, be sure to remember your benefits.*

6. Do you wish to reduce because of health benefits (whether or not by medical advice)?
   COMMENTS: *If health problems motivated you to reduce, you may need to consult with your physician regarding any of your expected health benefits. If you are already in good health, be grateful ... and be sure to remember your benefits.*

Desire for Identity

7. Did you start overeating because of peer pressure, or the desire to do what your friends do?
   COMMENTS: *This one fades with time, which varies from person to person. If you feel you can leave it in the past, put an "X" through 7 on your motivation map. If unsure, leave it alone; but if your original map had four or five circles in this gateway in the "Old You" category, "X" this one.*

8. Do you resent society's peer pressure against overweight people, and/or do you resent a relative or spouse who is pressuring you to reduce?
   COMMENTS: *You must internalize that it is your choice to reduce, regardless of social pressure against obesity. This can still work against you if someone catches you off guard with criticism against people who are overweight, so 8 remains.*

9. Do you seek the company of overweight people in order to feel okay?
   COMMENTS: *Choose your friends because of who they are, and not because of their size or weight. Your objective is to get this handled, so put an "X" through 9. If you have trouble with this, professional hypnotherapy is an option.*

10. Have you frequently snacked either as a reward or a way of giving yourself some attention (e.g. after completing tasks, getting off work)?
    COMMENTS: *Change the reward. Remember that it is easier to replace than it is to erase, so make a conscious choice to reward yourself with something other than food. Some clients will buy themselves flowers because they are "worth it"! While the new reward may satisfy you, failure to change rewards could make you vulnerable again, so 10 remains.*

11. Have you felt a strong sense of pride with your identity as an overweight person?
    COMMENTS: *A "yes" response here is rare; but if you circled 11 then your work is cut out for you; so 11 remains, and it is even more important for you to follow the program. Hypnotherapy might be needed.*

12. Does the anti-overweight social pressure make you want to reduce? (Note: Some people answer yes to both 8 and 12.)
    COMMENTS: *Although this is a motivator for some people to reduce, it can be a vulnerable one if you have a "rebel" button. Remember your benefits.*

13. Is someone you love motivating you to reduce (e.g. parents wanting to set a good example for their children)?
    COMMENTS: *Congratulations! This can be a strong motivator for some people, provided this gives you a positive feeling. However, if the feeling is negative, then put a circle around 8 and refer to those comments.*

14. Will you have a better self-image or professional image at your ideal weight, and/or a sense of pride, or feeling of victory?
    COMMENTS: *If you circled 14, then read my comments regarding rewarding yourself ... and you can double the effect of 14.*

Hypnosis and Self-Hypnosis

15. Have you frequently snacked while watching TV, reading, or driving?
    COMMENTS: *Be sure to have some water or a non-caloric beverage available to sip on as a substitute for snacks. Without a substitute you could be vulnerable, so this motivator remains.*

16. Have you frequently snacked in bed, or if your sleep is interrupted?
    COMMENTS: *The same comments as for 15 apply here, so 16 remains. If possible, train yourself to go back to sleep without getting up.*

17. Do you have a past success with hypnosis for any goal?
    COMMENTS: *If you have ever experienced a success with hypnosis (or a hypnosis tape or CD), then 17 belongs on your motivation map. Draw on that success. (Note: 17 applies to a past success with hypnosis.)*

18. Are you listening to the hypnotic CD, tape, or MP3 regularly?
    COMMENTS: *It is difficult to overcome years of programming with only one or two sessions, so make a recording (if you don't already have one) using the sample script provided in Appendix 7. Then continue listening to it daily for at least twenty-one days, or until the eating habits change. Circle 18 if you have not yet done so, and listen daily as instructed. If you prefer, you may purchase a CD from <http: www.royhunter.com/selfhelp.htm>.*

19. Do you fantasize your benefits often?
    COMMENTS: *You pass through hypnosis on the way to and from sleep every night. You can take advantage of some of this time by fantasizing your benefits. If you make a commitment to do this, you can circle 19 if not yet circled.*

Emotion

20. Everyone enjoys the taste of food . . . so circle this number.
    COMMENTS: *This number remains on your motivation map. Remember that it is easier to fight emotion with emotion, so it is vital for you to get emotionally involved with your benefits for attaining your ideal weight.*

21. Have you used food or beverages as a stress-coping technique?
    COMMENTS: *The stress management exercise in Chapter 8 is vital for you. This number remains on your map. Listen to the CD that came with this book and start using your peaceful place trigger when stressed instead of reaching for food.*

22. Do you feel guilt or shame regarding your weight?
    COMMENTS: *Forgive yourself, and put an "X" through 22. If you believe it is difficult to forgive yourself, then you might consider hypnotic regression.*

23. Are you emotionally excited about the benefits of your ideal weight?
    COMMENTS: *This could be your most important key to permanent success, especially if you circled 20. Make the commitment to get emotionally involved with your benefits, and circle 23 if it was not previously circled.*

Additional instructions: While it is not necessary to read the comments for those questions in the "Old You" category, go back now and read all the comments for questions in the "New You" category that you did not circle (2, 3, 5, 6, 12, 13, 14, 17, 18, 19, and 23). Some of these comments will tell you to circle the number on your motivation map if you can make the commitment to follow the recommendations. Circle the appropriate numbers *only* when the comments instruct you to.

You may also add the power of rewards (Question 14) in the following manner if you succeed in losing the desired weight. By planning and scheduling your rewards, you may circle 14 if not yet circled, or write another "14" on your motivation map and circle it. Here are my recommendations:

Appendices

(a) Every ten pounds.
(b) Half-way to your goal weight.
(c) Reaching your ideal weight.
(d) One year after reaching your ideal weight.
(e) Optional: each anniversary after reaching your ideal weight.

Buy something you want, or do something you enjoy . . . and spend some of the money that used to go toward junk food! Also remember that since it is your success that you are celebrating, *you* choose the reward.

Next comes the most interesting part.

Computing Your "Potential Advantage" Score

Now go back and count the number of remaining circled numbers in the "Old You" category, and enter this figure on your motivation map as your revised "Old You" score. Likewise, count the circled numbers in the "New You" category and enter this figure as your revised "New You" score. Most people who follow this program properly should have a higher revised "New You" score than in the revised "Old You" category. Record the difference as your "Potential Advantage" score.

If your Potential Advantage is 6 or more, you should be well on the way to success. Even if it seems easier than you thought possible, you must still remember the power of imagination and monitor what you imagine. Sometimes those who reduce easily can also gain it back quickly if they take success for granted.

If your Potential Advantage is 4 or 5, you still may be able to succeed without additional help beyond this workbook, but you must be consistent and persistent.

If your Potential Advantage score is 1 to 3, your work is cut out for you. While it is possible for you to succeed on your own, you have a higher probability of needing hypnotherapy and/or other professional help to reach and maintain your ideal weight.

If your revised "Old You" score is equal to or greater than your revised "New You" score, then you are a likely candidate for private hypnotherapy to discover the causes of your subconscious blocks if you want to enjoy long-term success. This is rare, but does occasionally happen.

Appendix 6

Script for Stress Management Download

This section contains the script to the stress management audio download, "What To Do When Your Buttons Get Pushed." If you would prefer to make a recording in your own voice, you may choose an induction from Chapter 4, followed by the script below. Then conclude your recording with the awakening script also shown in Chapter 4. (Note: If making your own script, pause at the three dots (. . .).)

Introductory remarks and the formal induction into self-hypnosis appear, followed by this script...

> Just imagine the place you are at now is so beautiful, so tranquil, so serene, and so relaxing, that it's easier and easier to go even deeper . . . just relaxing completely . . . into a very deep hypnotic peace . . . so calm, so peaceful, that it becomes even easier to imagine more vividly any beautiful, peaceful sights, sounds, feelings, or sensations . . . imagining such a wonderful harmony in your special, private place of peace, that it is as though you are becoming a part of the peace that you imagine . . . as though there's an inner peace, physically, mentally, emotionally, through every part of your being. And it just feels so relaxing, it's easier and easier to go deeper and deeper relaxed . . .Waaaaay down, into a very deep, inner peace . . . a very deep, deep, inner peace.
>
> You have the ability to REMEMBER your place of peace. Just touch your thumb to a finger that you choose as your PEACEFUL PLACE finger. While you do this, take a deep breath and think the word, "RELAX." You have the power to remember your place of inner peace whenever you touch your

Script for Stress Management Download

peaceful place finger OR whenever you take one deep breath and think the word "relax." Just do so now once again . . . take another very deep breath, and THINK the word "RELAX" as you exhale . . . relax . . .

Now, in the rehearsal room of your mind, where you can do anything you wish, rehearse your ability to use three different choices whenever your buttons get pushed. You may either express immediately in the here and now . . . or you may respond at a later, more appropriate time and place . . . or you may simply release it and let it go . . . YOU make the choice, according to your best wisdom, knowledge, understanding, training, experience, and intelligence.

Let's rehearse the first choice, because some situations are best handled in the here and now. Imagine a situation, either a real event from the past or a fictitious event, where someone pushes your buttons, and your BEST CHOICE is to respond NOW . . . and as you imagine the person pushing your buttons, just take one deep breath . . . and RELAX . . .

[Pause . . .]

. . . and now imagine yourself expressing appropriately, with a satisfying outcome . . . or a satisfying resolution. You may also touch your thumb to your peaceful place finger if you wish . . .

[Pause . . .]

Now rehearse your second choice, where it's best to wait until a later, more appropriate time and place . . . and as you imagine that situation, take a deep breath *[breathe close to microphone]* and RELAX . . . or you may touch your thumb to your peaceful place finger.

[Pause . . .]

Just imagine yourself choosing to wait until a better time and place, and you TOTALLY accept YOUR decision, so you are free to go about your other activities . . . And now move forward in time to that later time and place, and imagine yourself expressing appropriately . . . to a negotiated compromise or a satisfying resolution . . . a satisfying outcome!

[Pause . . .]

Your third choice is to simply release it, or let it go . . . releasing the other person from the apology without condoning the actions . . . And now imagine a situation where RELEASE is your best choice . . . And as you do, touch your thumb to your peaceful place finger or take one deep breath *[breathe close to microphone]* and RELAX . . .

[Pause . . .]

And as your inner mind indicates RELEASE, just take another deep breath and think the word RELEASE as you release the air from your lungs . . . and release that person as easily as you release the air from your lungs. You release that person from the apology they used to owe, and you release yourself! Just FEEL the release, and know that you have the power to do this whenever you choose.

[Pause . . .]

Your deep breath is also your peaceful place trigger, just as much as your thumb touching your peaceful place finger . . . and it's also your trigger for CHOICE . . . because YOU have the power of choice . . . And whenever you take one deep breath and think the word "RELAX," you are free to make the best choice, according to your best wisdom, knowledge, understanding, training, experience, and intelligence. YOU have the power of choice . . . and like a muscle that is used is stronger with use, your power of choice is stronger with use! . . . like a muscle that is used is stronger with use, your power of choice is stronger with use; and you LOVE your power of choice!

So whenever something happens that used to push your buttons, you simply take a deep breath . . . relax and remain calm, and make the best choice. Whenever you relax and think the word RELAX as you exhale, or touch your thumb to your peaceful place finger, it's an automatic reminder that you are free to think with a clear mind, and use your best wisdom, knowledge, understanding, training, and experience to make the best choice. And every day in every way you are more relaxed and calm and composed. You now are and ever shall remain FREE to be the BEST that you can BE . . . because it's SO much easier to be your best than it is to try to be perfect. Simply be your best.

You claim and attain your ideal self-empowerment, and you now allow your desire to become your reality . . . and you have the power to make it so . . . and so it is!

[Awakening . . .]

©2002, revised ©2007 by C. Roy Hunter, all rights reserved.

Appendix 7

Affirmations and Scripts

Instructions

The affirmations in this section provide you with a foundation for constructing your own personalized affirmations for HypnoCise. You may use these as you wish, modifying them and/or adding additional ones in accordance with the guidelines provided in Chapters 15 and 16.

If you wish to make a recording change the affirmations from the first-person format to the second-person format ("I am" becomes "You are," etc.). Additionally, note the inclusion of full scripts (in the second-person format) for weight management, smoking cessation, and smoking reduction. Should you wish to utilize one of these three scripts, you may either have someone read the script to you, or you may record the script in its entirety into a recorder or computer for playback. Note that the scripts are designed for the subconscious, and do not follow strict rules of grammar.

Affirmations for Confidence

1. Each day I go through my daily activities with a confident and controlled attitude.

2. I am calm, relaxed, and confident.

3. My new self-image makes it easier to go through all my daily activities with increasing confidence and success.

4. I enjoy peace, health, and greater happiness in all my endeavors.

5. Whenever I desire extra confidence, I simply take a deep breath, and feel more calm and confident as I exhale.

6. I am grateful for all that contributes daily to my increasing confidence.

7. I am an expert in my profession.

8. I handle all areas of my chosen profession easily and confidently.

9. The many and varied situations in which I find myself are always handled competently in a calm, relaxed manner.

10. I do all things well. I look my best in all situations, and work my best.

11. My conversation is natural and easy, and my confident attitude attracts success.

12. I always act, feel, and think as my new self-image.

13. My confidence increases daily.

14. I am now and ever shall remain as my new self-image.

15. I love myself now.

16. I claim and attain empowerment, and I now allow my desire to become my reality.

Affirmations for Learning and Study Habits

1. I am calm, relaxed, and confident about my personal learning processes. I accomplish more in shorter periods of time and my work shows an increasing accuracy and understanding. This is my self-image.

Appendices

2. Whenever I read or hear material I wish to know and remember, I find my memory is crystal clear. I easily recall whatever is desired or required. My mind is always calm, relaxed, efficient, and orderly.

3. When I study I have increasing ability to concentrate for longer periods of time as I choose, excluding all common distractions. My comprehension and recall improve daily.

4. I easily present whatever is desired or required, whether orally, in written form, or by demonstration. I always communicate easily and effortlessly.

5. My memory improves daily. My habits and attitudes reflect my confident self-image.

6. Every day in every way I find it easier to study, recall, and present information and remain in total self-control. I am now and ever shall remain as my new self-image.

7. I claim and attain empowerment, and I now allow my desire to become my reality.

Affirmations for Stress Management

1. I am calm, relaxed, and self-confident. I think of myself this way. It is easy to be efficient and effective and still be calm and composed.

2. Each time I retire, I fall into a deep, restful, and peaceful sleep. I awaken at my desired time happy, refreshed, and ready for new activity.

3. When I wish to sleep, I take several deep breaths and think the words "relax and sleep" and easily drift into a deep slumber.

4. Whenever something happens that used to push my buttons, I simply take a deep breath and remain calm. While exhaling, I

think the word "relax" and I am free to think with a clear mind and use my best wisdom, knowledge, understanding, training, and experience to make the best decision.

5. I like myself now, and I am in control of my emotions.

6. Every day in every way I am more relaxed, calm, and composed. I am now and ever shall remain as my new self-image.

7. I claim and attain empowerment, and I now allow my desire to become my reality.

Affirmations for Success

1. I am increasingly poised and successful in all situations. I know that my successful self-image improves and matures each day.

2. Every day I am influenced by whatever benefits me and my objectives. My activities add to my health, my strength, my energy, my prosperity, and my peace of mind, and every day in every way I get closer and closer to my ideal image.

3. I am happy and healthy.

4. My conversation is natural and easy, and my confident attitude attracts success. I use my talents wisely and efficiently.

5. I have my life plan well-defined and organized, and my priorities and goals are clear.

6. I work efficiently with determination to bring my desires into reality because I control my own destiny. I excel at what I do, and I remember to recognize and celebrate my successes.

7. My relations with people continually become more pleasing and effective. I talk to people easily and naturally on first acquaintance and I initiate the conversation. I expect to do this.

Any time I take a deep breath and think of this expectation, it gains strength and permanence.

8. What others might call problems are simply opportunities for growth. I know that the best answers present themselves in deep states of relaxation.

9. Through the power of love, I am abundantly successful. I am worthy of my success, and I accept my success naturally and gratefully. I am and ever shall remain as my new self-image.

10. I claim and attain empowerment, and I now allow my desire to become my reality.

Affirmations for Weight Management

1. I like myself and believe in myself.

2. I desire to be at my healthiest, most ideal weight because I am worth it.

3. I enjoy eating the right amounts of those foods that help me reach and maintain my healthiest, ideal body weight. By eating slowly, I am satisfied with appropriate amounts of the right foods, and I am pleasantly satisfied from meal to meal.

4. Every day in every way I find it easier to be totally self-motivated to do what is wise to help me reach and maintain my healthiest, ideal body weight.

5. I make wise choices about my health and eating habits.

6. I am totally satisfied with the wise choices I make regarding the foods I eat.

7. Every time I choose water or a non-caloric beverage in between meals, my choice satisfies me, because I love my power of choice. And like a muscle that is used is stronger with use,

my power of choice is stronger with use, so every wise choice increases my motivation and confidence.

8. With each passing day, my new slim, trim image becomes more and more real. I always think, act, and move as this new self-image. As my new image becomes more and more real in my mind, it becomes more and more real in my body.

9. I claim and attain empowerment, and I now allow my desire to become my reality.

Script for Weight Management

Read the script below into a recorder (or to the person entering self-hypnosis). The words in normal print are instructions for the person reading the script. Emphasize the words in CAPITALS, saying them slowly and with feeling. Pause briefly wherever you see three dots (. . .). Review the script at least once before using it, in order to become familiar with both its content and the instructions. Have your list of benefits and affirmations handy.

Begin with the progressive relaxation induction from Chapter 4, then continue.

> Now imagine you are already at your ideal, healthiest body weight. You LOVE how you look and feel. Imagine standing in front of a mirror, seeing a reflection of yourself wearing the size clothes you choose to wear. These clothes LOOK good, and they FEEL good, and they fit well on you. Now imagine doing something you totally enjoy doing at your ideal weight. Just BE there in your mind . . . and ENJOY.
>
> [Pause . . .]
>
> Imagine your personal benefits . . .
>
> [Take list of personal benefits and read them one-by-one, slowly.]

Appendices

Now imagine your MOST IMPORTANT BENEFITS SO VIVIDLY that you feel as though you already enjoy success . . . Imagine your benefits . . . SO VIVIDLY . . . that you FEEL as though you already . . . ENJOY . . . SUCCESS!

[Pause . . .]

The terms are so simple. You simply use your power of choice to CHOOSE what goes into your mouth . . . when, where, and how much. YOU decide what goes into your mouth . . . when, where, and how much . . . and you have an increasing satisfaction from the right amounts of those foods which help you reach your ideal, healthiest body weight . . . And you make wise choices about your health and eating habits. Also, whenever you choose water or a non-caloric beverage to satisfy an in-between meal snack urge, you are TOTALLY satisfied, physically, mentally, and emotionally, because YOU CHOOSE . . .

You LOVE your power of choice. And like a muscle that is used becomes stronger with use, your power of choice becomes stronger with use. Imagine using that power of choice right now to choose water or a non-caloric beverage. And when you've successfully practiced this imagery in your mind, either move a finger or take one deep breath . . .

[Pause . . .]

Very good. Like a muscle that is used becomes stronger with use, your power of choice becomes stronger with use . . . and every time you make a wise choice, it becomes even easier to make wise choices, because the BENEFITS are so satisfying, and you LOVE your power of choice!

[Note: If you eat too fast, slowly read next paragraph; otherwise, skip it.]

Also, whenever you eat, you eat SLOWLY . . . enough to ENJOY . . . the FLAVOR of EACH BITE . . . And when you have had enough food to give your body nourishment, you

Affirmations and Scripts

feel satisfied, physically, mentally, and emotionally. And every day it becomes easier for you to be TOTALLY self-motivated to do those things that help you reach your ideal body weight, because you love the benefits.

Now imagine you are already at your ideal, healthiest body weight. You LOVE how you look and feel . . . Imagine standing in front of a mirror seeing a reflection of yourself wearing the size clothes you choose to wear. These clothes LOOK good, and they FEEL good, and they fit well on you. Now imagine doing something you totally enjoy doing at your ideal weight. Just BE THERE in your mind . . . and ENJOY.

[Read your affirmations slowly, in second-person format.]

[Pause. Say the next paragraph slowly.]

Now imagine your MOST IMPORTANT BENEFITS SO VIVIDLY that you feel as though you already enjoy success . . . Imagine your benefits SO VIVIDLY . . . that you FEEL . . . as though you already ENJOY . . . SUCCESS!

You have chosen the benefits because you absolutely deserve them. KNOW that you deserve the benefits. You LOVE your power of choice and every day it becomes easier and easier for you to be TOTALLY self-motivated to make wise choices about your health and your eating habits . . . And like a muscle that is used becomes stronger with use, your power of choice becomes stronger with use . . . giving you a GREATER STRENGTH OF WILL THAN YOU HAVE EVER KNOWN BEFORE . . .

[Pause . . .]

And now, as I give you some silence, once again imagine your success SO VIVIDLY that all of these affirmations simply go deeper and deeper into your subconscious, becoming a part of you simply because you choose them.

[Pause . . .]

Now, I am going to count from one up to five and then I am going to say "fully aware." At the count of five, let your eyelids open and you are calm, refreshed, relaxed, fully aware, and normal in every way.

One . . . Slowly, calmly, easily, and gently you are returning to your full awareness once again.

Two . . . Each muscle and nerve in your body is loose, limp, and relaxed, and you feel wonderfully good.

Three . . . From head to toe you are feeling perfect in every way . . . physically perfect, mentally alert, and emotionally serene . . . and when you get behind the wheel of your vehicle, you are totally alert in every way, responding appropriately to any and all traffic situations.

Number four . . . Your eyes begin to feel sparkling clear, just as though they were bathed in fresh spring water. On the next number now, let your eyelids open and you are then calm, rested, refreshed, fully aware, and feeling good in every way.

Number five . . . Eyelids open now. You are fully aware once again. Take a deep breath, fill up your lungs, and stretch.

Once you have the above script recorded, listen to it several times weekly until you reach your ideal weight. Be sure to fantasize your benefits often; and seek help from a hypnosis professional if needed. Also, you might find it helpful to complete the motivation map presented in Appendix 5.

Script for Quitting Smoking

Read the script below into a recorder (or to the person entering self-hypnosis). The words in normal print are instructions for the person reading the script. Emphasize the words in CAPITALS, saying them slowly and with feeling. Pause briefly wherever you see three dots (. . .). Review the script at least once before using it,

Affirmations and Scripts

in order to become familiar with both its content and the instructions. Have your list of benefits handy, plus any personal affirmations should you choose to add them.

Begin with the progressive relaxation induction from Chapter 4, then continue.

> Your imagination is the rehearsal room of your mind . . . and you have TOTAL POWER, and TOTAL FREEDOM to DO anything you wish, and to BE anywhere you wish. In your mind, you can move through time and space . . .
>
> Now imagine this is one year from today, and you have already been a totally tolerant non-smoker for one year. Your lungs reward you for the fresh air you give them and you LOVE how you feel . . . physically, mentally, and emotionally.
>
> *[Pause . . .]*
>
> Imagine your personal benefits . . .
>
> *[Take list of personal benefits and read them one by one, slowly.]*
>
> Now imagine your MOST IMPORTANT BENEFIT SO VIVIDLY that you feel as though you already enjoy success.
>
> *[Read next paragraph slowly.]*
>
> Imagine your benefits . . . SO VIVIDLY . . . that you feel as though you already enjoy SUCCESS! If you choose these benefits for yourself, then indicate that choice to yourself right now by moving one of your index fingers or by taking one deep breath . . .
>
> *[Pause . . .]*
>
> You have used your power of choice to choose your benefits. The terms are so simple . . . you simply use that same power of choice to choose ONE DEEP BREATH any time an

old light-up trigger occurs, allowing ONE DEEP BREATH to become a TOTALLY SATISFYING REPLACEMENT for yesterday's fair-weather friend. The physical replacement for yesterday's breath of smoke is one deep breath of air. The mental replacement for yesterday's urge is your new friend, FREEDOM to focus your mind or imagination on whatever you choose, because you love your power of choice . . .

You LOVE your power of choice . . . and like a muscle that is used becomes stronger with use, your power of choice becomes stronger with use. Imagine using that power of choice right now by imagining a situation that used to trigger a light-up. Now take a deep breath and RELAX . . . CHOOSE something fun, enjoyable, beautiful, or pleasant to imagine. Indicate to yourself that you have successfully done that by moving a finger or taking one deep breath.

[Pause . . .]

Very good. Like a muscle that is used becomes stronger with use, your power of choice becomes stronger with use . . . and every time you take that one deep breath, it becomes easier and easier to choose the deep breath instead of the old slave master.

You are a non-smoker now, because the BENEFITS are so satisfying, and you LOVE your power of choice! Now once again imagine another old light-up trigger. As you do, take a deep breath and RELAX. Now imagine something fun, enjoyable, beautiful, or pleasant. As you do, you are already practicing your ability to use your new power and friend, FREEDOM, to be a non-smoker . . .

Whenever you use your power of choice to focus your mind on whatever you choose, yesterday's urges are simply forgotten . . . fading away into the mists of time, vanishing into the fog of forgetfulness, replaced with your new friend, FREEDOM . . . to focus your mind, thoughts, or actions on WHATEVER YOU CHOOSE, whether at work or play, at home or away from home, alone or with others. You have the power of choice.

Affirmations and Scripts

You LOVE your power of choice, and it was YOUR CHOICE to become a non-smoker . . . and it is YOUR CHOICE to put your mind or imagination on WHATEVER YOU CHOOSE. And YOUR DECISION is bringing you the benefits you have chosen . . .

[Include personal affirmations here if desired.]

[Pause . . . Speak slowly and with feeling.]

Now, once again, imagine your MOST IMPORTANT BENEFITS SO VIVIDLY that you FEEL as though you already ENJOY success . . . Imagine your benefits . . . SO VIVIDLY . . . that you feel as though you already . . . enjoy SUCCESS!

You have chosen the benefits because you absolutely deserve them. KNOW that you deserve the benefits. You LOVE your power of choice; and every day it becomes easier and easier for you automatically to take that deep breath at times you used to light up . . . and as you do, you feel more and more like a non-smoker with each passing day, as the deep breath becomes a TOTALLY satisfying replacement for yesterday's fair-weather friend.

Your new friend, FREEDOM, becomes so much more satisfying that you simply allow your subconscious to accept that you are now a non-smoker simply because you chose to be, and you love your power of choice . . . and every time you say, see, hear, or think the word RELAX, it automatically reinforces all these affirmations. Whenever you say, see, hear, or think the word RELAX, it becomes easier and easier to be totally self-motivated to act like a non-smoker and remain a non-smoker, because YOU CHOSE . . .

[Pause briefly . . .]

And now, as I give you some silence, once again imagine your success SO VIVIDLY that all of these ideas and suggestions simply go deeper and deeper into your subconscious, becoming a part of you simply because you choose them. And when you again hear my voice, it will be almost time to come back.

[Pause for about 30 seconds . . .]

Now, I am going to count from one up to five and then I am going to say "fully aware." At the count of five, let your eyelids open and you are calm, refreshed, relaxed, fully aware, and normal in every way.

One . . . Slowly, calmly, easily, and gently you are returning to your full awareness once again.

Two . . . Each muscle and nerve in your body is loose, limp, and relaxed, and you feel wonderfully good.

Three . . . From head to toe you are feeling perfect in every way . . . physically perfect, mentally alert, and emotionally serene . . . and when you get behind the wheel of your vehicle, you are totally alert in every way, responding appropriately to any and all traffic situations.

Number four . . . Your eyes begin to feel sparkling clear, just as though they were bathed in fresh spring water. On the next number now, let your eyelids open and you are then calm, rested, refreshed, fully aware, and feeling good in every way.

Number five . . . Eyelids open now. You are fully aware once again. Take a deep breath, fill up your lungs, and stretch.

Once you have the above script recorded, listen to it several times weekly until the frequency and severity of urges have almost vanished. This process usually takes a few weeks. Be sure to fantasize your benefits often; and seek help from a hypnosis professional if needed. Also, you might find it helpful to complete the motivation map presented in Appendix 4.

Affirmations and Scripts

Script for Smoking Reduction

Read the script below into a recorder (or to the person entering self-hypnosis). The words in normal print are instructions for the person reading the script. Emphasize the words in CAPITALS, saying them slowly and with feeling. Pause briefly wherever you see three dots (. . .). Review the script at least once before using it, in order to become familiar with both its content and the instructions. Have your list of benefits handy, plus any personal affirmations should you choose to add them. Notice this script uses the word "try" involving a cigarette, which implies failure. *Never* use the word "try" unless you do *not* want the subconscious to accept what immediately follows.

Begin with the progressive relaxation induction from Chapter 4, then continue.

> Your imagination is the rehearsal room of your mind . . . and you have TOTAL POWER, and TOTAL FREEDOM to DO anything you wish, and to BE anywhere you wish. In your mind, you can move through time and space . . .
>
> Now imagine yourself as a totally controlled smoker, and you light up ONLY when you consciously choose. Your lungs reward you for the fresh air you give them and you LOVE how you feel . . . physically, mentally, and emotionally. You find that only a few chosen puffs can give you far more satisfaction than letting the cigarette try to control you.
>
> *[Pause . . .]*
>
> Imagine your personal benefits . . .
>
> *[Take list of personal benefits and read them one by one, slowly.]*
>
> Now imagine your MOST IMPORTANT BENEFIT SO VIVIDLY that you feel as though you already enjoy success.

Appendices

[Read next paragraph slowly.]

Imagine your benefits . . . SO VIVIDLY . . . that you feel as though you already enjoy SUCCESS! If you choose these benefits for yourself, then indicate that choice to yourself right now by moving one of your index fingers or by taking one deep breath . . .

[Pause . . .]

You have used your power of choice to choose your benefits. The terms are so simple . . . you simply use that same power of choice to choose ONE DEEP BREATH any time an old light-up trigger occurs, allowing ONE DEEP BREATH to become a TOTALLY SATISFYING REPLACEMENT for yesterday's fair-weather friend. The physical replacement for any automatic light-up is one deep breath of air. You smoke ONLY when you consciously choose, because you love your power of choice . . . and when you do smoke, you pay total attention to each and every puff, so that a little satisfies more . . .

You LOVE your power of choice . . . and like a muscle that is used becomes stronger with use, your power of choice becomes stronger with use. Imagine using that power of choice right now by imagining a situation that used to trigger an automatic light-up. Now take a deep breath and RELAX . . . CHOOSE something fun, enjoyable, beautiful, or pleasant to imagine. Indicate to yourself that you have successfully done that by moving a finger or taking one deep breath.

[Pause . . .]

Very good. Like a muscle that is used becomes stronger with use, your power of choice becomes stronger with use . . . and every time you take that one deep breath, it becomes easier and easier to choose the deep breath instead of the old slave master . . . because YOU have the power of choice. You are MUCH smarter than the cigarette! You have a mind, and you can CHOOSE when or whether to smoke . . .

Affirmations and Scripts

You smoke only when you consciously choose . . . and the BENEFITS are so satisfying . . . and you LOVE your power of choice! Now once again imagine another old light-up trigger. As you do, take a deep breath and RELAX. Now imagine something fun, enjoyable, beautiful, or pleasant. As you do, you are already practicing your ability to use your new power and friend, FREEDOM, to CHOOSE . . .

Whenever you use your power of choice to focus your mind on whatever you choose, yesterday's urges are simply forgotten . . . fading away into the mists of time, vanishing into the fog of forgetfulness, replaced with your new friend, FREEDOM . . . to focus your mind, thoughts, or actions on WHATEVER YOU CHOOSE, whether at work or play, at home or away from home, alone or with others. You have the power of choice. You LOVE your power of choice, and it is YOUR CHOICE to tell the cigarette what to do . . . whether to get lost or get smoked . . . and it is YOUR CHOICE to put your mind or imagination on WHATEVER YOU CHOOSE. And YOUR DECISION is bringing you the benefits you have chosen . . .

[Include personal affirmations here if desired.]

[Pause . . . Speak slowly and with feeling.]

Now, once again, imagine your MOST IMPORTANT BENEFITS SO VIVIDLY that you FEEL as though you already ENJOY success . . . Imagine your benefits . . . SO VIVIDLY . . . that you feel as though you already . . . enjoy SUCCESS!

You have chosen the benefits because you absolutely deserve them. KNOW that you deserve the benefits. You LOVE your power of choice; and every day it becomes easier and easier for you automatically to take that deep breath at times you used to light up . . . and as you do, you feel more and more in control . . . and the deep breath becomes a TOTALLY satisfying replacement for yesterday's automatic light-ups . . . Your new friend, FREEDOM, becomes so much more satisfying that you simply allow your subconscious to accept that you smoke only when you consciously choose, and you love your

Appendices

power of choice . . . and every time you say, see, hear, or think the word RELAX, it automatically reinforces all these affirmations. Whenever you say, see, hear, or think the word RELAX, it becomes easier and easier to be totally self-motivated to be an occasional smoker, because YOU CHOSE . . . and if and when you ever decide to quit totally, it will be when and if YOU CHOOSE . . .

[Pause briefly . . .]

And now, as I give you some silence, once again imagine your success SO VIVIDLY that all of these ideas and suggestions simply go deeper and deeper into your subconscious, becoming a part of you simply because you choose them. And when you again hear my voice, it will be almost time to come back.

[Pause for about 30 seconds . . .]

Now, I am going to count from one up to five and then I am going to say "fully aware." At the count of five, let your eyelids open and you are calm, refreshed, relaxed, fully aware, and normal in every way.

One . . . Slowly, calmly, easily, and gently you are returning to your full awareness once again.

Two . . . Each muscle and nerve in your body is loose, limp, and relaxed, and you feel wonderfully good.

Three . . . From head to toe you are feeling perfect in every way . . . physically perfect, mentally alert, and emotionally serene . . . and when you get behind the wheel of your vehicle, you are totally alert in every way, responding appropriately to any and all traffic situations.

Number four . . . Your eyes begin to feel sparkling clear, just as though they were bathed in fresh spring water. On the next number now, let your eyelids open and you are then calm, rested, refreshed, fully aware, and feeling good in every way.

Affirmations and Scripts

> Number five . . . Eyelids open now. You are fully aware once again. Take a deep breath, fill up your lungs, and stretch.

Once you have the above script recorded, listen to it several times weekly until you find yourself *very* rarely lighting up out of habit – and only lighting up when you consciously choose. This process usually takes a few weeks. Avoid lighting up out of stress!

Also, here is a very important tip: keep your supply of cigarettes out of arm's reach, which will force you to consciously choose whether or not to light up. In addition, if and when you choose to smoke, make sure that you pay attention to the cigarette. Do *not* smoke while driving, reading, or watching TV. Additionally, be sure to fantasize your benefits often; and seek help from a hypnosis professional if needed.

Glossary

abreaction: emotional discharge, usually due to remembering past pain

affirmations: positive statements designed to change subconscious programming

age regression: guiding a hypnotized person backwards in time by his/her age (*Warning:* Only those trained in regression therapy should do this)

alpha: a state of the mind where brainwave activity slows down to a range of 7–14 cycles per second, during which we experience hypnosis, and which we pass through daily on the way to and from sleep

altered consciousness: synonymous with alpha; terminology used to refer to the state of mind we experience during hypnosis, meditation, or any form of trance

anchoring: establishing a trigger which, when activated, will trigger certain responses; this happens randomly in life, but can be suggested during hypnosis; *see also* trigger

aversion suggestion: suggestions given that emphasize negative aspects of a habit, such as finding the smell of smoke horrible

awakening: the act of bringing a person up out of trance and into full conscious awareness

beta: that state of mind we are in during most of our waking hours, the thinking mode

deepening: in hypnosis, this refers to attaining a more profound trance state

Glossary

delta: that state of mind we enter during deep sleep of total unconsciousness

direct suggestion: suggestions given as commands ("take a deep breath")

ego states therapy: *see* parts therapy

expectancy: having expectations of a certain outcome

expectation: another word for expectancy

eye-fixation: induction involving staring at an object

false memories: fantasies that are experienced during a mishandled regression which are believed to be repressed memories rather than fantasies

FMS: False Memory Syndrome (having false memories)

gestalt therapy: involves role-playing (often used for release)

HypnoCise: a word coined by the author to describe a combination of imagery, meditation, self-hypnosis, and properly constructed affirmations

hypnosis: a trance state which is guided by someone or something other than the person experiencing the trance (there are numerous definitions by different experts)

hypnotherapist: a trained professional who uses hypnosis to help people with self-improvement and/or for therapeutic purposes

hypnotherapy: the use of hypnosis for self-improvement and/or for therapeutic purposes

hypnotist: anyone who guides another person into hypnosis

ideomotor responding: having a client answer questions via finger movement

imagery: using the imagination to fantasize or remember events

indirect suggestion: permissive suggestions ("you can take a deep breath whenever you wish to relax")

induction: a technique that guides (induces) a person into a hypnotic state

initial sensitizing event (ISE): an emotional event that is the origin of a problem, creating a sensitivity to feelings; such as claustrophobia being traced back to being locked in a closet at age three

neuro-linguistic programming (NLP): a modality of change that evolved from the teachings of Milton Erickson

old tapes: a term frequently used to describe memories that are replayed in the imagination in a manner that may influence our behavior and/or attitudes

original sensitizing event: alternate name for initial sensitizing event (ISE)

parts therapy (PT): a complex hypnotic technique where the therapist talks with various parts of the mind, such as the inner child and inner adult – also called ego states therapy (*Warning:* Only those trained in parts therapy should use it)

past life therapy (PLT): a regression into a real or imagined past life; also known as past life regression (PLR)

post-hypnotic suggestion (PH): a suggestion given during the trance state which is acted upon after emerging from the trance

progressive relaxation (PR): a type of induction involving the progressive relaxation of various parts of the body

rapport: a comfortable feeling between client and hypnotist resulting in a level of trust that produces greater ability to respond to suggestion

Glossary

reframing: using the imagination to imagine a different outcome of a past event, such as combining gestalt therapy with regression therapy to facilitate release; also used in NLP with guided imagery

regression: going back in time during trance to remember past events, and replaying them in the imagination, often with accompanying emotions

self-hypnosis: a self-induced trance state

stage hypnosis: the public use of hypnosis purely for entertainment purposes

subconscious: that part of our mind which is the seat of imagination, emotion, artistic abilities (and other skills), and which takes care of numerous functions without our conscious awareness, such as the automatic functions of our organs and so on

subject (of hypnosis): the term used by many to describe a person who is in hypnosis (Note: The word "client" is used with increasing frequency by hypnotherapists)

systematic desensitization: the use of programmed imagery in a systematic way to help desensitize someone from an anxiety or phobia

theta: that state of the mind we are in while dreaming

time distortion: the term for a unique phenomenon where we lose conscious awareness of how much time has passed (e.g. 5 minutes can seem like 20 minutes, or vice versa)

trigger: something seen, heard, felt, and so on, which "triggers" a response, urge, memory, or emotion (e.g. turning the ignition key might trigger a smoker to light up a cigarette)

Bibliography

Brown, B. 1978. *Stress and the Art of Biofeedback*. New York: Bantam Books.

Coué, E. 1922. *Self Mastery through Conscious Autosuggestion*. Montana, KS: Kessinger Publishing Company.

Damon, D. 2005. *The Amazing Stone-Deaf Hypnotist: Dr. Rexford L. North*. Merrimack, NH: HypnoClassics.

Darnton, R. 1968. *Mesmerism and the End of Enlightenment in France*. Cambridge, MS: Harvard University Press.

Elman, D. 1970. *Hypnotherapy*. Glendale, CA: Westwood Publishing.

Gawain, S. 1990. *Creative Visualization*. San Rafael, CA: New World Library.

Hill, N. 1966. *Think and Grow Rich*. New York: Hawthorn Books.

*Hunter, R. 2000. *The Art of Hypnosis: Mastering Basic Techniques* (3rd edn). Dubuque, IA: Kendall/Hunt Publishing.

*Hunter, R. 2007. *The Art of Hypnotherapy* (3rd edn). Dubuque, IA: Kendall/Hunt Publishing.

LeCron, L., and Bordeaux, J. 1947. *Hypnotism Today*. North Hollywood, CA: Wilshire Book Co.

McGill, O. 1981. *Hypnotism and Meditation: The Operational Manual for Hypnomeditation*. Glendale, CA: Westwood Publishing.

Parkhill, S. 1995. *Answer Cancer, Answers for Living: The Healing of a Nation*. Deerfield Beach, FL: Health Communications.

Russell, J. 1988. *Psychosemantic Parenthetics*. Escondido, CA: Institute of Hypnotechnology.

Siegel, B. 1986. *Love, Medicine & Miracles: Lessons Learned about Self-Healing from a Surgeon's Experience with Exceptional Patients*. New York: Harper and Row.

Spanos, N., and Chaves, J. 1989. *Hypnosis: The Cognitive Behavioral Perspective*. Buffalo, NY: Prometheus Books.

Bibliography

Tebbetts, C. 1985. *Miracles on Demand* (2nd edn). Dexter, MI: Thompson/Shore.

Tebbetts, C. 1977. *Self-Hypnosis and Other Mind Expanding Techniques*. Glendale, CA: Westwood Publishing.

Teitelbaum, M. 1965. *Hypnosis Induction Technics*. Springfield, IL: Charles C. Thomas.

Vitale, J. 2008. *The Attractor Factor* (2nd edn). Hoboken, NJ: John Wiley & Sons.

Zanuso, B. 1986. *The Young Freud: The Origins of Psychoanalysis in Late Nineteenth-Century Viennese Culture*. Oxford and New York: Blackwell.

Note: The Art of Hypnosis and *The Art of Hypnotherapy* are now published by Crown House Publishing.

Index

abreaction, 281
achievements (as goals), 133, 165
action plan, 124, 147, 148, 149, 150, 152, 186, 189, 195, 200, 217
affirmations, 9, 120, 177–178, 180–181, 182, 183, 185–194, 195, 197, 199, 200–203, 204, 262–280, 281
   active wording, 187
   attitude, 62–63, 167, 170, 186, 200, 216, 217, 262
   editing, 189–194
   description, 16
   designing, 182, 281
   positive statements, 177, 185, 189, 281
   present tense, 186, 188
   structure, 178, 189, 200
   writing down, 131
alpha, 12, 13, 16–18, 47, 49, 50, 51, 53, 54, 76–78, 82, 87, 89, 90, 102, 135, 137, 138, 143, 148, 151, 152, 153, 199, 203, 226, 281
altered consciousness, 11, 281
anchoring, 60, 61, 88, 101, 119, 281
anxiety, 24, 39, 82, 93, 95, 97, 119, 163, 218, 284
archery/darts, 168
authority, 65–69, 81–82, 87, 88–89, 91, 232–233, 238, 246, 251
aversion suggestion, 281
awakening, 203, 258, 261, 281

baseball, 63, 66, 71, 167, 168, 179
basketball, 167, 169
benefits (of a goal), 4, 8, 74, 81, 124, 147, 148, 149, 150, 152, 153, 154, 155, 162, 165, 167, 172, 186, 188, 189, 200, 201, 202, 204, 205, 211, 234, 240, 247, 254

Bernheim, Hippolyte, 35
best time (for self-hypnosis), 223
beta, 12, 13, 50, 53, 95, 135, 138, 281
bowling, 170
Braid, James, 14, 33, 34
brain waves, 12, 13
business motivation, 77, 159, 161, 217
buttons, see stress

cause and effect, 147, 148, 149, 200
celebrating your success, 75, 90, 123, 125, 127, 129, 166, 265
change:
   resistance to, 3, 85, 150, 215
   see also subconscious programming
Charcot, James, 35–36, 37
choice(s):
   dealing with stress, 62, 97
   power of, 7, 10, 89, 97, 114, 121, 130, 138, 211, 238, 249, 251, 260, 267, 268, 269, 271, 272, 273, 276, 277, 278
cigarettes, see smoking
combining programming methods, 88, 90
computer, mental, 59, 61
confidence, 9, 97, 119, 125, 166, 197, 218, 262–263
conflict, subconscious, 3, 92
consulting, 162, 194, 220
control (during hypnosis), 12, 14, 15, 21, 37, 76, 226, 249
Coué de Châtaigneraie, Émile, 38
courses, see hypnosis courses
creative daydreaming, see daydreaming
cults, 73, 81

Index

daydreaming, 145–174
deepening, 14, 51, 53, 54, 281
delta, 13, 102, 282
desire for identity, *see* identity
direct suggestion, 282

ego, 6, 65, 69, 71, 73, 74, 75, 76, 90, 144, 221, 226, 231, 282, 283
Elliotson, John, 32
Elman, Dave, 40
emotion(s), 11, 21, 61–62, 65, 78–81, 82–83, 87, 89, 90, 93–95, 97, 110, 150–151, 153, 178–179, 199–201, 205, 231, 234, 241–242, 247, 255
   motivating power of the mind, 78, 82, 151, 205
   negative, 62, 78–79, 80–81, 82, 83, 94, 109–111, 178, 200, 203
   subconscious gateway, 67, 78
Erickson, Milton, 40, 283
Esdaile, James, 34
ethics, 14, 44, 221
expectancy, 18, 19, 180, 282
eye-fixation, 282

failure, 3, 5–6, 82, 110–113, 117
false memories, 119, 282
FAQs, 222, 229
Faria, Abbé Jose Castodi de, 32
fear, 61, 78, 80–82, 88, 97, 185, 226
fixed gaze, 32, 33
forgiveness, 90, 113, 114, 118
Franklin, Benjamin, 29
Freud, Sigmund, 26, 36

Gassner, Father Johann Joseph, 27, 30
goals, 4–5, 8–9, 10, 72, 76, 81, 91–92, 109, 110, 111, 121, 123, 124, 131–133, 134, 135, 137–144, 149–155, 162, 163, 165, 166, 167, 188–189, 195–198, 200–205, 215–218
golf, 63, 98, 134, 148, 167, 170

group identification, 72, 73
gymnastics, 171

habits, 3–4, 21, 59–64, 65–67, 70, 71, 77, 80, 81–83, 85, 87, 88–89, 91, 92, 109, 133–134, 147, 149–159, 163–165, 179, 186, 190, 197, 249, 254, 263–264, 266
happiness, 123, 124, 132, 137, 140, 143, 144, 200, 262
Hell, Father Maximilian, 27
hockey, 172
HypnoCise, 199–206, 282
hypnosis, 11, 15, 23, 24, 32, 38, 45, 65, 76, 85, 87, 89, 90, 150, 224, 226, 229, 230, 235, 240, 241, 248, 254, 282, 284
   benefits, 3, 4, 41, 44, 77, 125, 147–148, 152–154, 155, 156, 157, 159–160, 161–162, 163–164, 165, 167, 172, 177, 186, 188, 189, 198, 201–202, 204–205, 210, 211, 227, 233, 234, 238, 240, 241, 242, 246, 247, 252, 253, 254, 255, 267–270, 271–274, 275–279
   courses, 3, 220
   description, 12, 16
   origin of word, 24
   subconscious gateway, 67, 78
   to facilitate change, 4
   training, 42, 44, 67, 75, 92, 111, 120, 148, 216, 220, 221, 224, 230, 259, 260, 261, 265
   see also stage hypnosis
hypnotherapy, 40, 44, 173, 215, 239, 252, 253, 282
   certification, 163
   finding a hypnotherapist, 154, 220
   legal recognition, 44

identity, 65, 69, 87, 89, 90, 233, 235, 238, 239, 246, 248, 251, 252
   subconscious gateway, 67, 78

Index

imagination, 10, 17–18, 19, 21, 23, 29, 30, 39, 52–54, 61, 76, 81, 82, 94, 98–99, 100, 110–111, 120, 126–127, 128, 149, 150, 151–153, 170, 181, 193, 200, 203, 205, 211, 229, 236, 243, 249, 256, 271–273, 275–277
language of subconscious, 18, 21, 54, 76, 150, 151, 168, 205, 229
winning over logic, 3, 4, 12, 111, 134, 137, 143, 191, 200
indirect suggestion, 283
induction(s), 30, 32, 33, 37, 49, 51–53, 102, 283

job performance, 161, 162, 217

key word, 195–198, 202, 203–204

law:
    of awareness, 182–183, 203, 229, 281, 284
    of cause and effect, 147– 149, 200
    of conflict, 3, 4, 39
    of expectancy, 180–181
    of justification, 111–112
    of reversed effect, 181–182, 185, 190
legislation, 44, 70
Liébeault, Ambroise-Auguste, 35
love of self, *see* self-esteem

McGill, Ormond, 41, 43
magnetism, 27
manipulation, 81, 83, 89
memory, 163, 187, 217
mental confusion, 102
mental mini-vacation, 93–100, 120, 163, 199
mental misdirection, 52-53
mental states, 12
mentor(s), 65, 69, 71, 82, 90, 180, 188
Mesmer, Franz Anton, 27

mind, 3, 5, 6, 9, 11, 12–14, 16, 17, 20, 48, 50, 54, 59, 60, 61, 62, 63, 65, 67, 69, 71, 73, 76, 78, 81, 82, 85, 91, 94, 95, 98, 99, 100, 102, 103, 104, 109, 110, 111, 117, 120, 126, 127, 129, 134, 135, 138, 143, 144, 147, 149, 150, 151, 152, 153, 157, 158, 160, 162, 163, 164, 165, 166, 167, 168, 169, 170, 171, 172, 173, 177–184, 185, 187, 188, 189, 191, 193, 195, 196, 197, 199, 201, 202, 203, 205, 211, 226, 229, 231, 245, 259, 260, 261, 264, 265, 267, 268, 269, 271, 272, 273, 275, 276, 277, 281, 282, 283, 284
    control, 3, 4, 5, 7, 9, 12, 14, 15, 21, 62, 63, 65, 69, 74, 75, 76, 77, 79, 81, 82, 83, 91, 93, 94, 95, 96, 99, 105, 119, 148, 156, 158, 179, 185, 186, 196, 199, 208, 226, 238, 246, 249, 251, 265, 275, 277
    four states of, 12–13
motivation, 3, 5, 6, 7–8, 9, 41, 44, 65, 73, 74, 77, 80, 85, 87, 88, 89, 90, 91, 92, 117, 148, 149, 150, 159–160, 161, 163, 164, 165–166, 167, 172, 173, 178, 189, 197, 199, 204, 209, 215, 216, 217, 218, 220, 225, 226, 231–244, 245–257, 267, 270, 274
music (during self-hypnosis), 18, 28, 47, 201, 203, 223–224

negative thinking, 9, 109–110, 119
North, Rexford L., 41

pain, 32, 41, 78, 114, 116, 183, 219, 281
peaceful place, 48–49, 54, 95, 99–101, 102–103, 105, 120, 163, 207, 224, 228, 229, 255, 258–261
peak performance, 125–130, 166, 167, 168

Index

peer pressure, 69–71, 72, 73, 75, 233, 239, 246, 252
positive attitude, 63, 134, 186, 197, 199, 200, 210, 253, 281
possessions (as goals), 133, 165
post-hypnotic suggestions, 229
price of success, 124, 147, 149, 186, 200
programming the subconscious, *see* subconscious programming
Puységur, Marquis de (Armand-Marie-Jacques de Chastenet), 31

quintuple whammy, 85–82

rebellion, 68, 87, 88, 89
recognition:
    rewards, 73, 74
regression, 37, 67, 70, 86, 118, 119, 238, 244, 255, 281, 282, 283, 284
relaxation:
    progressive, 47–50, 51, 52, 54, 283
repetition, 61, 65, 66, 81, 87, 88, 91, 101, 231, 232, 235, 237, 245, 248, 250
    subconscious gateway, 65–66, 67, 78
responsibility, 7, 113, 251
rewards, *see* recognition

sales, 63, 67, 73, 77, 80, 95, 97, 110, 132, 133, 147, 148, 161, 162, 178, 179, 180, 191, 197, 224
    motivation, 65, 73, 74, 77, 80, 85, 87, 88, 89, 90, 91, 92, 117, 148, 149, 150, 159–160, 161, 163, 164, 165, 166, 167, 172, 173, 178, 189, 197, 199, 204, 209, 215, 216, 217, 218, 220, 225, 226, 231, 232, 233, 234, 235, 236, 237, 238, 239, 241, 242, 243, 245, 247, 248, 249, 250, 251, 252, 253, 255, 257, 267, 270, 274

slumps, 63, 110
self-criticism, 117
self-esteem, 62, 74, 75, 81, 82, 90, 105, 109, 117, 121, 125, 126, 161, 166, 174, 208, 218
self-pity, 110, 112, 116
Siegel, Bernie, 8, 42
skiing, 172
sleeping, 93, 101, 105
smoking, 4, 10, 59, 66, 68, 75, 88–90, 156, 181, 234, 240, 241, 242, 279
    cessation, 69, 75, 86, 154–155, 216
    reduction, 156, 216, 262
soccer, 172
solution (affirming), 185, 186, 190, 203
sports enhancement, 134, 166, 168, 197, 218; *see also* individual sports
stage hypnosis, 15, 284
states of mind, 12, 199
stress:
    release options, 95–96
study habits, 148, 163–164, 197, 217, 263
subconscious, 3–4, 5, 6, 7, 8, 9, 10, 11, 12, 13, 17, 18, 21, 28, 48, 54, 57–105, 106, 109, 110, 111, 115, 119, 120, 121, 123, 124, 134, 147, 148, 149–150, 151, 152, 154, 155, 156, 159, 160, 162, 165, 167, 168, 177, 178, 179, 180, 181, 182, 183, 185, 186, 187, 188, 189, 191, 193, 195, 196, 197, 198, 199, 200, 202, 203, 204, 205, 208, 209, 210, 211, 215, 216, 218, 219, 222, 225, 227, 229, 231, 236, 243, 245, 249, 250, 257, 262, 269, 273, 275, 277, 278, 284
    language of, 18, 21, 54, 76, 110, 150, 151, 168, 205, 229

programming, 4, 5, 6, 7, 8, 9, 57, 60, 62, 63, 64, 65, 66, 67, 68, 69, 70, 71, 72, 73, 74, 76, 78, 79, 80, 82, 85, 86, 87, 88, 90, 91, 92, 94, 96, 98, 100, 101, 102, 104, 106, 109, 112, 134, 150, 151, 189, 199, 200, 205, 208, 209, 211, 245, 254, 281, 283
resistance to change, 3, 85, 150, 215
selling success to, 149, 152, 156, 202, 227
subject (definition of), 37
success, 5, 9, 15, 18, 19, 21, 34, 40, 54, 62, 63, 65, 71, 75, 77, 81, 82, 86, 88, 89, 90, 92, 94, 97, 110, 111, 112, 116, 123, 124, 125, 126, 127, 128, 129, 131, 144, 147, 149, 150, 152, 153, 155, 156, 158, 159, 161, 164, 165, 166, 170, 178, 180, 186, 188, 195, 197, 199, 200, 202, 205, 211, 217, 225, 226, 227, 231, 234, 236, 240, 241, 242, 243, 247, 249, 254, 255, 256, 257, 262, 263, 265, 266, 268, 269, 271, 273, 275, 276, 277, 278
defining, 123, 124, 125, 127, 129, 132, 197

suggestions, 14, 15, 16, 17, 30, 33, 37, 55, 67, 69, 86, 97, 110, 129, 177, 180, 183, 185, 187, 202, 204, 229, 237, 244, 250, 273, 278, 281, 282, 283
accepting, 15, 17, 112, 114, 115, 150
rejecting, 72, 196
swimming, 155, 166, 171

Tebbetts, Charles, 24, 41, 43, 44, 65, 69, 180, 224, 245
television, 4, 16, 17, 77, 87, 89, 90, 155, 182, 226, 234, 240, 247, 254, 279
theta, 13, 102, 203, 284
time distortion, 49, 203, 284
triggers, 60–61, 62, 66, 87, 88, 119, 167, 187, 202, 232, 237, 245, 250, 251, 281, 284

weight management, 90–91, 156–58, 196, 216, 217, 245–257, 262, 266, 267
Winkler, Arthur, 42, 187
workshops, 230

About the Author

C. Roy Hunter, M.S., FAPHP is the published author of several books, and an experienced trainer with a strong background in sales. He first started practicing hypnotherapy in 1983, and began teaching professional hypnosis in 1987.

The first edition of *Master the Power of Self-Hypnosis* (Sterling Publishing, 1998) was considered by many professionals to be one of the best books available about self-hypnosis. His *The Art of Hypnosis* (3rd edn, Crown House Publishing, 2010), is required reading at many schools of hypnosis around the world. Additionally, two other books about advanced hypnotherapy techniques come highly recommended by professional hypnotherapists.

Roy was inducted into the International Hypnosis Hall of Fame in April 2000 for his written contributions to the field of hypnotherapy, and he has been honored by three different hypnosis organizations for lifetime achievement in the profession.

He maintains a commercial hypnosis website at: <http://www.royhunter.com>.

Appointed EU Representative: Easy Access System Europe Oü, 16879218
Address:Mustamäe tee 50, 10621, Tallinn, Estonia
Contact Details: gpsr.requests@easproject.com,
+358 40 500 3575

www.ingramcontent.com/pod-product-compliance
Lightning Source LLC
Chambersburg PA
CBHW070753230426
43665CB00017B/2334